THE YACHTSMAN'S VADE MECUM

The Yachtsman's Vade Mecum

PETER HEATON

FOURTH EDITION

ADAM & CHARLES BLACK

LONDON

FIRST PUBLISHED 1961

SECOND EDITION 1969

THIRD EDITION 1971

FOURTH EDITION 1978

A. AND C. BLACK LTD.

35 BEDFORD ROW, LONDON WC1R 4JH

COPYRIGHT © PETER HEATON 1978

ISBN 0 7136 1859 0

Dedicated to
Porky and Pippy

British Library Cataloguing in Publication Data

Heaton, Peter
    The yachtsman's vade mecum.—4th ed.
    1. Yachts and yachting
    I. Title
    797.1′24   GV813
    ISBN 0–7136–1859–0

Printed in Great Britain by offset lithography by
Billing & Sons Limited, Guildford and London

CONTENTS

CHAPTER I

THE ORIGIN OF YACHTS AND THE THEORY OF SAILING

PAGE

Origins in Holland; King Charles II; the *Mary*; yachts of the Cork Water Club; origins of yachting in the United States; Viking ships; Arabian ships; 'lateen' rig; the theory of sailing; maximum speed of a ship; basic principles of design; net registered tonnage; Thames tonnage

CHAPTER II

THE HULL, SPARS, SAILS, RIGS, AND RIGGING OF A SAILING YACHT

The parts of the hull; building materials; the mast and spars; standing rigging; purchases, running rigging; sails; the cable; Sloop rig; Cutter rig; Yawl rig; Ketch rig; Schooner rig; Bermudan rig versus gaff

CHAPTER III

ON BUYING A YACHT AND THE FOUR PRINCIPAL TYPES OF SAILING YACHT

The right boat for the job; take advice; surveys; the cruising yacht; the racing yacht; the dinghy; the ocean racing yacht; short history of ocean racing

CHAPTER IV

UNDERWAY

Bending on and hoisting the mainsail; bending on and hoisting the jib; getting under way in various conditions of wind and tide; getting under way when yacht is (i) at anchor and (ii) moored alongside a quay; sailing to windward; tacking; the genoa jib; heeling; reaching; running; gybing; use of the spinnaker; rolling and broaching to; balance; relation of sail plan to hull; trim and ballast

LIST OF FIGURES

CHAPTER I

THE ORIGIN OF YACHTS AND THE THEORY OF SAILING

'A YACHT? You mean one of those big white boats with funnels and full of people in white flannels and co-respondent shoes!' 'Certainly not, I mean a proper yacht that sails!' This strangely evocative word 'yacht' has different meanings for different people. To some, like our first speaker, it conjures a vision of a large white vessel with one or more yellow funnels, containing suites of rooms and staffed by a large and immaculate crew. To others, it means a slim racing yacht with a towering mast supporting a gleaming white mainsail. To a third person, it means a sporty little racing dinghy, while to a fourth, it indicates a small, trim motor yacht, such as are found on large rivers and in harbours the world over. Of the many differing views, all are right. They are all yachts (although some would disagree about the dinghy), and each represents to his owner the acme of sailing or motor-cruising pleasure. Yachting today is a world-wide sport, giving delight to millions and employment to nearly as many. Yachting brings peace of mind, a sense of adventure, an opportunity to match one's strength with natural forces, and is one of the most health-giving, invigorating pursuits indulged in by man. It teaches self-confidence as well as humility, and philosophy as well as initiative; and there is great beauty in sailing. It may truly be said that the designing, the building, and indeed the sailing of a yacht, extracts from human beings the highest degree of art of which they are capable.

How did this fascinating sport begin?

It is generally accepted that the use of small, privately owned vessels (yachts) for pleasure purposes began in Holland. It was the English King Charles II who, in 1660, imported the sport from Holland, where he had been in exile. It is not known exactly when yachts were first used in Holland, but there is evidence to show that they existed at a very early date; originally as naval vessels. Attached to the fleet of every Dutch Admiral was an admiralty yacht, an 'admiraliteit yaght'. The word 'yaght' is Dutch, and a Dutch-Latin dictionary published in Antwerp in 1599 shows 'yaghte' or 'yaght schip' as meaning a swift, lightly built vessel of war. A 'yacht schip' was a swift vessel, used originally for war, but which was soon to be used also for commerce and pleasure cruising.

Of course the Dutch were by no means the first people to use small vessels for pleasure. We can delve far back into history to find examples: Cleopatra's barges, the *Isis* and *Thelamegus*, built by Ptolemy Philopator in 222 B.C.; the galley of Hardicanute; the pleasure vessel given to Athelstan, the Saxon King of England, by the King of Norway in A.D. 925; the *Rat of Wight* built in 1588 for Queen Elizabeth at Cowes; and the *Disdain*, the pleasure boat built for the young Prince Henry by Phinean Pett to the order of King James I. The list could be greatly extended. However, although no hard-and-fast definition of yachting has ever been agreed upon, it is, I think, unquestionable that the sport as we know it (together with the word 'yacht') came from the Low Countries. During the seventeenth century, merchants in Holland made use of yachts in the rivers and canals and on the North Sea and the Zuider Zee. As the Dutch nation's wealth increased, so did the fleet of yachts, until by the middle of the century pretty well every person of any standing possessed a yacht. Yachting became a social sport; the possession of a yacht was a social asset.

The young Prince Charles of England, who was then living in Holland in exile, became infected with a taste for the sport. From quite an early age, we are told, the sea and sailing ships had held a fascination for King Charles, and while in Holland, the trim, easily handled little vessels made an ineradicable impression upon him. An account of a cruise published in 1660 by Adrian Vlackett, *In Graven's Hage*, reports that 'the King found his yacht so convenient and comfortable, that he remarked, while discoursing with the Deputies, that he might order one of the same style, as soon as he should arrive in England, to use on the river Thames'.

When, on the 8th May 1660, Charles was proclaimed King of England in Westminster Hall, the Dutch at once placed at his disposal a number of yachts to take the King and his entourage from Breda to The Hague (where he was to embark for England). There is a painting by the Dutch artist Verschieer, which shows the yacht in which the King made the journey to Rotterdam. She was rigged with a sprit mainsail and staysail. She carried lee boards and, in the custom of the day, her sides were pierced with circular gun ports. The picture hangs today in the Rijks Museum in Amsterdam. Referring to the *Mary*, the name given to this particular yacht by the King, Samuel Pepys, on the 15th August 1660, wrote in his Diary as follows:

. . . to the office, and after dinner by water to White Hall, where I found the King gone this morning by five of the clock to see a Dutch pleasure-boat below bridge where he dines, and my Lord with him.

The *Mary* was 52 feet long and 19 feet in the beam, carried 8 guns, and was manned by a crew of 30 men. She was the prototype yacht which served as a model for the many yachts shortly to be built to the order of the King, his family, and certain members of the Court. Some of the yachts built for members of the royal family were used by them for a year or two, after which they passed into general use. Both Charles II and James II placed their yachts at the disposal of the ·Admiralty during periods of emergency, and when, in 1665, England found herself at war with Holland, almost all yachts were turned over to the Admiralty, and pleasure sailing ceased. This was indeed a low period for the new sport, but it never died out altogether, and in the reigns of George I and George II royal yachts were in frequent use, and in 1720 in the reign of George I the first yacht club in the world was founded, in the harbour of Cork in Ireland.

There, early yachts were not much like the craft we know today. The royal yachts at the start of the eighteenth century were ketch-rigged and carried a squaresail on a yard surmounted by a topsail.

The yachts of the Cork Water Club (the first yacht club) were cutters, but once again, far removed from the slim modern vessel that we know today by that name. They were solid, bluff-bowed vessels, with long bowsprits which carried a large jib.

They possessed a good-sized fore-staysail, and a large mainsail, loose-footed and laced to a gaff at the head. They were carved and gilded at the stern and carried two or three gun ports on each side forward.

It is not my purpose here to trace the history of yachting, but simply to indicate its origin. Yachting in the United States of America began also with the Dutch. In 1664 New York was occupied by the British, but most of the Dutch settlers continued to live there, and the building of yachts and their employment and enjoyment was doubtless carried on as it had been before the coming of the British.

Of course, leaving out the question of yachts, sailing craft have existed since the dawn of the history of man, when man discovered that the wind could be made to propel a craft on the surface of the water by the simple act of driving that vessel in front of it. In ancient Egypt the Nile vessels used this method to sail upstream before the wind. By doing this, they were able to sail against the current, and then when they wanted to return, all they had to do was to lower the sail and come back with the current.

Of the early navigators, the Vikings have been shown by historical documents to have possessed the knowledge and ability to make a boat sail to some extent to windward (against the wind). There is no doubt that by trimming the large square-sail of a Viking ship well fore and aft, the ship could be made to 'work up to windward', although her performance in this respect would not begin to compare with that of a modern yacht. Nevertheless, by sheeting the sail as flat as possible, it could be, and undoubtedly was, done. The long slim lines of the clinker-built Viking hulls would, of course, help in windward performance, although proportionately they did not have much depth by modern standards.

However, it is a fact that the fore-and-aft rig, which enables a yacht satisfactorily to go to windward, is a modern invention by comparison. Probably the first people to develop the fore-and-aft rig were the Arabs—their baggara or dhow being the father of all 'fore-and-afters', and certainly of all lateen-rigged craft. To this day in the Mediterranean may be seen many vessels carrying the lateen rig. With the lateen rig, the sail is hoisted on a very long, raking yard. When hoisted to its full extent, the after end or peak of the sail stands high above the comparatively short mast. The sail can be sheeted into a fore-and-aft position to almost the same degree as a modern 'Bermudan' sail, and with this rig the Arab boats are quite efficient performers to windward.

But, although 'lateeners' can sail to windward, they are not true 'fore-and-afters'. A real fore-and-aft rigged vessel may be distinguished by the fact that the forward edge of the sail is secured to a mast or stay about which it pivots. Seamen, being by nature conservative, were slow to change, and hundreds of years were to pass before the fore-and-aft rig acquired much recognition. But all the time there was gradual improvement in the design of ships. The deepening of keels, the lowering of the high poops and forecastles of the ship of the sixteenth century —all increased the sailing efficiency of ships, until by the seventeenth century they had come to look very much more as we know them today and the fore-and-aft rig could be said to have come to stay. The early Dutch state yachts carried fore-and-aft mainsails, and headsails, in addition to the normal squaresails.

And so we come back to the advent of yachting as a sport and have therefore established that from the start yachts employed the fore-and-aft rig. It should at once be admitted that many yachts right up to recent times have been 'square' rigged, but the point is that, by the time of the coming of yachts to Great Britain and America, the fore-and-aft rig and the principle of sailing to windward had been generally accepted. Which brings us to the interesting question—how *can* a yacht sail to windward—*against*, in fact, the very force which drives it?

No boat will, of course, sail *directly* against the wind, but it can be made to sail at an angle to it, say from 45 to 50 degrees, and by sailing for a while at 45 degrees to the right of the wind and then by altering course and sailing 45 degrees to the left of the wind, the ship will advance towards the wind in a series of zigzags. This process is called tacking (the reason for this name will be explained later). We have still not quite answered, however, the question of how a boat can be made to sail against the wind, even at an angle of 45 degrees. To understand this, we must borrow an illustration from the science of flying. It was discovered at an early stage in the history of flying that it was not the pressure *underneath* an aircraft's wings that lifted it into the air, but the vacuum on the *upper* surface of the wings. This vacuum or negative pressure was caused by the air flowing

What happens to the wind on the lee side of the sail.

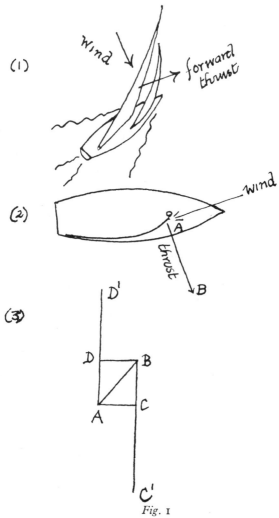

Fig. 1

off the wings' curved upper surface. The same argument applies to the sails of a sailing boat. The wind blowing over the curved leeward surface of a sail creates a negative pressure which imparts a forward lift. In Fig. 1, AB represents the direction and the wind on the weather side of the sail.

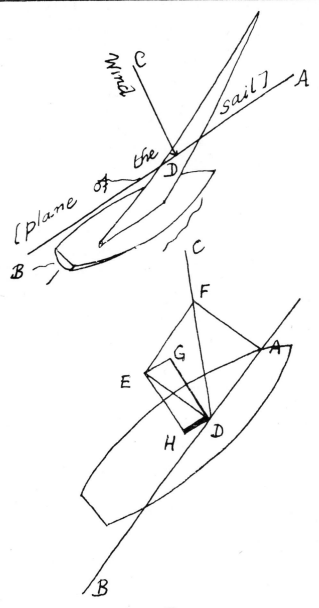

Fig. 2

force of this forward lift. We now employ a geometrical device known as the parallelogram of forces to represent this forward lift AB as two forces acting at right angles to each other. Looking again at Fig. 1, let AB be the forward lift we have mentioned. Let AD¹ be the line of the ship's keel extended. Draw BC¹ parallel to the keel of the ship. Draw a line from A at right angles to the ship's keel to cut BC¹ at C. With centre A and length BC cut AD¹ at D. Join DB. You then have the necessary parallelogram of forces. Now the hull of the vessel is shaped so that it offers very little resistance to that part of the forward drive represented by AD and a lot of resistance to that part represented by AC. The result is that the boat will move along AD, except in so far as its lateral resistance is overcome by AC. This failure of lateral resistance is called lee-way. When close-hauled, all craft make a certain amount of lee-way, that is to say, they 'fall away' to leeward instead of keeping absolutely on their course. The amount of lee-way varies greatly with the hydrodynamic efficiency of the hull and the aerodynamic efficiency of the sail-plan, and, of course, it is affected by wind and sea conditions.

At the moment, we are considering the problem of a vessel sailing to windward. On this 'point' of sailing, experiments in wind tunnels have shown that 75 per cent of the driving force comes from the negative pressure on the leeward side of the sails. It is only when going to windward that negative pressure comes into the picture. When a boat is sailing at more than right angles to, or away from, the wind, negative pressure does not apply.

To continue with the argument: we have seen that the forward lift given by the wind acting on the leeward side of the sails is translated into forward thrust and lee-way, and that this provides 75 per cent of her momentum—what of the other 25 per cent?

Fig. 2 shows a vessel, close-hauled, on the port tack. AB is the sail and CD the wind (we are assuming for the purposes of this illustration that a representative part of the wind strikes the sail at D).

Let CD be the force of the wind and AB the plane of the sail. From A draw AF at right angles to the plane of the sail (AB) to cut CD at F. From F draw a line parallel to AD and with centre F and radius AD cut this line at E. Join ED (which will be parallel to FA). Here then is the new parallelogram of forces ADEF. The wind force CD has been resolved into two forces at right angles to each other, AD and DE. AD represents the wasted force running aft along the surface of the sail. ED represents a force acting at right angles to the sail. Resolve ED, by means of a parallelogram, into another pair of forces at right angles, GD and HD. GD is of no use to us as it merely tries to drive the hull sideways (in other words lee-way), but HD is the driving force. Notice how small it is compared with the amount of force that is wasted in various directions. This diagram also illustrates why a ship heels over when going to windward. The force GD heels the yacht and tries to push the boat sideways. The hull, however, is so shaped that it offers great resistance sideways and little resistance forwards, so that the small forward-acting force HD is able to drive the boat ahead through the water, while the large sideways-acting force GD does no more than heel the boat and cause a little lee-way.

In these explanations, the term 'wind' refers to the 'true' wind, that is to say, the actual direction of the wind. To the person sailing the boat the wind appears to come from a different direction, and this is called the 'apparent' wind. Once the boat starts to move forwards through the water, the wind *appears* to move more and more ahead, continuing to draw ahead until the water resistance set up by the hull to any forward movement exactly balances the forward-acting force. When this point has been reached, the only way in which a further increase of speed can be obtained is by increasing the amount of sail carried (assuming the force and direction of the wind to be constant), and so pushing back the point of balance between the drive from the wind and the resistance of the water to the hull.

But a ship has a maximum speed, and no matter how much sail you set, how hard you drive her, she will not materially exceed this figure (unless she is of the type of craft that can 'plane'—but of that more later). This speed may be found from the following formula: '$1\cdot4\sqrt{\text{Load Water Line (in feet)}}$ = maximum speed in knots'. A ship's hull moving through the water meets with resistance, both from the inertia of the mass of water which the hull has to push out of the way, and from the friction between the immersed surface of the hull and the water itself as the vessel moves ahead. This latter is called skin friction, and it is due to this that most of the resistance is set up when a hull is moving slowly. If, however, it begins to move faster, the resistance due to pushing the mass of water out of the way, in other words 'wave making', increases while the skin friction remains much the same. This resistance first increases as the square of the speed until a point called the critical speed is reached. This critical speed is that shown in the formula given above and called the 'maximum speed in knots'.

Now, the less of a hull there is immersed in the water, the smaller will be the mass to push out of the way, and the less wave-making resistance. Therefore, the lighter displacement a yacht has, the less wave-making resistance she has, and this resistance can further be reduced by giving the hull sweet gradual curves and pointed ends, or the same principle as the 'streamlining' of an aeroplane or a racing motor-car.

So much for wave-making resistance. With regard to re-ducing resistance due to skin friction, this presents a harder problem. We have seen that a ship's speed depends upon the water-line length, so the only way we can reduce the amount of skin friction is once again to cut down the wetted surface—in other words, lighten the displacement. But, and it is a big but, if a hull has no lateral resistance, she would make tre-mendous lee-way when sailing to windward, so we must be careful at this point. However, it is a curious fact that resistance to lee-way is dependent more upon the depth of the keel than the length of it. To give an example, the centreboard of a racing dinghy is deep and short in length. You would not really im-prove the dinghy's windward performance if you increased the length of a centreboard that was shallow, whereas if you in-creased the depth of it, you most certainly would. So we have come to the conclusion that to be fast, a hull must have the following properties: a long water-line, a light displacement (small wetted surface), a deep, narrow keel, and a slim, streamlined shape. With regard to the latter, all yachts must have stability, which is dependent partly on breadth or beam, so then our ideal fast craft should not be over-narrow. If we apply these principles to our design, we get a racing type of yacht (see Fig. 3). The various types of yachts are discussed in Chapter III, but it suffices to say here that the basic principles of yacht design remain the same. The hull must have the properties listed above in varying relative proportions according to the uses to which she is going to be put.

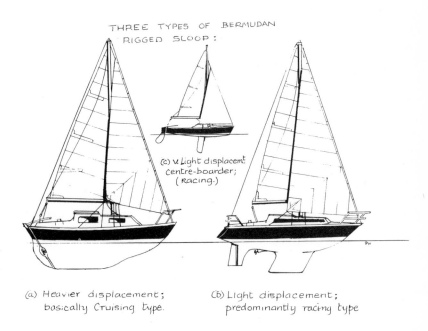

THREE TYPES OF BERMUDAN RIGGED SLOOP:

(c) V. Light displacem‡ centre-boarder; (Racing.)

(a) Heavier displacement; basically Cruising type.

(b) Light displacement; predominantly racing type

Fig. 3

So far we have studied why sails propel a yacht and what is the optimum shape for such a yacht so that her sails may drive her as easily as possible. Most yachts today are about three times as long as they are broad; the length being the length along the water-line when the ship is normally loaded (the load water-line—L.W.L.). The draught of a yacht (unless she is a centre-board craft) will be approximately one-fifth of the L.W.L. Thus, roughly speaking, for a yacht whose displacement tonnage (the weight of water she displaces when afloat) is 2 tons, the measurements will be: L.W.L. 20 feet, beam 7 feet, draft 4 feet. For a large yacht, say, of $8\frac{1}{2}$ tons' displacement, the proportions would be about as follows: L.W.L. 27 feet, beam 9 feet, draught 5 feet. So far we have mentioned displacement tonnage, but in addition to this term, there are two other terms (also tonnage) by which yachts are distinguished—the Net Registered Tonnage and the Thames or Yacht Measurement Tonnage. The Net Registered Tonnage is the measurement of the carrying capacity of the vessel less allowances for spaces used in the navigation and handling of the ship. If your yacht is a registered British ship, the figure of so many tons Net Register will be carved on her main beam. This figure will be recorded in Lloyd's Register of yachts, and it is on this figure that harbour dues, etc., are paid. The Thames (or Yacht Measurement) Tonnage is not strictly a weight. It is a figure obtained by a formula and used to express the actual size of a yacht. The formula is: when L=length on deck from the fore side of the stern to the after side of the stem post, and B=the extreme beam:

$$\frac{(L - B) \times B \times \frac{1}{2}B}{94} = \text{Thames Tonnage.}$$

For example: if L=20 and B=7, the Thames Tonnage will be about $3\frac{1}{4}$ tons; and when yachting people speak of a '3 tonner', it conjures at once in their minds the image of a little vessel of just such proportions as these.

A major design development in recent years has occurred in the profile. The rudder, which used to be a moveable extension of the keel is now frequently separate, hung on its own right aft, often with a skeg ahead of it. Cruising/Racing yachts compete against each other using a rating indicating their speed potential. This is the International Offshore Rule (I.O.R.). Advertisements for yachts for sale often give this I.O.R. Rating, sometimes the Thames Measurement tonnage, and sometimes just a few measurements; like length, beam and draught.

CHAPTER II

THE HULL, SPARS, SAILS, RIGS, AND RIGGING OF A SAILING YACHT

NOWADAYS boats may be built of a number of materials: wood, steel, plywood, glass-fibre reinforced plastic. The last is by far the most commonly found. However, many wooden craft are still built and indeed many yachtsmen prefer them; and to understand thoroughly wooden building teaches us a very great deal about the general shape and construction of a yacht. We will therefore begin by considering a typical wooden-built vessel and take a look at glass-fibre later.

Let us imagine we are standing in front of a small yacht. Assume that we know nothing as yet of yachts, but we are fortunate in having with us a friend who is going to show us the parts of the little vessel. We will begin with the hull. This is the boat's body. It is made up of planking (in a wooden vessel) laid on timbers (or frames) which are like the ribs of a human being. The hull is built on a long, tough piece of wood called the keel. Attached to the bottom of this, is another piece of wood. This is called the false keel. Rising from the keel on either side are the timbers. To these timbers are attached the planks which form the hull. Planking of a yacht may be fastened on to the timbers in three principal ways, called clinker (or clencher) building, carvel building, and diagonal building. There are other methods of construction, which will be discussed later, which employ the use of metal alloys, synthetic materials, or the moulded type of hull used widely in the building of racing dinghies. For the purpose of learning our way about the yacht, however, let us stick to these three principal ways of joining the planks to the frames of the vessel.

First, then, we will take the clinker method of building. Here the planks are fastened so that they overlap one another.

They are held to the timbers by nails, preferably of copper, which are driven through the planks and then 'clenched' over washers called roves. In carvel construction, however, the planks are laid edge to edge. The edges meet in a V shape with the widest part of the V towards the water. To prevent the water getting into the boat, the V spaces are fitted with material known as caulking cotton. Then stopping (like putty) is put on top of that and the whole hardened down. Two or three good coats of marine paint complete the process, and the hull does not leak. In the last of our types of building, 'diagonal', the boats have two skins. The planking of one skin runs diagonally across the hull in the opposite direction to the planking of the other. Sometimes the inner skin is diagonal while the outer skin runs parallel with the keel. Diagonal built boats do not require caulking and are very strong. They are, however, for obvious reasons, much less simple to repair than clinker or carvel boats.

Now, let us look at our boat. To take the 'blunt end' or stern first. The plank across the stern is called the transom. At the back end of the keel and underneath the boat is the rudder. The rudder is a shaped board, straight along the forward edge and curved along the after edge, and attached to a rod, known as the rudder post, about which it pivots. If the rudder post is fastened outside the transom, the rudder is said to be 'outboard' but if it is an 'inboard' rudder post, it moves in a hollowed space called the rudder trunk. At the top of the rudder is the 'head', and fastened to this is the tiller, an arm which extends forward, and by means of which the rudder is moved from side to side, causing the ship to change direction in the water. The part of the keel immediately in front of the rudder is called the deadwood.

Now, let us walk round to the front of the boat. This is called the bow, and the foremost part of it consists of a strong piece of wood termed the stem. The bow can be a number of different shapes. It may be straight stemmed, or spoon shaped, with varying degrees of 'overhang'. As we have seen, the back part of the boat is called the stern. The stern may also be a variety of shapes, the principal ones being transom, canoe, or counter. (See Figs. 4 and 5.)

The front part of the boat is called the forward (pronounced

TYPES OF STERN.

1. TRANSOM.

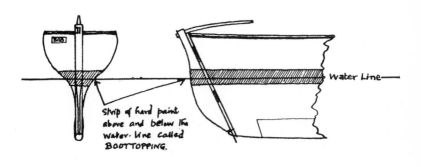

Water Line——

Strip of hard paint above and below the Water-line called BOOTTOPPING.

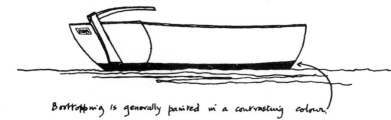

Boottopping is generally painted in a contrasting colour.

2. CANOE.

short overhang.   long overhang.

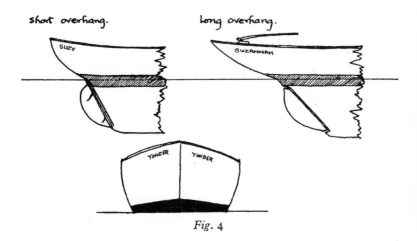

Fig. 4

for-ard) part, and anything in the general direction of the bow is said to be fore or forward. Anything in the general direction of the stern is said to be aft or after. It would be correct to say that the anchor is 'forward' of the mast, but incorrect to

TYPES OF STERN

3. COUNTER

Two Types of modern (short) Counter.

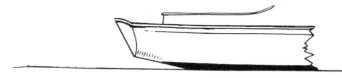

Old-fashioned long Counter.

Fig. 5

say the rudder is 'aft' of the mast. In the second case, the right expression is 'abaft' the mast. Anything inside the vessel is 'inboard', anything outside her is 'outboard'.

The deck is the term given to the layer of planking that covers the top of the boat extending from one side to the other. In all boats, except open boats and half-decked boats, the deck has a hole in it aft where the helmsman and crew sit. This is called the cockpit. The boat may or may not have a cabin; if it is decked all over except for the cockpit, it probably will. Sometimes, in fact, generally speaking with small vessels, the deck has a raised part in the centre of the boat called the coach roof. This gives extra head-room in the cabin below. In larger yachts, this is unnecessary. In very large yachts, particularly motor yachts, of, say, 500 tons or so, there will be more than one deck, just as there are in passenger liners. Any horizontal layer of this nature in a ship is called a deck. The under-side of the deck is called the deck-head. The deck consists of planks running fore and aft fastened onto beams which run in a gentle vertical curve from one side of the ship to the other. Around the edge of the cockpit runs the coaming, and where the cabin top is raised, this coaming extends forward to form the sides of the coach-roof. Onto these sides is built the coach-roof itself, the beams of which will also run in a vertical curve, which, though gentle, may be more pronounced than the deck beams.

Where the coach-roof or skylights are built onto the deck, the deck beams are cut down to allow for the space required in the decks, and two strong pieces of wood are fastened at right angles to these 'half-beams'. These two pieces of wood are called 'carlines'.

In yacht building today, more and more use is being made of synthetic materials, and of alloys in the construction particularly of masts. Alloy hulls, too, are to be found in increasing numbers. But many people still prefer wood. In the construction of wooden yachts, the following materials are in general use:

Grown timbers—oak.
Steamed timbers—American elm, rock elm, oak.
Keels—elm, oak.
Planking and Decks—afromosia, mahogany, mevanti, pitch-pine, Oregon pine, Columbian pine, yellow pine, sapele, teak, utile, western red cedar.
Masts—Californian silver spruce, sitka spruce, Douglas fir.

Now to return to our hull. We saw earlier that the planking of the hull is fastened to timbers. These timbers may consist of grown frames (frames that grow in the right shape naturally— like the crooks of oak) or steamed timbers (frames made from wood which has to be bent into shape under steam). The planking is fastened to them by screws or, more usually, by boat nails, sometimes of galvanised iron, but in yacht building far more generally of copper. The nails are driven through, then a washer, called a rove, is placed over the end and the latter knocked back (clenched) over the rove. In small yachts of, say, from 2 to 4 tons, usually all the timbers are steamed and placed at about 6 inches apart. In larger craft it is usual to find two steamed timbers at 6-inch intervals between a grown frame. The timbers are attached to the keel by means of floors. These are generally of either oak or iron.

Sometimes yachts are built in what is called 'composite construction'. This means, generally speaking, that the frames are of metal while the planking (or skin) is of wood. To give stability to a yacht, a shaped piece of metal is set into the keel at the very bottom. This is known as the ballast keel and is made of lead or iron. It is fastened to the keel by long keel bolts. In boat building, great care has to be taken to see that the correct metals are used and that the metals are not placed near one another, which would set up electrolytic action in the water and rapidly cause corrosion. An example of this would be if a copper sheathing (a covering of the underwater body against marine worm) were to be fastened by means of iron nails. (I have known this to be done, with curiously unhappy results!) The tops of the timbers are fastened to two strong planks called deck shelves. These run on either side of the ship, from right aft, forward. Also running forward from aft and attached on the inboard side of the vessel, but much lower down towards the keel, are two similar pieces of wood termed the bilge stringers. The beams in front of, and behind and nearest to, the mast are called the main beams. To these, right-angled pieces of stout wood (usually oak) or of metal are attached to give strength. Those which connect the beams to the timbers or frames are called hanging knees. Those which connect the beams to the deck shelf are called lodging knees. Many yachts are built in wood using synthetic resin glues; a process which is called 'hot' or 'cold' moulding, the latter being the most common. It makes use of thin wood veneers glued in strips. Such a method produces a strong and light hull, but it is expert's

work. Easier for amateur building are the kits of sheet plywood, cut ready to shape, and which can be glued (and
screwed) together. But you can buy the whole hull if you
want (in wood or in G.R.P.) and complete the rest; a good
method of saving money and needing only modest carpentry
skill. Aluminium alloy is not for amateurs, but as the lightest
of all building materials, it has plenty of supporters. High
tensile steel and reinforced concrete may also be used.

Let us now take a look at the construction of a boat in reinforced plastics. This is a relatively new method, but great
advances have been made in it; and new techniques are continually being developed. It disposes of the evils of rot and worm
—great advantage. A method which gives great strength is that
of resin–glass construction, using a resin–glass laminate which is
laid up either by hand or by spray.

In moulding a hull a polyester resin is used. This starts in
the form of a clear, sticky fluid. To make this set hard a catalyst
must be added, a process known as curing. This takes about 14
days, during which time various other substances are added in
order to make the resin strong, to make it opaque and to give
it the desired colour. Glass fibre can be woven into various types
of cloth. It is made up of a lot of filaments of spun glass; each
filament being about one ten-thousandth of an inch in thickness.
For boat building the fibres are usually cut into lengths of two
or three inches and made into what is termed a random mat;
the strands in the mat being arranged at all different angles to
take strains in all directions and give strength. Glass fibre itself
is immensely tough, having a tensile strength of several times
comparatively that of steel.

To make a yacht hull in reinforced plastic we use a prepared
mould. It is the mould that gives resin–glass the smooth finish
which it would not have on its own. The hull is 'laid up wet' inside the mould, the smooth surface being to the outside. With
boats of more than 20 feet in length the mould will usually be
split in two longitudinally and the two halves are later bolted
together. The inside of the mould must be waxed to prevent the
hull from sticking to it.

Next a coat of resin is applied to the mould and allowed to gel.
After this comes a coat of resin into which is laid a ready-made

sheet of fibre-glass mat which must be carefully pressed into every corner of the mould. The process is then repeated until the desired thickness is achieved.

Now wooden stringers, ribs, etc., may be moulded in. These parts can also be of metal or plastic covered with resin–glass laminate. Again, thwarts, gunwhale capping, can now be moulded in; or again, bulkheads, cabin top, decks—all pre-moulded, (depending on the type and size of the vessel).

The hull will by now be as far forward as it is possible to take it at this stage and must be allowed to set for about 14 days.

Designers of yachts who intend to use reinforced plastic construction can arrange for water and fuel tanks to be moulded into the hull; quite an advantage. I have described briefly the resin–glass laminate method of building but, as I said, plastic construction methods are in a state of continual development; for example, the use of plastic foam slabs reinforced on either side with resin–glass—a method called the sandwich method which is favoured by some for reasons both of strength and buoyancy.

Now let us consider the mast and spars. These may be made of wood or metal. New boats will usually have metal (alloy) masts. The mast is a round or oval-shaped pole fixed vertically in the ship and on which are hoisted the sails. The top of it is called the truck. Where it passes between the main beams of a wooden deck, it is strengthened by two pieces of wood wedged between those beams called partners. The mast is held in place at this part of it, by wooden or rubber wedges.

The mast has a projection on its lower end which fits into a groove in a strong piece of timber fixed to the top of the keel. This is called the mast step. The part of the mast between the deck and the mast step—that part, in fact, inside the vessel—is called the mast housing.

The second largest spar is the boom. One end of this is attached to the mast so that it may pivot from it freely. The metal attachment by which it is secured to the mast is called the gooseneck. With wooden masts, this fits into a metal hoop on the mast called the mastband. In gaff-rigged vessels, the next largest spar is the gaff. The gaff has a jaw fitting at its lower end which rides up and fits round the mast, allowing the gaff to pivot as freely as the boom. The top of the sail is laced to the gaff. Vessels which carry the large balloon sails, called spin-nakers, will carry also a spar used to spread it known as the spinnaker boom, the function of which will be elaborated later. In some boats, a spar projects forwards from the bow, to which is attached the topmast-stay, sometimes called the jib-stay be-cause on it is set the jib. This projecting spar is called the bow-sprit. As with the mast, the inboard part of the bowsprit (that part of it which lies inside the area of the ship's deck) is called the housing. The bowsprit is held in position inboard between two stout pieces of oak called knight heads. It has an iron band on the outboard end of it, to which are secured the foretopmast-stay, and the bob-stay, a stay running downwards from a point underneath the bowsprit to a point low down on the stem or bow of the boat. Nowadays, with smaller and 'inboard' sail plans, bowsprits are seen much less frequently.

In the days of square rig, the sails were known by the mast or stay on which they were set. For example: the mainsail was the sail set on the mainmast, the fore-staysail was the sail set on the fore-stay, the topsail on the topmast. Nowadays, the terms are employed more loosely, and in the case of a sloop (with a single headsail in front of the mast) the sail forward of the mast will frequently be called the jib, although, in fact, it is set from the fore-stay, and should, correctly, be called the fore-staysail.

Now, let us examine the rigging of our boat. Rigging is of two kinds: standing rigging and running rigging. The defini-tions are self-explanatory. Standing rigging is rigging that stands throughout the season (apart from minor adjustments). Running rigging is rigging that runs through blocks and is continually being hauled on or 'eased' (slackened). To take standing rigging first: this is made of flexible steel wire (the best being stainless). It is whippy and immensely strong. Experiments in the aircraft industry have produced wire of great tensile strength, and modern wire rigging is of far smaller diameter than it used to be. Uffa Fox, a well-known author-ity, says that the combined strength of the topmast and main shrouds should equal the displacement of the yacht. When wire passes round a spar, or a block, or is joined to a rigging screw, it will have to be spliced. The standing rigging is held to the deck by means of lanyards or rigging screws. Which you have is a matter of taste. Rigging screws are of several kinds, but they all operate on the same principle. There are two male screw members, with threads running in opposite directions and a female screw member between them and which, when turned one way, approaches the two male members and separates them when turned the other way. In some rigging, the female member consists of two vertical struts joined at the ends. This is a poor type, as it gives no protection to the threads of the male members. Another type is a long thin band with holes in it, through which a bar may be inserted in order to get the leverage to turn it. But the best type of rigging screw consists of a barrel that has a nut cast in the centre of it, as well as a hole, so that it can be turned with an adjustable spanner. There should be some method of preventing the rigging screw from turning back of its own accord when under strain. The most commonly found method is by wire passing through the holes in the female member. Other methods are by inserting other pins through the female members, or by means of locking nuts at either end of the female member. This last method is the best. Rigging screws are made of gun-metal or galvanised iron and sometimes of strong alloys. The other method of attaching standing rigging to the boat's deck is by lanyards. The wire rigging is here spliced round a wooden or lignum vitae block called a dead-eye. A second dead-eye is shackled to a chain plate on the ship's side. In the dead-eyes are holes through which the hemp lanyard is passed several times and hauled taut, then turned round its own part and secured with the appropriate knot (for example, a clove-hitch—see 'Ropework and Ship's Husbandry', p. 229).

The chain plates are attached to the hull by bolts. They are, or should be, long enough to extend across several planks, and the bolts should pass through timbers, as well as planking for real security. They can be either outside or inside the planking. It is rather more expensive to have them inside but it gives the hull a smoother appearance. Next, let us consider the shrouds. The object of the shrouds is to secure the mast. Were they not there the mast would bend and break under the severe strains enforced upon it when the sails are full of wind. If the ship is

Bermuda-rigged, there are usually two or more sets of shrouds, one main pair running to a point about half-way up the mast, or in the case of a large vessel, about a third of the way up it, and another pair running either to the top of the mast or to a point about two-thirds of the way up it, in the case of a larger craft. This latter pair of shrouds do not, like the main shrouds, run directly from the deck to the mast, but are spread out from it by 'spreaders' set at right angles to the mast, so that up to the spreaders the shrouds are parallel with the mast, while above them they make an angle with the mast of the same degree as the main shrouds. In the case of large craft, a third pair of shrouds run up to a second pair of spreaders about two-thirds of the way up the mast. These proportions may be varied greatly, of course, with individual yachts, and the proportions and patterns of rigging I have stated are solely for the purpose of giving a general idea of the positioning of the shrouds about the mast. The number of spreaders depends, generally speaking, on the height of the mast. The shrouds are attached to the hull by the chain plates. Shrouds should be set up taut. The degree of tautness has always been a subject for controversy. Generally speaking, the tendency of inshore racing craft to have very taut rigging has spread to ocean racers and many types of cruisers, but there are still many who favour the old idea of elasticity. In the old square-rigged ships, the shrouds were never set up too tight for this reason. The old maxim used to be that shrouds should look taut to the eye, but not feel too taut with the hand. When a mast bends under pressure of wind, the windward shrouds which take the strain will be very taut, when the leeward shrouds will be appreciatively slack.

Next in order let us consider the stays. Running from the bow (or the outboard end of the bowsprit if there is one) to the top of the mast is the foretopmast-stay, and running from the stem head (whether there is a bowsprit or not) to a little over half-way up the mast, is the fore-stay. We have already seen that the stay connecting the bowsprit end with the stem is called the bob-stay. The foresail will be hanked (by means of hanks or spring hooks) to the fore-stay. This stay *should* be good and taut. Not only must it support the mast from forward, but when the foresail is full of wind it will cause the fore-stay to bend to leeward. This gives a slight curve to the leading edge of the sail, and it is clear that this curve should be as small as possible if the foresail is to function efficiently. A good general rule is that when the windward runner is set up and the foresail set, the fore-stay should be quite taut. When the vessel is under way, and sailing close-hauled and the foresail has wind in it, the fore-stay will take the slight leeward curve we have mentioned. When the mainsail is lowered and the runners are slackened off, the fore-stay can feel less taut to the hand. But only by trial and error can you determine the best degree of tension for your own particular craft.

The same principles apply for the foretopmast-stay, on which may be set the jib.

It is as well to remember, as a general picture, that by tightening the fore-stays you bend the mast forwards, and vice versa. If they are too slack, not only will the sails have too marked a curve in their leading edges, but the pull of the runners and the weight of the mainsail (when sailing close-hauled) will make the mast bend aft. Bending is not the same as raking, which is the term given to the angle the mast makes (usually aft) with the vertical from the deck. The question of rake is a matter of some controversy amongst designers.

Finally—the runners. Although most modern yachts, with mast-head rig and standing backstays, do not have runners, you are still likely to find boats which do, and we must consider them here. These have a dual function. Firstly, they support the mast against the forward pull of the mainsail when the wind is abaft the beam, and secondly, when sailing to windward, they help to keep the fore-stay taut, and thereby to prevent the jib's leading edge from curving to leeward. The runners lead from two points on the after side of the mast (opposite the point on the forward side from which the forestay runs) to two points on the deck on either side of the cockpit.

If a vessel has more than one headsail and the jib is set on a topmast-stay, there may well be another pair of runners higher up the mast to take this additional pull. Frequently, in this event, the two runners join half-way down on either side of the mainsail in a single line. These extra runners are normally only found where the topmast-stay runs to a point some feet below

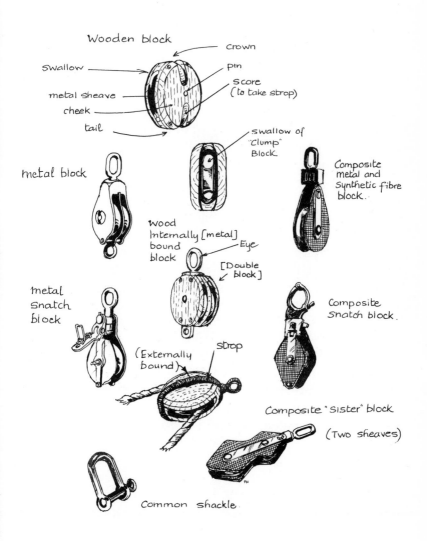

Wooden block
Crown
Swallow
Pin
Score (to take strop)
metal sheave
cheek
tail

metal block

swallow of "Clump" Block

Composite metal and Synthetic fibre block.

Wood Internally [metal] bound block
Eye
[Double block]

metal Snatch block

Composite Snatch block.

(Externally bound)
Strop

Composite "Sister" block
(Two sheaves)

Common shackle.

Fig. 6

the top of the mast. Where the stay runs to the top, the forward pull on the mast is taken normally by another stay, called the standing back-stay, which runs from the after side of the top of the mast to a point on the transom right aft. Standing back-stays are tightened by means of a rigging screw near the deck. Of course, it is only possible to have a standing back-stay when the boom stops short of the counter, or if a small bumpkin, projecting beyond the counter, is fitted. The expression 'standing back-stay' differentiates it from the running back-stays, an alternative name (commonly found in the U.S.A.) for runners. Runners are tautened or slackened either by metal levers, or by winches or by rope tackles or purchases. Levers have the advantage of putting exactly the same tension on the runner each time. The advantage of a purchase is that the degree of tension can be varied at will, *e.g.*, they can be eased off a little in light airs, so as to slacken the fore-stay and so give the fore-sail a little more fullness. Where a purchase is used, the normal method is to have the eyes in which the runners terminate working on tracks or wire spans running fore and aft along the side decks. When sailing, the weather runner is kept taut and the lee runner slack. In most yachts there is at least one pair of winches, of the horizontal rotating drum type, situated one on either side of the cockpit. The fall of the runner purchase can be brought to the winch if the force of the breeze prevents one getting the proper tension on it. The third method of tautening or setting up a runner is by means of purchases. With this, we progress from standing to running rigging. Indeed runners provide a perfect transition from the one type of rigging to the other, since they are part standing—and part running.

First of all then—purchases. Purchases give increased power to the man hauling on a rope. They consist of a length of rope running through two or more blocks. A block consists of an outer shell of wood or metal or plastic. In the hollow interior, called the swallow (see Fig. 6), a pulley revolves about a pin. A wooden block, with a rope or wire strap round its exterior, fitting into grooves at the top (crown) and the bottom (tail) of the 'shell', is called a 'common' block. An 'internal bound' block has an iron strop inside the shell. The best wooden blocks are made of ash internally bound, and most people agree that

Increasing power by the use of tackles.

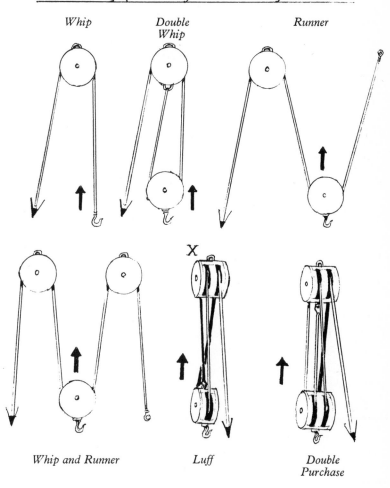

Whip *Double Whip* *Runner*

X

Whip and Runner *Luff* *Double Purchase*

Fig. 7

they look the most attractive when clean, bright, and properly varnished. They are, of course, expensive. The blocks with straps round (externally bound) are much cheaper. Blocks for small yachts are nowadays also made from strong synthetic fibre, a very good and proved brand of which is the Tufnol block.

When buying wooden blocks, they are described by their length. The length of a block should be three times the circumference of the rope, if the latter is to run easily; and nothing is more annoying than a rope which is too large for a block and which consequently sticks, particularly in wet weather! In the case of wire rope, the diameter of the sheave should be five times the circumference of the rope.

Now a rope is run through a block for two reasons: to alter the direction of the pull, and to increase the power of that pull. The object of a purchase is to give the man exerting the pull additional mechanical power. Look at Fig. 7: the single whip, it will be noticed, gives no additional power; it simply changes the direction of the pull. The runner, however, is the single whip reversed. Here the single block can move. One end of the line is fixed and the other is the hauling part. By attaching the hook on the block to whatever is required to be lifted or moved, the power gained is double. This is the simplest form of purchase or tackle. Look now at Fig. 7 again. Here are shown: a whip and runner combined, a double whip, and a luff tackle, and a double purchase and a double whip and runner. A double whip, it will be seen, consists of a single wire rove through two single blocks, the standing part of the line being made fast to the tail of the upper block, the lower block being the moving block. This gives double power. A luff tackle gives the hauler three or four times the power, depending on whether the single or the double block is the moving block. If the double block is the moving block, the power gained is four times. (Twice as much as a runner.) The principle of the whole thing is quite simple. Where a single block is used which does not move, only the direction of pull results. As soon as a moving block is rigged, power increases to the hauler in direct proportion to the number of moving blocks, or (as in the case of a luff tackle) the number of sheaves in those blocks. The most usual tackles used

THE CLEAT.

Wooden cleat
viewed from above.

viewed from side.

Belaying a Rope round a Cleat.

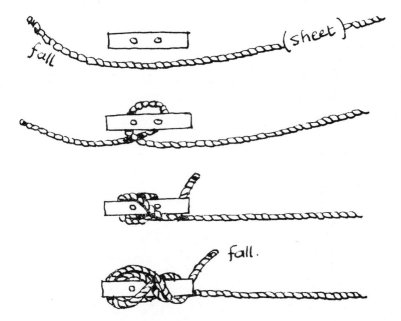

fall

(sheet)

fall.

[The fall may be coiled alongside, or if
the cleat is on a mast, coiled and
hung on the cleat.]

Fig. 8

to set up runners or back-stays on a yacht, are the double whip in small yachts, and the luff in larger yachts. Blocks and tackles are also used in the arrangement of the main sheet, by means of which the mainsail is trimmed. Main sheets are generally of two kinds, single-ended or double-ended, usually the latter. With a single-ended main sheet, one end of the sheet is secured to the boom or to the deck, and the other end leads to a cleat in the cockpit or on the outside of the cockpit coaming. With a double-ended sheet, both ends of the sheet lead to the cockpit. The advantage of this is that the sheet can be trimmed or let fly on either side of the cockpit. It is, however, less simple than the single-ended sheet.

The main sheet usually has the lower, centre block travelling on a horse. This enables the boom to be trimmed to a point on deck directly beneath it, thus making the sail flatter and of a better shape, aerodynamically speaking. In the case of a gaffsail, it stops the gaff sagging away to leeward.

If the yacht has an outboard rudder, the 'horse' will have to run over the top of the tiller. The size of tackle required depends on the size of the mainsail, but as a rough guide: a mainsail of 500 to 600 square feet can be trimmed properly with a four-part purchase.

The main sheet can be rigged in a variety of ways. A good double-ended form is a double block on the boom with a single block running on a horse and two single blocks on deck, through which the two running parts are led.

Now to take a look at the halliards. This is the name given to all the ropes with which the sails are hoisted. This name is derived from the days of square rig when the sails were attached to 'yards', and it was the yards which were hoisted by the 'haulyards' (halliards). On Bermudan-rigged craft, there is one halliard for the mainsail, and one for as many headsails as there are. On a gaff-rigged vessel, the mainsail requires two halliards, as there is a halliard to 'peak up' the gaff in addition to one to hoist the inboard end of it. Headsails, that is, the sails in front of the mast, are hoisted by the head. When the sails are hoisted, the halliards are prevented from slipping back by twisting them round a cleat (see Fig. 8)—a procedure known as belaying from the old days when halliards were twisted round belaying pins. Cleats are generally made of wood and are found on the mast, on deck in various positions, and on the sides of the cockpit coaming aft. In a gaff-rigged craft (I take this example as it is more complicated than Bermudan), the peak halliard would probably be a single block on the gaff and another on the mast. The standing part of the halliard would be shackled to an eyebolt on the mast. In other words, a whip and runner (power of two). A jib or foresail halliard will, in a small yacht, say, 5 tons, be a single whip giving no added power. If the headsails are larger, a good method is to have a block on the head of the sail, through which the halliard passes, the standing part being secured on deck. This gives a power of two.

Attached to the bottom inboard corner of each headsail are two ropes called sheets, by means of which the sails are trimmed. Attached to the outboard end of the boom and running through blocks to give leverage, and so to the cockpit, is the main sheet, by means of which the mainsail is trimmed. Running from the outboard end of the boom to a sheave or block high up on the mast, and so down to a cleat at the foot of the mast, is the topping lift. This is used to keep the boom off the deck when the mainsail is not hoisted, and to raise the boom slightly on occasion; like when hoisting the mainsail (so that the sail may be well and truly hoisted) or when rolling badly when sailing before the wind.

Next let us turn our attention to the sails. For the purpose of our illustration we will assume that our boat is a gaff-rigged sloop (see Fig. 9). Once again I take gaff rig as an example. Although far less common, it is more complicated, and so serves as a more thorough illustration. There are, we see, two working sails. A large, four-sided sail hoisted abaft the mast, called the mainsail, and a small, triangular sail forward of the mast called the fore-stay-sail. (Also called frequently, but as we have seen earlier, erroneously, the jib.) The mainsail is fixed to the boom and to the gaff, and along its forward edge to hoops which slide up and down the mast. The top of the mainsail, which is attached to the gaff, is called the head. The bottom of the sail, attached to the boom, is called the foot. The forward edge with the mast hoops is called the luff, and the remaining (after) edge, the leech.

The corner between the luff and the head is called the throat. The corner between the head and leech is called the peak. The corner between the luff and the foot is called the tack, and the corner between the leech and the foot is called the clew.

In the four corners of the sail, small brass rings are sewn. These are called cringles. About 18 inches or so above the foot of the sail there is a row of short lengths of line fixed at regular intervals in the sail and extending on either side of it. These are

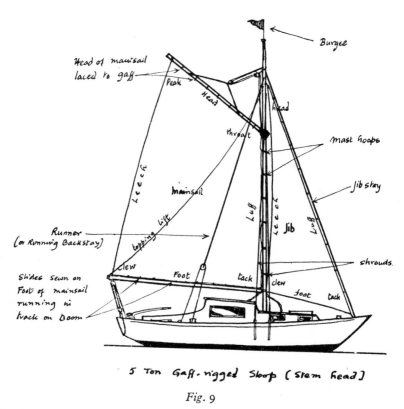

Head of mainsail laced to gaff

Peak

Head

Head

Burgee

throat

mast hoops

Jib stay

Leech

mainsail

Luff

Leech

Jib

Luff

luff

topping

Runner (or Running Backstay)

shrouds

clew

Foot

tack

clew

foot

tack

Slides sewn on Foot of mainsail running in track on Boom

5 Ton Gaff-rigged Sloop (Stem head)

Fig. 9

the reef points by means of which the sail is reefed, as we shall see later. There are usually three of these rows each about 2 feet above the other. There are further cringles in line with each row of reef points in the luff, and in the leech of the sail. They are known as reef cringles.

We have talked so far of a gaff mainsail. In the case of a Bermudan (or triangular) mainsail, the parts of the sail are the

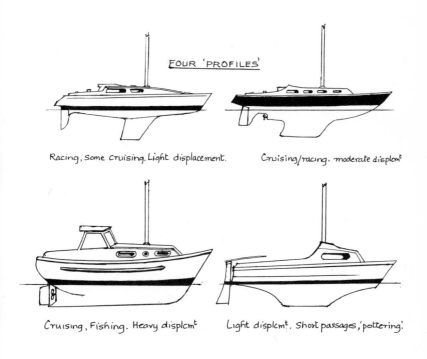

FOUR 'PROFILES'

Racing, some cruising. Light displacement.

Cruising/racing. moderate displcmᵗ

Cruising, Fishing. Heavy displcmᵗ

Light displcmᵗ. Short passages, 'pottering'.

Fig. 10

same, except that there is no throat and no peak, simply a head, which is the name given to the top corner (the corner between the luff and the leech). Bermudan mainsails do not have hoops but metal slides along the luff which run in a track on the mast.

In Great Britain we term this sail a Bermudan sail, deriving the name from the triangular or 'leg o' mutton'-shaped sails of the early sailing craft indigenous to that lovely island. In the U.S.A., however, the same rig is called a marconi rig, so named because the complex nature of the mast rigging of this type of rig resembles a wireless mast. A further point of dispute is that some people call the sail 'Bermudian'. So far as I know, there are no statutes controlling this terminology! There is much controversy between devotees of the two rigs. It has been proved by wind-tunnel experiments that the maximum driving power of a sail is developed along its leading edge. The high narrow Bermuda sail-plan which has a longer leading edge than a gaff-sail has more driving power to windward, and is superior to the gaffsail in this respect. On the other hand, from a cruising standpoint, working to windward in these days of auxiliary power is not the absolute criterion. Furthermore, if the wind is abaft the beam, the gaffsail develops more drive than the Bermudan. The Bermudan sail has no gaff to sag underway and is easier to reef and calls for less man-power in handling. On the other hand, the gaffsail with its hoops runs easily up the mast, while a warped track on a Bermudan mast can be a disaster. In general, the Bermudan sail's development is 10 per cent more efficient than a gaffsail of equivalent area, but with the former, the tall mast can be a big responsibility in a seaway. However, almost all ocean racers have Bermudan sails these days and lose very few masts.

The headsails are termed in the same way as a Bermudan mainsail. The headsails are hoisted by halliards which run through blocks high up in the fore part of the mast. They are attached to the fore-stay (in the case of the fore-staysail) and the topmast-stay (in the case of the jib) by means of spring hooks (called, sometimes, 'hanks').

To help the mainsail to keep a regular flat, unbroken curve, there are battens let into the after end of it. These stop the leech curling inwards and ruining the aerodynamic shape of the sail. Battens are long, thin, whippy strips of wood or plastic, which slide into pockets in the leech, and are then tied into position by wires that run through cringles and through holes in the outboard end of the battens. Another method is to have a slot above the batten pocket in the sail through which the batten enters before dropping securely into the pocket.

Having learned the names of the principal parts and fittings of a ship, we can now turn our attention to a few of the essential items of gear. The first, and perhaps most obvious of these, is the anchor, together with the anchor chain, called the cable. In the chapter that deals with moorings, etc., the various types of anchors are dealt with in detail. Suffice to say here that there

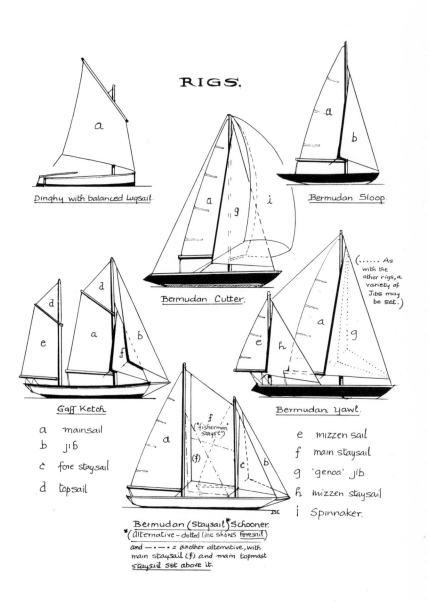

RIGS.

Dinghy with balanced Lugsail.

Bermudan Sloop.

Bermudan Cutter.

(...... As with the other rigs, a variety of Jibs may be set.)

Gaff Ketch.

Bermudan Yawl.

a   mainsail
b   jib
c   fore staysail
d   topsail

e   mizzen sail
f   main staysail
g   'genoa' jib
h   mizzen staysail
i   Spinnaker.

Bermudan (Staysail) Schooner.
* (alternative - dotted line shows foresail)
and —·—·= another alternative, with main staysail (f) and main topmast staysail set above it.

Fig. II

will probably be two anchors aboard our boat—a large anchor and a small one, called a kedge. The large anchor is attached to the cable. The small anchor is unattached, but when required to be used, is secured to a long length of light line. Being light, it is much easier to pull up than the big fellow, and is very useful if you have to anchor for a short while anywhere—to pick up someone from shore in the dinghy, to have lunch in an attractive cove, to wait for the tide to turn, for safety in foggy weather, or a hundred other such reasons.

The cable is a length of chain. The length of it, and the size of the links varies with different-sized vessels. In a 6-tonner cruising yacht, say, there would probably be about 25 fathoms of chain. (One fathom = 6 feet.) One end of the cable is shackled onto the ring of the anchor, and the other end is fastened to a ring bolt on the keelson. The cable is stored below decks in the 'cable locker', and runs up to the deck through a navel pipe or chain pipe. Attached to the stem head is a metal roller or a fair-lead, through which the cable runs out when the anchor has been thrown over the side. In some yachts there are fair-leads near the stem head on both port and starboard sides. Large yachts with high gunwales have holes cut round these fair-leads to permit the cable to run through. Although ordinary fair-leads will suffice, it is far better to have a roller.

Among other items of gear we should expect to find on board are: a boathook for picking up mooring buoys, etc.; a deck mop; cork, rope, or rubber fend-offs, or fenders, for protecting the vessel when lying alongside; mooring ropes; and lengths of light line including a lead line (which will be explained later). Navigation (red and green, port and starboard) lights may or may not be permanently fixed in suitable positions reasonably high above the water-line, but they should be on board with the gear.

There should also be in a cruising vessel the necessary gear for cooking and eating, sleeping below decks. Finally, there will probably be an engine. If there is, don't touch it until you have studied the handbook on it, and even then, don't touch it until you have learned to sail. An engine is of invaluable use to the experienced yachtsman, but is a menace to a learner. The temptation to 'turn on the mechanical topsail' is very strong.

You should never be dependent on your engine. Learn first to handle your ship in all situations under sail. It is, after all, the fun of the whole thing to use your art and skill to make the wind do the work.

Now, we have so far dealt with the simple sloop rig. Considered from the viewpoint of aerodynamic efficiency, the simple sloop, or cutter, rig is the best. If ability to sail well to windward were the sole criterion, the sloop and the cutter have the advantage. There are, however, other considerations: suitability of rig to size of craft, ease of handling, accommodation below decks and the question of man power (crew) for example. (The largest sail area that one man can reasonably handle is 500 square feet.) There are five principal rigs found in yachts today: sloop, cutter, yawl, ketch, and schooner. There are modifications of these rigs, of course, like the single sail cat-boat of North America, or the balanced lug, or the wishbone ketch, and occasionally one finds square-rigged yachts. Broadly speaking, however, the rigs of yachts today fall into these five categories. Let us examine each one in turn.

The Sloop (Fig. 11). This rig has much to commend it. It is the simplest of rigs, consisting of a large mainsail and a single headsail. The mast being stepped nearer the bows than in a cutter, for example, enables the cabin below to be larger. This is a great point in favour of the rig for small vessels up to 5 tons (yacht measurement). The sloop rig is the easiest to handle, there being only one pair of headsail sheets. But there are disadvantages. In larger vessels, the forward positioning of the mast tends to make the vessel plunge in steep head-on seas. Furthermore, it is difficult to heave-to (see chapter on bad weather) in a sloop, because of the position of the mast in the ship.

The Cutter (Fig. 11). This is really the most efficient rig. The balance of the two headsails and mainsail makes for a beautiful performance to windward. The cutter rig is both handy and fast. But in larger yachts the size of the mainsail becomes a problem, and this is the disadvantage of the cutter.

The Yawl (Fig. 11). This represents an attempt to solve the problem of the large mainsail by dividing it into two sails, a mainsail and a very small mizzensail. It is popular in the larger cruising yachts and ocean racers. Like the sloop, the main mast being positioned slightly farther forward assists the accommodation below decks. The mizzensail has several separate uses too, and is particularly useful in holding the vessel's head to windward when hoisting the mainsail or riding out a gale to a sea anchor (see bad weather). Disadvantages? It is generally agreed that it is not as fast as a cutter to windward or quite as 'close-winded', and in very large yachts the mainsail is big enough to require just as much crew as a cutter, which, in turn, bring us to:

The Ketch (Fig. 11). This is an attempt still further to reduce the area of the mainsail, by making the mizzensail larger, and making the two sails much nearer the same size. However, although suitable in some cases for large cruising yachts, it must be conceded that this rig lacks the power of a cutter or a yawl when it comes to windward work.

The Schooner (Fig. 11). There is something romantic about the schooner rig. It has always been associated with pirates and smugglers and the South Pacific Islands. It is certainly a very beautiful rig aesthetically and is extremely popular in America. It is, however, a poor performer to windward, but makes up a lot if the wind is on or abaft the beam. It is a good rig for off-shore sailing, because in bad weather the mainsail can be stowed, and a trysail set on the mainmast. This has the effect of turning the schooner into a ketch, and brings the largest sail amidships, where it is most easily handled. The masts to some extent support each other, being joined aloft by the rigging.

Now a word on the old question of Bermudan rig versus gaff. This is so much a matter of personal taste that I think the best policy will be to state simply the case on both sides and leave it to the reader. Wind tunnel and other experiments have proved that the maximum driving power of a sail is developed when going to windward, along its leading edge. The high, narrow (high aspect ratio) sail-plan of the Bermudan rig must, by this token, have more driving power, and, when going to windward, is in this way superior to the gaff rig. Furthermore, there is no gaff to sag to leeward. The sail is easier to hoist and lower, and it is easier to reef and, generally, calls for less manpower to handle it.

The gaff rig, on the other hand, develops more drive when

the wind is on or abaft the beam. Further, in these days of auxiliary power, windward efficiency in a cruising yacht is not as important as it used to be. There are plenty of vessels built to-day, tough, seaworthy craft which embody many up-to-the-minute features, are constructed in glass reinforced plastics, and employ the gaff rig as being the most suitable for a certain type of Motor Fishing Vessel design.

The Bermudan mast being very tall can be a big responsibility in a seaway. However, it is only fair to add that almost all ocean racers nowadays have Bermudan rig, and many long off-shore passages are safely made with this rig in all weathers. The gaff rig still has it supporters, but for the majority to-day, it is Bermudan every time.

To enter into a discussion on the aesthetic merits of the two rigs would be inappropriate here, and with this wise, if cowardly, reservation, I will turn to another, possibly equally contentious matter; the growing popularity of the 'multi-hull'. By multi-hull yachts I mean the twin-hull type known as a catamaran (see Fig. 16) and the three-hull type called a trimaran. The chief advantage of these is a gain in average speed. This is achieved by designing the vessel so that a large area of sail can be carried without additional ballast weight. It is not a new idea and was known to the Pacific Islanders at the time of their discovery, and doubtless before that. Over the years experiments with these craft have resulted in the production today of fast, safe, seaworthy vessels, with, in the cruising form, fine craft with a remarkable degree of comfort below decks. The rig is usually either sloop or ketch. There is no doubt that with a reaching wind the multi-hull is faster than the single-hull yacht, and with sails correctly trimmed the former will cheerfully sail herself for hour after hour. On a close windward leg, however, the single-hull boat wins, as the lightweight multi-hull is slowed by the short head seas and she is much slower in stays. But when the wind is aft the multi-hull wins again; the twin hulls of the 'cat' cutting along in their twin grooves. Multi-hull craft sail very upright with little angle of heel and, of course, they can take the ground easily and float off as the tide makes—all points in their favour. When it comes to bad weather, though, and riding out gales there are many who prefer the single hull. I said the subject was contentious!

CHAPTER III

ON BUYING A YACHT AND THE FOUR PRINCIPAL TYPES OF SAILING YACHT

THE new-comer to yachting is faced with a bewildering array of widely differing types of yacht. Of course, in choosing a boat, finance obviously plays an important part. Dinghies cost less than half-deckers. Half-deckers cost less than small cabin cruisers. Small cabin cruisers cost less than ocean racers; and so on. But there are also other important considerations to bear in mind when choosing a boat. For example, the kind of cruising ground near your home, or, at all events, the locality in which you want to do your sailing, must inevitably affect your choice of a boat. If you live on the east coast of England and would be doing most of your sailing in those waters, you should choose a boat of shallow draft which is able to take the ground easily, because in many parts of the east coast there are delightful creeks and havens which, by reason of their shallow depth, can only be visited by shallow-draught yachts. On the other hand, if you are a west country man, who is going to find himself afloat in the deep water and the long rolling seas of the western part of the English Channel and the Atlantic Ocean, the best sort of boat for you would be a deep-draught vessel. Again, if your aim is cruising, comfort both at sea and in port is of importance. If your aim is sheltered-water racing, comfort doesn't really come into it. If ocean racing is your chief interest, comfort and room below must, to some extent, give way to the needs of the sport.

In short, you want to take advice. There are many pitfalls for the new-comer to yachting, and not the least of them are concerned with the choosing and buying of a boat. As a quick glance at the yachting periodicals will show, there are always lots of boats for sale. One can spend a ridiculous amount of

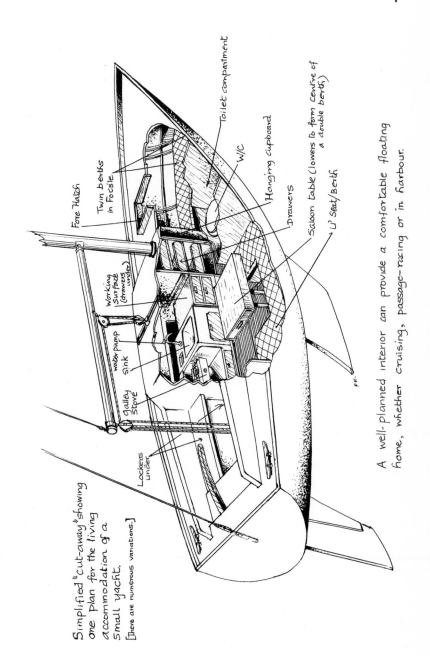

Simplified "cut-away" showing one plan for the living accommodation of a small yacht.
[There are numerous variations.]

Fore Hatch

Twin berths in Focsle

Working Surface (drawers under)

water pump

Sink

galley Stove

Lockers under

Toilet compartment

W/C

Hanging cupboard

Drawers

Saloon table (lowers to form centre of a double berth)

U Seat/Berth

A well-planned interior can provide a comfortable floating home, whether cruising, passage-racing or in harbour.

money travelling many miles to look at boats which appeared perfectly good on paper. What is much more serious, however, is a fact that a beginner may like a certain boat for, shall we say, her roomy cabin, without realising—perhaps not even bothering to look—that, before he can get her to sea, he must completely renew all the running and all the standing rigging, and possibly all the sails. By the time he gets his boat afloat, she will have cost him half as much again, if not twice as much.

So the first thing your sailing friend can tell you is whether or not your prospective boat is worth the expense of a survey. I cannot be too emphatic about the necessity of a survey. Structural weaknesses, rotten keel bolts, dry rot, and so forth, frequently only come to light under the scrutiny of a really experienced professional surveyor. Now the point here is—surveyors cost money. The charge varies, depending upon value; distance the surveyor has to travel; complexity of the survey, etc., and if the vessel is lying afloat must be added the cost of hauling her out, to examine the hull properly. Obviously, if the beginner is going to employ the services of a surveyor for every boat he likes the look of, he may soon find himself in the unhappy position of having spent the money he had earmarked for his yacht on a long list of unsatisfactory survey reports.

Here, then, is where your yachting friend can help. He will be able to tell you whether the boat of your dreams is generally sound, whether her sails are in reasonable condition, also her rigging; whether she looks well-balanced and would behave herself in a seaway—in fact, whether she is or is not worth the expense of a survey.

It is unhappily true that many of the boats for sale are not worth buying. An old boat can be painted to look almost like new, but once the germ of dry rot has got a hold of a ship, it is never completely certain that it has been eradicated. It is a mistake to be in too much of a hurry to buy a boat. The man selling you the boat will as likely as not tell you of her unique attractions and mention two or more rival purchasers, who, at that moment, are filling their fountain-pens and hunting for their cheque books. If this is the case, my advice is let them have her. No boat is perfect. All are a compromise. The hull may be exactly what you require, but the rigging unsatisfactory in some respects. Or again, the rigging may be modern and well-nigh perfect, the vessel may sail like the wind and handle like a thoroughbred, but when you go below, you are lucky if you have got kneeling head-room. The more boats you examine with your sailing friend, the more experience you will acquire in evaluating for yourself the points of each vessel. You will come to appreciate certain basic principles of design. For example, we have noted in Chapter I the normal proportions for a modern yacht—namely, that her water-line length is three times her breadth and her draught about a fourth of her waterline. It may be of use here, therefore, to the prospective purchaser of a yacht to discuss certain types of yacht and their essentials. But before leaving the question of the buying of a boat, I would just like to make one point more and make it emphatically.

Remember that you, as the buyer, have the upper hand. You can make the seller an offer. He is (presumably) eager to sell his boat, and by making an offer, you have placed him in something of a quandary. If he does not accept your offer, he may have lost the opportunity of a sale. On the other hand, you, remembering that there are as good fish in the sea as ever came out of it, can try somewhere else. Once you have found a boat that you, or you and your sailing friend together, really like and believe to be sound, make an offer subject to survey. There are many reasonable surveyors of yachts who advertise in the yachting press, and here again your sailing friend will no doubt prove helpful in the choice of a surveyor. If the vessel in question was brought to your notice by a firm of yacht brokers, you must make your offer through them. If your offer, subject to survey, is accepted by the owner of the vessel, you may obtain legal option of her by paying either the owner or his agent, 10 per cent of the agreed price. For survey, the vessel must be hauled out, if she is afloat or in a mud berth, so that the surveyor may examine her bottom and draw one or more keel bolts for inspection. This cost of hauling out is your liability. As I have indicated earlier, a good survey is not cheap, but I would emphasise that it is absolutely essential.

Now if the survey report is bad, you are of course under no liability to buy the boat. You have, it is true, incurred the

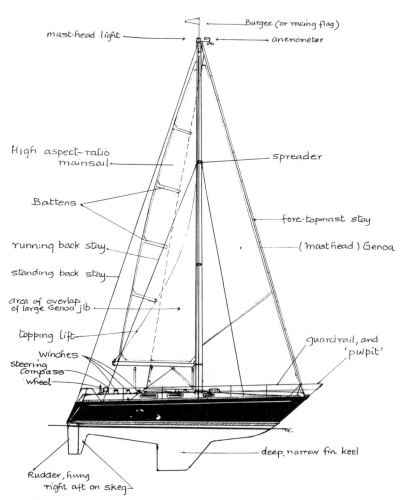

Burgee (or racing flag)

mast-head light

anemometer

High aspect-ratio mainsail

spreader

Battens

fore-topmast stay

running back stay

(masthead) Genoa

standing back stay

area of overlap of large Genoa jib

topping lift

guardrail, and 'pulpit'

Winches

steering Compass

Wheel

deep, narrow fin keel

Rudder, hung right aft on skeg

A fine type of Offshore Cruiser-racer. Fiberglass hull. Length 40 to 41 feet, say, twelve and a half metres. Approx I O R rating 10·2m (33·5 feet).

Fig. 12

expense of hauling out, the surveyor's fee and travelling expenses. However, if your sailing friend has examined the vessel carefully before you have made your offer, the chances of the survey report being completely bad are small; and if the surveyor has found certain faults, you can bring these to the owner's notice, and if he is a reasonable man he will put them right at his own expense; or alternatively, you can reduce your offer. In either case, the suveyor's fee will be well spent. In the somewhat unlikely event of there being no faults at all, it is still a satisfactory feeling to know that an expert has examined your ship and passed her AI—increasing, if possible, the pride of ownership, which by now will be near to boiling point.

Having dealt briefly with surveying and the purchase of a yacht, let us now turn our attention to some different types of vessel and examine the pros and cons. For the purposes of our examination, I have divided these as follows: the cruising yacht, the racing yacht, the dinghy, and the ocean racing yacht.

THE CRUISING YACHT

In any cruising boat the first requisite is that she shall be suited to the area in which she will be sailed. What should be the size of the cruising boat? This is a difficult question to answer, as there are a lot of limiting factors. The cost of maintaining a boat gradually increases with size, until we come to the vessel requiring paid hands, whereupon the expense suddenly goes up. When considering size, we are confronted with the familiar law of diminishing returns. In a boat less than thirty feet over all, one can enjoy fairly good cruising. In a boat forty feet over all, one may have more enjoyment and safety, but at a higher cost. A boat fifty feet over all may be luxurious, but the additional cost is frequently not proportionate to its value. The man of restricted means should not buy too large a boat. A cruising vessel should be as small as possible and still accommodate sufficient hands, give full head-room, and carry a dinghy on deck. Being able to carry a dinghy on deck is the limiting factor which determines the bottom of the size range. On any long cruise, towing a dinghy is nearly impossible, and cruising without a dinghy should be forbidden. Most dinghies are of no real value as a lifeboat, as in a sea which would wreck the cruising boat the dinghy would be useless; however, there should always be a means by which to leave the vessel in the case of fire or explosion (or leak which cannot be located!), and the dinghy provides this, as well as the essential communication with the shore when in port.

The first consideration in building cruising boats is strength. In bygone days the scantlings, planking, and deck of cruising vessels were all much heavier than those of racing craft. Now the purpose of weight is strength, but strength is possible without weight. Often a lightly built boat that is well built is stronger than a heavier-built boat which has been poorly constructed. We can establish the rule that a cruising boat should be strong, but that strength and weight are not the same and should not be confused. It is a good plan to have a deck as strong as the planking, because a boat with a lightly built deck may give way if a heavy sea should come aboard. Most cruising boats have short ends, for long overhangs fore and aft usually make bad sea boats. It is certainly a great effort, in a heavy sea, to drive a long-ended boat to windward. Another good reason for short ends is that a short-ended boat will usually lie at anchor more quietly.

However, you should not have 'too short' ends. The main purpose of forward and aft overhangs is so that the builder can draw out the lines, making all the water-lines longer and straighter than they would be otherwise. Also the sailing length of a vessel increases as she is heeled. A long-ended boat increases the sailing water-line length with the angle of heel. The added length allows her more stability, which increases in proportion to the need for it. Do not be in too great a hurry, therefore, to choose a boat with very short ends. An average overhang is preferable for cruising conditions.

The traditional cruising yacht had a long keel. Most racing boats, on the other hand, were built with a short, deep keel. A long-keel boat that will stay on her course without being constantly steered, is an easier boat to sail. The helmsman is free to leave the wheel or tiller, knowing the boat will hold her course, at least for a while. A long keel usually means a rather deep forefoot. A deep forefoot was always among the first considerations if the boat was to be used for off-shore work. A boat intended for off-shore use, must be the type that can be hove-to easily. But modern off-shore racers make very long passages in all weathers with fin keels, short ends, and high freeboard. This is the pattern of the 70s; a small underwater profile, fin keel and rudder right aft, and this trend has undoubtedly spread to cruising boats. Between the 'old' and the 'new' lie also many 'compromises'.

Rudders are hung right aft, usually on a skeg, or aft of the keel. Outboard rudders are found on some of the latest cruising boats. They are advantageous in long cruises, for in the case of an accident they can be repaired without having to haul the boat out, and the pintles and gudgeons can quite easily be examined.

Modern boats are usually built with large beam. This has the merit of giving good accommodations below decks, allowing plenty of working space on deck, and plenty of space for a dinghy to be stowed. In general, the large beam adds greatly to comfort and convenience. However, beam should always be considered in relation to length. The longer and straighter the water-lines of the boat, the more 'sea kindly' that boat will be. So beam should never be out of proportion.

The problems of accommodation and living on board will be studied in a later chapter, but we should consider one aspect of them here—the matter of head-room. There are two types: sitting head-room and standing head-room. One must be satisfied, on very small boats, with just enough head-room for the crew to sit upright on a bunk. One should look for full head-room on larger boats, for anything less than very full head-room is not enough. You may have more impression of space below in a boat of 5 feet 6 inches of head-room than in a boat of 5 feet head-room, but for obvious reasons, there will be more bumped heads and headaches in the boat of 5 feet 6 inches. The late E. F. Knight in his classic, *The Falcon on the Baltic*, said in defence of boats with only sitting head-room, 'If one wants to assume an erect position, one can always go on deck'. I do not personally agree. If I am to live aboard a cruising boat, I like to be able to stand upright in some part of her.

Every cruising yacht should have a self-draining cockpit. There is always the risk of pooping when running off before a heavy sea, and there should, therefore, be a method for getting rid of the water. A well-constructed self-draining cockpit will keep the water out of the boat. Without a self-draining cockpit, the boat must be pumped after every heavy rainstorm, although this is not a strong point. In extremely heavy rainstorms, over a long period, she would become water-logged, and damage would result.

THE RACING YACHT

If it is racing that claims your interest, before you decide on any one class of racing boat, take note of the most popular classes in the area in which you will be doing your sailing. It is best to have a boat which is popular in the vicinity because then you are certain to have a large fleet to race against. You will get better sport, and you learn more quickly. A racing yacht, however splendid she may be, is less valuable if she is the only one of her kind in the locality, or if there are only a very few similar yachts.

In this matter again, advice from the local yacht club is invaluable—because in the long run it is the many and varied local conditions which are most important when deciding on the most suitable small racing yacht in any given area. A primary decision you will have to make is whether you want a keel or a centreboard yacht. The keel boat is usually considered more seaworthy, and if well designed, it is practically impossible to capsize. It should not be categorically stated, however, that all keel boats are more seaworthy than all centreboarders. A centreboard yacht with large beam and enough freeboard can be a very stable vessel. Some light-ballasted centreboarders will plane, reaching far greater speeds than the fastest keel yachts, but these belong rather to the dinghy classes, which we will be discussing later.

However, keel yachts are not so affected by a choppy sea and are more forceful in driving through it. They give a feeling of

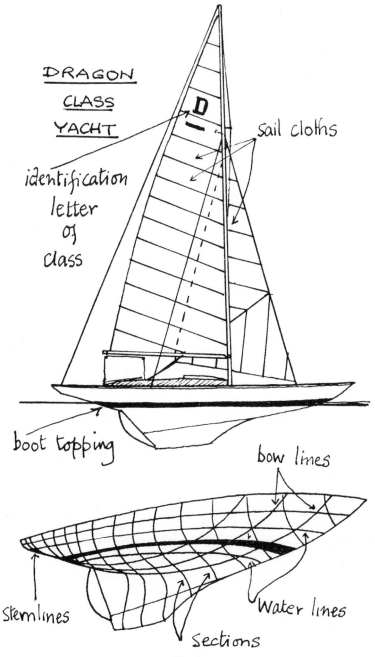

DRAGON
CLASS
YACHT

identification
letter
of
class

sail cloths

boot topping

bow lines

stemlines

Sections

Water lines

Fig. 13

power, which the lighter centreboard yachts seem to lack.

Of course, each type of boat has its advantages, and the new prospective owner must make the decision according to his own preference, the money he wishes to spend, and in the light of advice as to the conditions in the waters where he will be sailing. Centreboard boats are generally found amongst the shorter, smaller craft. Keel yachts are, of course, useless in very shallow water. It is simple to pull up the board and move away if a centreboard yacht touches ground, which would be much harder and at times impossible in a keel boat.

The tiresome question of cost enters, of course, into this business of choosing a boat and must be considered much further than the initial expense of buying the vessel. Some classes have strict rules, and prospective owners can determine the expected cost of a year's racing. For example, these controls will limit the amount of times a boat may be hauled out in a season, how many new sails can be bought, and sometimes there is a limit on initial cost of the yacht and sails. In other classes, there are no stringent rules. There is no limit on the number of sails bought, no rules concerning hauling-out, and spars and fittings may be altered as desired. Hulls may be constructed very light. To win in such a class one must go to considerable expense on both the first outlay and on upkeep in the years to follow. However, maybe a few years later, despite your extravagance, a faster boat of similar design is built, or possibly your boat has started to lose shape under the strain of racing due to her light build. She is not the winner now and her value has gone down. There is naturally, a certain excitement in racing in such a class if your means will allow. The new construction methods and equipment offered by such classes, make for ease of handling and general racing efficiency. On the other hand, if you are a beginner and of limited means, it is much wiser to enter a class of strict controls, which lessens the cost and retains the design of the yachts, so that it is not always the newest boat with the newest suit of sails that wins.

Be cautious of bargain prices for yachts. When buying a boat, as in anything else, you generally get what you pay for. Less expensive boats are likely to have poorer construction, wood, and fittings. Not all of these faults will be noticed by the beginner, but after a season or so, they will become more apparent. You will find your boat slower than those which were a bit more expensive. Because you have spent more on certain paint work, chromium hardware, etc., you cannot be assured of more speed. It is excellent workmanship that is worth paying for. The least expensive yacht is not often the best buy.

It is not possible to lay down hard and fast rules for distinguishing between a good and a bad boat. It needs years of practice, and even then an experienced yachtsman can only explain up to a certain point why he has made such a choice. For various indefinable reasons, he just *knows* she is a good boat. To sum up; the best way for the new-comer to yachting to select a good boat is to find an experienced yachtsman who is a local authority, and explain to him the type of boat he prefers, what he will use her for, where he plans to sail her, and the amount he is prepared to spend. When the experienced man has offered his advice, it should be *followed*!

THE DINGHY

Dinghy racing today is enormously popular. There are the 'International' classes—for example, the International Cadet, Finn, 505, Flying Dutchman, 14-Foot Restricted, Lightning, Snipe, 470, Vaurien and Tornado (Catamaran) Classes, etc., and the 'National' classes, *e.g.*, Albacore, 18-Foot Restricted, Enterprise, Firefly, Graduate, Hornet, Merlin-Rocket, Osprey, Solo, 12-Foot Restricted classes, etc., as well as scores of 'other' classes, like the Yachting World G.P. 14, Gull, Mirror, Wayfarer, etc. And then there are the Catamaran Classes, growing greatly in popularity, of which the National Shearwater and the Yachting World Catamaran are two for good examples. The choice of Dinghies is vast, impressive and exciting!

The dinghy classes do not lie well at moorings and should be hauled out of the water when not in use. This and their relaunching is not at all a difficult matter, owing to the lightness of the boats. To help the new-comer to decide in his choice of a dinghy, as with other classes of yacht, a sailing friend, or

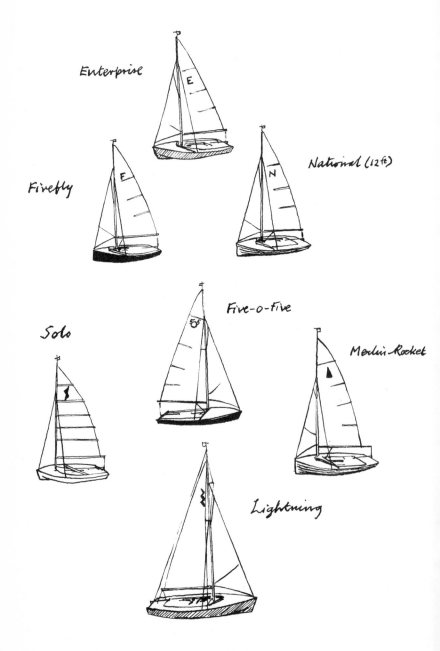

Enterprise

Firefly

National (12ft)

Solo

Five-o-Five

Merlin Rocket

Lightning

Fig. 14 *Some Dinghy Classes*

possibly a local club, is again an essential. Although dinghies are much cheaper than their larger sisters, nevertheless an important factor in choosing a dinghy is the amount of money you are prepared to spend. Once bought, however, a dinghy is a very cheap proposition from the maintenance point of view. Since racing dinghies, like other class racing boats, provide the best sport when there is good competition, the choice of the local club and the waters in which you will be racing, is in itself, expremely important. It is the practice at many racing dinghy centres to remove the masts from the dinghies when they are ashore and wheel the hulls away from the water on trolleys into sheds. A very great number of racing dinghies are taken by their owners to the open races for their classes held at various parts of the coast-line. They are taken on a trailer behind a car. It should be mentioned here that pretty well all the dinghies we have been discussing may be used for moderate cruising, but the Swordfish and the National 18 footer make the best family boats for picnicking and such purposes. You will find when you come to buy a second-hand dinghy that the condition of most of them is good because racing dinghy owners treat their boats, as a rule, extremely carefully. The way in which a dinghy has been stored in the off season affects greatly her value. So make enquiries as to the conditions under which she has been stored. Make enquiries, furthermore, as to how the boat of your choice has been performing during the previous season in races. If you are buying a new dinghy, it will have to be measured by one of the Royal Yachting Association class official measurers, who will issue a certificate that the boat has been passed for a race in her class. Second-hand boats should also have a certificate endorsed each year of the dinghy's life that the dinghy has been tested for buoyancy. All dinghies in order to qualify for the certificate to race in their class must undergo this test for buoyancy, carried out by filling the boat to the gunnel with water after a specified weight of iron has been placed in the hull and which weight is required to be supported by the water-logged boat for a specified time.

You may, of course, wish to acquire experience of dinghy racing by crewing for a season for a good helmsman. A really first-class crew is an invaluable asset, and the satisfaction of crewing for a really good helmsman and in winning races with him, is tremendous. Nevertheless, most crews probably regard this as a first step to becoming expert helmsmen themselves. The sailing of a racing dinghy, although the principles involved are the same for all craft, is something which can only be learnt by

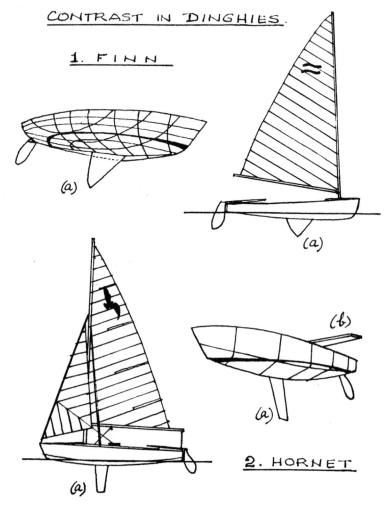

CONTRAST IN DINGHIES.

1. FINN

(a)

(a)

(b)

(a)

2. HORNET

Note: (a) centreboards, (b) sliding seat
[for crew]

Fig. 15

experience. It has been said with some truth that if you can sail a dinghy, you can sail anything. This is simply because a

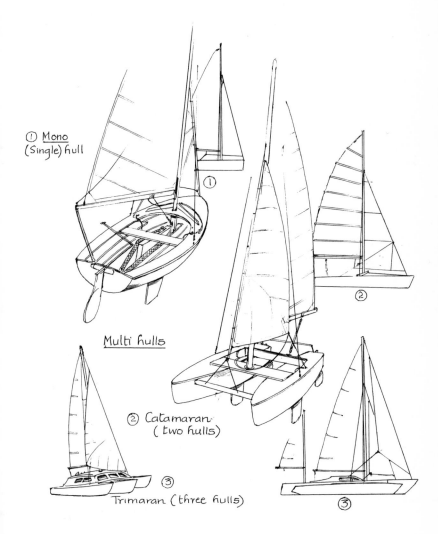

① Mono (Single) hull

Multi hulls

② Catamaran (two hulls)

③ Trimaran (three hulls)

Fig. 16 *Mono and Multihulls*

dinghy reacts so swiftly and violently to every gust and flaw in the wind, that the helmsman who is not continually on the alert to take advantage of these shifting conditions of wind, will soon find himself falling astern in the race. Such ability can only be acquired by continual experience of racing against other boats under varying conditions. If you have decided to take up dinghy racing, one of the first things you should do is to join a suitable club, if you do not already belong to one. By suitable, I simply mean that the locality of the club, the ease with which you can reach it, and the facilities which it offers, appeal to you. A list of the names and addresses of all yacht clubs in the British Isles may be obtained from the Secretary of the Royal Yachting Association at Victoria Way, Woking, Surrey. The Royal Yachting Association (R.Y.A.) is the body responsible for organising yacht races throughout the British Isles. Clubs which are affiliated to the R.Y.A. pay an annual subscription, and, in addition, there is a private membership of individuals. The excellent work of the R.Y.A. in the interests of yachtsmen of every class cannot be over-emphasised. I will leave the racing yacht for the present as the subject of racing is more fully dealt with in Chapter IX.

THE OCEAN RACING YACHT

Ocean racing is, in some ways, the most glamorous form of yacht racing. Certainly, to the general public, the idea of voyaging, let alone racing, in a small yacht across oceans or large expanses of water, is an idea fraught with risk and danger. And yet long-distance voyages, be they races or not, are not nearly as hazardous as might by some people be supposed.

We need only refer to the records of naval history to learn of the innumerable and successful ocean voyages which have been made in the past. These generally followed some shipwreck or mutiny, so that any thorough and careful preparation for the passage was quite impossible. There are, indeed, many reliable accounts of long passages in small open boats. In just the past hundred years, so many small yachts have crossed the Atlantic that it would be a fearsomely long job to give a complete account of each venture.

Now, both the joyful and the sad accounts of these long

journeys have proved that more important than the size or type of boat, is sufficient shelter, food, fresh water, and warmth. These requirements, added to sufficient strength of his craft, are essential to the seaman if he is to survive in a long passage. It is likely that the proportion of ships of under 60 tons which have been wrecked during transatlantic voyages is no higher than the proportion of losses in larger craft. The majority of these disasters have come about because the crew was not sufficiently experienced for the undertaking, or because the ship had been poorly found, or leaked due to old age or bad condition; but probably most often because of the lack of experience.

In ocean racing, it is true to say that the land holds more perils for the seaman than the sea. For this reason there is less risk in a long passage than in a short one, since the ship is then spending more time away from the dangers of land. It is after the seaman has made his landfall that he may mistake his position and run into breakers in shoal water. He may also get becalmed and find that the tide or current has pushed him onto a reef. By studying the misfortunes and losses of many small craft, one can see that it was most unusual for them to founder while at sea, and that they seemed to be practically unsinkable so long as they remained in deep water. Having, therefore, calmed ourselves with this hopeful fact, let us now consider just when and where ocean racing began.

For a good many years, long-passage races have taken place all over the world, as isolated events or for wagers, mainly in the Baltic. But it was in the United States, a country famous for the enthusiasm and size of its 'boat-minded' public, that the first regular organised series of races began. In 1904 six boats, ranging from 19 to 30 feet, raced a little under 300 sea miles from Brooklyn northwards to Marblehead. Then in 1905, twelve boats raced from Brooklyn southwards to Hampton Roads, also a distance of just under 300 sea miles. These two races aroused such interest that in 1906 a race to Bermuda was organised and was held for the following five years over a course of nearly 650 miles. During these years, there were entries of three, twelve, five, five, and two boats. This race was not held again until 1923, by which time the Cruising Club of America had been formed. It was then held for boats of at least 35 feet water-line length. About twenty-two small boats entered the race. In 1924 the race was held again and was then held every second year thereafter (with the exception of the war years). There have never been less than fourteen entries, with a maximum of forty-three.

During this time, particularly in the years between these Bermuda races, there were quite a few shorter deep-water races, which were also held in the United States. Most of these races were held between Maine and Virginia, over a course of from 200 to 300 miles. They included the Brooklyn Challenge Cup races, Larchmont to Gloucester, Block Island to Gloucester Harbor, New London to Cape May, and Cape May to Givson Island; these five being the best known among the races.

The Start of an Ocean Race.

Fig. 17

Several English boats sailed across the Atlantic to enter in the Bermuda races. As a result of the success of these races and the rising interest and enthusiasm of Englishmen, who either raced their own boats or crewed on American boats, a similar race was organised in England. The first such race was held in 1925 which was over a course of 615 miles and which presented a tougher race for both craft and crew than any race over the American courses, even though there was less of a run in the open waters of the Atlantic. The race started from Ryde in the Isle of Wight, went round the Fastnet Rock at the south-western corner of Ireland, and then back to Plymouth. This course was chosen because, to some extent, of its 'toughness'. One could nearly always be certain of a long beat to windward, most likely on the outward leg, due to the prevailing winds. It is this 'toughness' that makes the Fastnet a popular race with Americans, many of whom have entered yachts in it and continue to do so.

The first Fastnet race in the summer of 1925 had seven entries—their water-line lengths varying between 33 and 48 feet. It was at the end of this race that the Ocean Racing Club was formed. This famous club became known as the Royal Ocean Racing Club in the year 1931, by grant of a royal warrant.

In 1926 the race was held again with nine entrants. Among these were four from the previous Fastnet race, and one American boat, *Primrose IV*. Two entries had the misfortune of being caught in a strong westerly wind which prevented them from getting round the course. Even so, with the close of this race, the Fastnet had become a 'classic', and ever since has been the traditional main race of the Royal Ocean Racing Club. The following year the Fastnet race was held in most adverse conditions. The race had only just started when a gale blew up, and out of the fifteen entrants only two boats were able to get round the course. One of the entrants, *Jolie Brise*, had entered in the two previous races, and three other competitors had been in the 1926 race. Amongst the ten new-comers was an American boat, *Nicanor*, which had sailed across to take part in the event.

Largely as a result of this last race, the club made certain stipulations for all future Fastnet races. A low limit of 35 feet L.W.L. was fixed, and for vessels below that limit, a shorter race was organised, known as the Channel Race. The race was then held each year from 1928 to 1931, during which time the conditions varied and much knowledge was gained as to the most suitable boats and gear for the event. The entries in these races, including both American and French, were twelve, ten, nine, and seventeen, and those that failed to complete the course numbered three, three, five, and one respectively.

Meanwhile the Fastnet race continued to be held in alternate years. In 1931 an American new-comer to the race, *Dorade*, won, and caused something of a sensation by her fine design and labour-saving devices. By this time it seemed a better arrangement to have the Fastnet race held every second year. The reasons for this change were mainly the same as in the case of the Bermuda race. Furthermore, for economic reasons in England there were fewer suitable boats for the competition. So in 1933 the next Fastnet was held with six entrants. The 39 feet L.W.L. American boat *Dorade* was again the winner. The 1935 race was held with seventeen starters, and once again the winner was an American boat, the 40 feet L.W.L. *Stormy Weather*, designed by Olin Stephens. The following race in 1937 had thirty entries, including twenty English boats, six from Germany, and one each from America, France, Holland, and Dantzig. The winner was the Dutch boat, *Zeearend*, which was also a Stephens design. The next and final Fastnet race before the war was held in 1939 with twenty-six entries, including three German, two Dutch, and one French. There was no American boat for the first time in nine years. After the war the race was revived in 1947 as a biennial event. A new and shorter race was organised in 1949 and was held at the same time as the Fastnet. It was held for boats above 24 feet L.W.L. and 19 ft rating over a course of 300 miles. The low-limit rating for the Fastnet of that year was fixed at 27·5 feet.

Now, during the time between the first Fastnet and the beginning of war in 1939, English yachtsmen were slowly but very surely becoming keener and keener on ocean racing. The encouraging and organising of shorter races led to more experienced crews and the building of more modern types of cruising ocean racing yacht. The Royal Ocean Racing Club, the main organising body for deep-sea racing in the United Kingdom, schedules several such races each year and they have covered a good deal of the mid-western seaboard of Europe: Norway, the Baltic, Germany, Holland, North Brittany, the French Biscay coast, and Spain. Since some of these shorter races are point to point, they involve a journey back home, and therefore take up more time than the Fastnet race itself. Nevertheless, they are very popular, since the yachtsman can arrange his summer holidays to coincide with these races, and at the same time it is a means of his visiting some foreign shore and enjoying the hospitality of its local yachtsmen. Furthermore, the expense of a yachting holiday abroad need be no greater than at home, indeed it is often much cheaper and much healthier!

We already have some idea of the wide scope of the activities of the Royal Ocean Racing Club. Generally, the races given by the club cover a total mileage of well over 3000 miles a year. The number of members in 1951, including British and Foreign, was nearly 1200, and yachts of at least a dozen different nationalities have competed in races given by the R.O.R.C. The races are open to both members and non-members. One of the more important qualifications for membership of the club is that the candidate is an amateur, and has entered in at least one of the club's 'qualifying' races and is declared sufficiently competent by the Committee.

Now, with the revival of the Bermuda races and the mounting interest in deep-sea racing, a transatlantic race was bound to take place. By 1936 four different transatlantic races were organised. They were all over a course of about 3000 miles. The first race was held in 1928 when nine yachts raced to Spain. The second was to Plymouth in 1931 with ten boats. The third race was to Norway in 1935 with six entries, and the fourth to Cuxhaven in 1936. This last race was mainly a German State organised and subsidised event. It consisted of one Dutch boat, one boat from Dantzig, and seven German boats returning after the Bermuda races. Since all these races were from west to east, they were favoured by the prevailing westerly winds. However, they had to, of course, get out there or return home again when the going would not be as easy. Any transatlantic race, therefore, demanded a great deal of time, as well as expense, so that a regular transatlantic race was quite impossible to organise. The big problem in ocean racing is not the difficulties or dangers entailed but rather the need for sufficient time and—alas! sufficient money. Assuming one is fortunate enough, taking into consideration a due proportion of foul winds, to average 5 knots, even then, in order to cover about 3000 miles, the crew must be prepared to spend at least 3 to 4 weeks away from home, business, et cetera. Further time must be spent in preparing and practising for the race, as well as a rest on arrival, to say nothing of a somewhat 'leisurely' return! We can now see that it would be wise to allow at least 3 months for the round trip in such an ocean race. Occasionally, to save time, a small boat is taken one way on a steamer. This is an expensive proposition, including fares, dismantling, shipping, re-rigging, and outfitting; and still most of the crew must be prepared to spend at least 6 weeks away.

It might be argued from this that transatlantic races are not likely to occur regularly with a great many entries.

Yet Transatlantic ocean races have tended to follow a pattern. They have been from West to East, starting from a port in the United States or Bermuda. The first race, in which only three yachts competed, took place in 1866. From then there was a long interval until after 1945 when there have been transatlantic events every few years; for example in the 1960's races took place in 1960, 1963, 1966, 1968 and 1969, and the pattern continues. The smallest yacht to win a transatlantic is *Samuel Pepys*, 24 feet on the water-line, entered by the Royal Naval Sailing Association, and skippered by Commander Errol Bruce R.N. This race was from Bermuda to Plymouth and took place in 1952. In 1951 the R.C.N. San Sebastian and C.N. International La Habana organised a race from Havana to San Sebastian, a course of 4080 miles and the longest transatlantic race to date. The shortest being the Newport to Cork (Ireland) race, a distance of some 2668 miles, but still 'long' by normal ocean racing standards.

Since this book was first written, crossing wide areas of ocean single-handed has become almost familiar. The single-handed Transatlantic races (which recall the honoured name of Sir Francis Chichester) need no elaboration here. The possibilities of ocean sailing in small yachts have never been greater and the future never more exicting.

Ocean racing, or deep-sea racing, has developed along very similar lines in the United States and in England. The first type of cruising boat in both countries was the heavy cruiser; that is the gaff-rigged fisherman, or the pilot-cutter type, which in both cases gradually developed into a lighter-built type of boat, with lighter displacement, moderate overhangs, and the

Bermudan rig. The more recently built boats show that much improvement has been made in equipment. Such essentials as dinghy stowage and water-carrying capacity have been well provided for in the more recent lay-outs and accommodation schemes. But at the same time, because of an increase in income tax and living expenses ashore and the cost of building and maintaining a boat, most of the new boats are of a smaller size. For the same reason, there are more boats run by syndicates or partnerships. Also, to encourage those whose means will not run to new or moderately new vessels, in both the United States and England, there are certain allowances made for the older types of boats which compete for separate trophies, awarded in addition to the main trophies for 'open' competition. Furthermore, in both countries a minimum-length limit has been fixed for entrants, as a result of experience on the more extensive courses, and the main event has been a biennial affair. In both cases, too, it has seemed a good plan to divide the racing fleet into different classes according to size. A system of handicapping which would be suitable for vessels of all sizes in all possible weather conditions would be quite impossible to devise.

Today yachts are handicapped under the International Offshore Rule (I.O.R.). This came into force in 1970 when it superseded the Royal Ocean Club Rule and the Cruising Club of America Rule. It is widely used, not only for Ocean and Transocean races but for the 'Ton Classes' and for inshore racing. It is a complex but extremely effective rule under which a yacht once having been measured accordingly, can race anywhere in the world.

The longest ocean race in the world is the Transpacific. This race dates from 1906. In 1945, the Sydney-Hobart race was introduced (a course of about 630 miles) which has since become firmly established as a classic, and which produces a testing variety of weather conditions! Ocean racing is now so world-wide that to cover every one here would defeat my object in giving a 'potted' history. Wherever there is open water, in the seas and oceans of the world yachts will today be found competing under the I.O.R.

In 1957 the R.O.R.C. introduced the first series of combined inshore-offshore racing, known as the Admiral's Cup. The courses consist of the Channel Race, two inshore (Solent) races and the Fastnet Race.

Countries compete with teams of three yachts, and a points system on the four races decides which team is the winner. In 1975 nineteen countries participated! There are now similar contests in other parts of the world. There is the Southern Cross Cup (which includes the Sydney-Hobart Race); The Onion Patch Trophy (which includes the Bermuda Race) and the 'Rio Circuit' of Brazil. The Southern Cross is the most like the Admiral's Cup, having two offshore races, and two inshore, and is held every odd year.

In February and March of each year is held an exciting and increasingly popular series off the Florida coast, called the Southern Ocean Racing Conference (S.O.R.C.). It lasts six weeks (with intervals to recover breath between races). This series which started in 1941 was originally known as the Winter Circuit.

Ocean racing has indeed come a long way from Thomas Fleming Day's Bermuda Race of 1906. The adoption of the new International Offshore Rule makes it possible for yachts to race against each other truly internationally. In 1966 a Round Britain Race took place (the idea of Colonel H. G. Hasler who was largely responsible for the first singlehanded trans-atlantic). The race was for yachts with a crew of two only. Since then it has attracted a large entry (in 1974; 66 yachts—43 monohulls, and 23 multihulls).

The modern ocean racer, descended from the work-boat type of the earlier races, has arrived, by virtue of such yachts as *Dorade* and *Myth of Malham* (both revolutionary in their day), at the efficient, sleek, functional vessel she is today. To old hands some modern ocean racers may look too beamy, too short-ended and even under-canvassed! But their great performance proves their worth!

I mentioned earlier Sir Francis Chichester and the single-handed transatlantic races, and I cannot leave this subject without paying tribute to the seamanship and courage and splendid spirit of singlehanded sailors like Chichester, Alec Rose, Robin Knox-Johnstone, Chay Blyth, Frenchmen Eric

Tabarly and Alain Colas and women too, like Sharon Adams of the U.S.A. and so many other nationalities—American, German, Swiss; the list is by now remarkable. As a result, very long distance cruises and races in yachts are now a regular occurrence perhaps particularly, the singlehanded Transatlantic which attracts a large entry. But although some relatively inexperienced yachtsmen have tried their hand at singlehanded very long distance racing, nowadays there are usually qualifying conditions to determine the experience and fitness of both the contestants and their boats.

If I have digressed somewhat into a historical survey of ocean racing, I hope the reader will forgive me. It is of interest to any yachtsman who may be thinking of indulging in this branch of the sport to learn something of how it originated; and, in fact, what is really meant by the term 'ocean racing'. This I have tried to do. For the rest; anyone interested in the sport cannot do better than contact the Royal Ocean Racing Club and ask to be placed upon the amateur crew list—but here a word of warning. Do not do this unless you are of some use as a crew or you will be unpopular. It is wisest to have some cruising or racing experience (or both!) first. A cruising yacht, as has been shown, can, if she be over 24 feet on the load water-line, enter for an ocean race, and particulars may be had from this excellent Club (whose headquarters are in St. James's Place, London, S.W.1). If your vessel is smaller than that, and you are bitten by the 'off-shore bug', do not despair—a smaller but virile body, the 'Junior Off-shore Group' can still minister to your needs.

But, once again, and at great risk of boring by repetition, if you can do so, ask a friend who goes ocean racing for more details than I have room for here. You'll be surprised how many such friends there are!

But enough of theory and history and speculation; let us assume the deed is done. We have bought, stolen, or otherwise acquired a boat. Let us now bend on our sails and hoist them preparatory, at long last, to getting underway!

CHAPTER IV

UNDERWAY

Now at last we come to the question of getting our ship under-way. Let us assume we have a small sloop of about 5 tons, Thames measurement. There she is, lying peacefully yet ex-pectantly at her moorings on a sunny July day. As we row across to her in our smart new dinghy we experience that feeling of anticipation and excitement that all who sail will agree never stales with use. As we come alongside, we take care not to scratch the new paintwork. We jump aboard and make fast our dinghy by its painter aft, where it drops back obediently on the tide. At last we are here, afloat in our own ship and 'ready for sea'! And it is now that we realise that before we can get under-way something extremely important has to be done, in fact, it is more than important, it is essential—we have to hoist the sails!

In very small craft, dinghies and such like, mainsails are generally, in fact almost always, taken ashore after use each time and bent afresh before each sail. The same, of course, applies to the jib. However, in a boat of about 5 tons such as we are considering, it is very likely that the mainsail would be left bent to the main boom and covered over when not in use with a snug-fitting canvas cover, which laces through eyelets along its under side. For the purpose of our illustration here, however, let us assume that our mainsail and jib are new sails, lying in their sail bags in the cockpit of our boat, where they have been placed by the sailmaker. They would not normally live there but probably up in some dry stage stowage in the fo'c'sle. How-ever, here they are all to hand and the first thing we must do is to bend on the mainsail. We shake it carefully out of its bag. It will be done up by strips of canvas, which we cast off. Let us assume it is a Bermudan mainsail, because, although there are quite a large number of gaff-rigged craft about, I think it is fair

66

to say that there are considerably more of the Bermudan type. In Chapter II we gave the gaffsail pride of place, so it is only fair that the Bermudan should have its turn now. Very well then, we know that the Bermudan sail has three sides, a side or edge which runs up the mast called the luff; a bottom edge which runs along the boom called the foot; and the third, trailing edge called the leech. There are various ways in which these edges may be fastened to the boom and to the mast. Quite a common practice in very small craft is to attach the luff to the after edge of the mast by running the luff rope, which is the rope sewn inside the sail, up through a groove built into the mast itself. The groove holds the sail by the luff rope, the sail itself projecting aft through a slit at the end of the groove. The same principle is sometimes used on very light craft in the boom. However, by far the most common, and in my own personal opinion the best method is by using slides which run along a track. These slides may be of two kinds: they may run either outside a track or inside it. This is very much a matter of personal choice, I prefer the latter. Of course, the size of your mainsail, that is to say, the length of the foot and the luff, determines the number of slides, but in the case of our 5-tonner they will probably be about 1 foot 6 inches apart. Along the luff and along the foot at these intervals will be small brass-bound holes, called cringles. Now there are various schools of thought as to how the slides, which are of metal, should be attached to these cringles, the most common way is to fasten them with marline, but there are other methods. Quite a commonly found way is by the use of D-shaped shackles made of a light alloy. I have tried these and found that the shackles bent; I may, however, have been unlucky, but it is probably safer to use brass or galvanised iron. However, there are many theories and it would be burdening this book with unnecessary detail to go into them all, and anyway this sort of controversy provides a good source of argument for boat-minded people on winter evenings.

Now hoisting a Bermudan mainsail is fairly simple. You simply shackle the end of the main halliard on to the headboard of the sail and pull, making sure that the slides on the luff run up the mast track. A little grease here will save a lot of headaches. I learnt a bitter lesson in the English Channel once when trying to reef in bad weather, and the slide had stuck aloft and refused to come down. In the end there was nothing for it but a harassing climb up a tall and swinging mast. A word of caution, though. Not too much grease so as to make your slides greasy or they will dirty your sails. Before hoisting our mainsail, we must bend the foot to the boom. This again, in the case of a Bermudan sail with slide and tracks, is not complicated. To the corner of the sail between the foot and the leech is made fast a light line known as the outhaul. We fit the slide nearest the outhaul into the inboard end of the track of the boom and, fitting the other slides after it one by one, we slowly pull the outhaul towards the outboard end of the boom. The next thing to do is to secure the two corners to the ends of the boom. Now we learnt in Chapter II that the outer corner is called the clew and the inner corner is called the tack. There will be a ring-bolt, or similar fitting at the inboard end of the boom, to which the tack must be fastened either by shackle or light line. But there may be one of several methods of fastening the clew down to the outboard end of the boom. The reason here is that whereas in the case of the tack we simply secured it, in the case of the clew we are not only securing the outer bottom corner of the sail to the boom, but we are stretching the foot of that sail along the boom with a certain degree of tension. In the case of a new sail this tension should be very slight indeed. Many a good mainsail has been ruined by stretching it too rapidly. It is not necessary here to catalogue the various ways in which tension is put on the foot of the sail; quite a common way is for the outhaul to pass down through a block at the end of the boom through, down, and along the under side of the boom where it belays round a small cleat. In very small craft, however, the outhaul is usually passed through a ring-bolt on the outboard end of the boom, back through the hole in the clew, back through the ring-bolt and so on three or four times, pulled taut and made fast. Great care should be taken not to stretch a new sail too quickly. The foot of the sail should only be pulled to the end of the boom 'hand tight'. It won't reach the end of the boom, but it will stretch out further and further with use.

Now you may find that your sails are not fastened to the boom by slides and tracks at all, but by a lacing of light line. In this case you pass the lacing through the small brassbound holes (cringles) in the foot of the sail, starting from inboard and working out. You make one end of the line fast to the large brassbound hole in the tack and take a half-hitch round the boom at the first smaller hole. Then pass through the hole or cringle, take a half-hitch round the boom and pass through the second cringle, and so on. The head of a gaff-rigged sail is laced to the gaff itself in precisely the same manner, starting at the throat

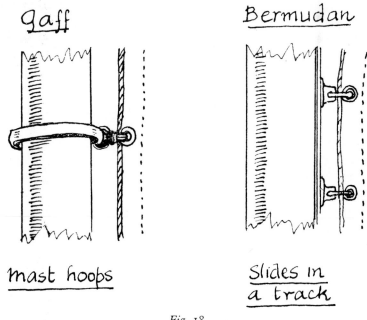

Fig. 18

and working outwards, making a half-hitch round the gaff at each cringle, then passing through the cringle and so on until the peak cringle is reached. In the case of the luff of a gaffsail it is generally found that mast hoops are used rather than slides. The cringles in the luff of the sail are seized to the mast hoops by passing tarred twine, or nylon line, several times through the cringle, round the hoop and finally round itself between the edge of the sail and the hoop, where it is tied with a reef-knot (see Fig. 18). Mast hoops are not practicable in the Bermudan rig because the lower spreaders and main shrouds would prevent the hoops from running up the mast. In the case of gaff-rigged vessels, the shrouds run much higher up the mast and, of course, the luff of a gaffsail is not nearly so long as a Bermudan luff.

Bermudan sails (and some gaffsails) have pockets sewn into the leech, running towards the luff and more or less parallel with the cloths of the sail (see Fig. 3). Into these are pushed thin whippy pieces of wood or plastic material, called battens, whose purpose is to stiffen the leech of the sail and prevent it from curling and spoiling its aerodynamic efficiency. The battens vary in length; the longest ones going in the middle and lower parts of the leech, and all the battens should be a little shorter than the pockets, otherwise, if the inboard end of the batten comes hard up against the end of the pocket, a hard line will be formed running down the sail when the latter is fully hoisted. We haul away on our main halliard then and the mainsail runs up the mast, flapping gently in the wind. We do not hoist so high that the small wrinkles which have appeared along the luff of the sail disappear. This would be a sure indication that the mainsail is hoisted too taut. The wrinkles should be there, and they should run parallel to the luff.

Now that our mainsail is hoisted, we can hoist the jib. Head-sails (jibs, fore-staysails) are bent on simply by snapping on the spring hooks, which are bent to cringles in the luff on to a stay, the jib-stay in the case of the jib; the fore-stay in the case of the fore-staysail. The jib halliard is attached to the head of the jib by means of a shackle or spring hook. The tack is secured to a ring-bolt or similar fitting in the deck at the lower end of the fore-stay. Whereas the main sheet, by which we control the mainsail, is attached to the outboard end of the main boom, the jib sheets are fastened to the clew of the jib itself by means of spring hooks or shackles. The sheets lead back through blocks or fair-leads to the cockpit, where they can be belayed round convenient cleats. (See Fig. 19.) In large craft the sheets are doubled to give added power to the crew tending them.

Additional power in the handling of sheets may be obtained from the use of sheet winches, metal drums, working on a ratchet principle. The sheet is led to the handiest winch, two or more turns taken, and the winch rotated with a lever or handle while the hauling part of the sheet is heaved on. (See Fig. 20.)

THE JIB SHEETS.

A turn has been taken round the winch and the sheet made fast to a cleat

Moveable fairleads alter the angle the sheet makes with the sail. Their position is most important for efficiency.

Jib, sheeted to port

A "figure of eight" knot tied in the end of the sheet will present the sheet flying out through the fairlead.

The lee jib sheet takes the whole strain; the weather sheet lying slack along the deck.

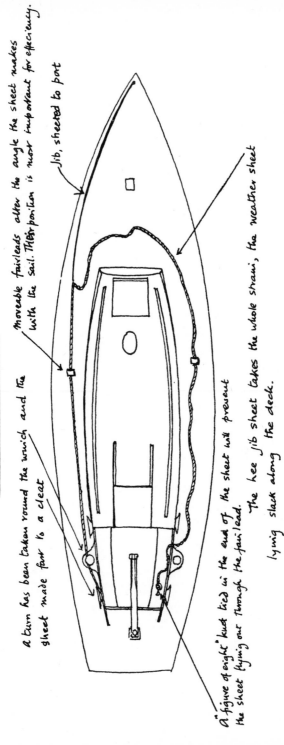

Fig. 19

Now we have learnt how to bend and hoist our sails, so let's get about the business of sailing our ship. But just before we do this there is an important matter to be decided. Before we can leave our moorings and start sailing we have to decide which we are going to hoist first, the mainsail or the jib, and why!

Fortunately for us there is a rule of thumb for leaving moorings, which concerns the direction of the wind in relation to the tide. It is this. If wind and tide are in the same direction, the mainsail should be set before dropping moorings. With wind and tide in opposition, get away under jib and hoist mainsail later.

With wind and tide in the same direction, the yacht will behave like a weather vane. The mainsail is easily hoisted and will

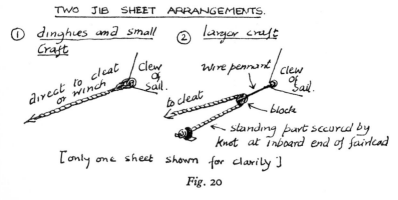

Fig. 20

flap gently in the breeze. If wind and tide are opposed to each other, and the current is strong enough to cause the boat to lie stern to wind, it will be difficult to hoist the mainsail, which will be blowing all round the shrouds as the wind fills it, and what is more, the ship will immediately start to sail. In these circumstances, drop moorings, hoist the jib, and sail away under it until you are able to turn head to wind and then hoist your mainsail with ease. You will not be able to beat to windward well under jib alone, unless you have a racing type of yacht. (In normal conditions, a racing boat can sail to windward under headsails alone.) But you will most likely have to sail down wind and find room to turn. Now, before getting underway, notice the positions of the other vessels and be quite sure you know what the tide is doing. When you have decided on a plan of action, put it into practice confidently and without hesitation.

Let us consider some problems you might meet with in getting underway. Although nothing can take the place of experience, it is very helpful to endeavour to visualise different situations.

There is no tide and plenty of room to manœuvre ('searoom'). Your yacht, a small Bermudan sloop, is riding head to

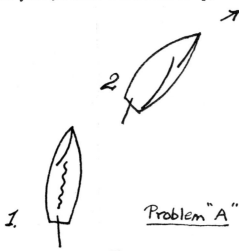

Fig. 21

wind. Your mainsail is hoisted and you have the jib ready for instant hoisting.

Assuming you wish to get away to starboard (on the port tack, that is, with the wind blowing on the port-hand side of the sails), first hoist the jib, but don't drop your moorings. Have the port jib sheet hauled in (Fig. 20 (1)).

Now the question is: is the yacht lying quietly or is she sheering about—first on one tack, then on the other? Should she be sheering about, wait until she has just finished a starboard 'tack', move the tiller to port (hard-a-starboard),* and the wind, blowing on the port side of the jib, will push the bow away to starboard. Then let go moorings. With the mainsail full and the boat sailing, slack the port jib sheet, and haul in the starboard sheet, steady your helm, and trim the main sheet

* If the tiller is moved to port, the rudder will move to starboard, and the ship will turn to starboard. Hence the term 'hard-a-starboard'. This does not, of course, apply in the case of wheel steering, when the wheel is moved in the same direction as the rudder is required to turn.

(Fig. 21 (2)). If the vessel is not sheering about, haul her ahead on the buoy rope (with the helm hard-a-starboard), and while the bow pays off to starboard, let go the moorings.

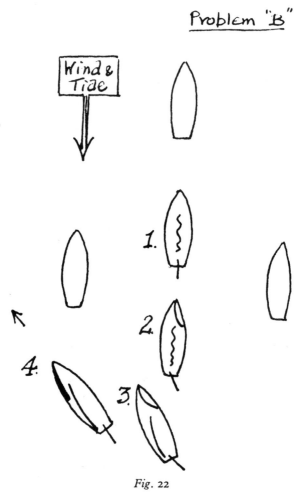

Fig. 22

This is rather more complicated. The yacht is lying head to wind and tide, but she has other craft close enough to her on either hand to make it unwise to 'cast' for one tack or another across their bows, as the tide would almost certainly cause her to touch one in her efforts to sail clear. So the answer is—hoist the mainsail, and have the jib ready for hoisting. Having done this, let go the mooring and let the tide carry her astern. When she has dropped astern enough to give sufficient room to make a cast, hoist the jib, and sheet it in. Let us suppose that we want to cast to port. We sheet the jib in to starboard therefore. Now when the wind strikes the jib, the yacht will start moving astern faster than the tide. At this, we move our tiller to port, because we remember that when our boat is going astern the rudder will have the opposite effect to when she is going ahead. The rudder then goes to starboard, with the result that the stern swings to starboard, and the bows to port, and the wind blowing on the starboard side of the jib helps this effect. When the yacht has paid off in this way on the port tack, sheet in the jib on the port side, she will then be sailing properly on the starboard tack, and you can easily clear the other craft (see Fig. 22 (4)).

This time, let's assume that the anchorage is distinctly crowded. Our boat is at A (Fig. 23); B, C, D, and E represent other craft at their moorings. We are going to try and get away to port. That will mean we will be sailing on the starboard tack. With B so close, it is more than likely that once again the tide will carry us onto her bows, and we should not be able to 'weather' (or pass clear ahead of) her. D is also in the way, and the vessel at E prevents us from dropping astern.

Now, it is perfectly possible, while still on our moorings, to make a tack or two, and in this way we can gain a bit of ground up to windward. Right! Hoist the mainsail and jib. Sheet the jib to starboard and *helm* hard-a-port. Our boat will instantly sheer away towards B until she is brought up by the mooring chain tightening. Her bow is now brought round (note Fig. 23). Slack away the starboard jib sheet and move the helm hard-a-starboard, helping her round. Now she is on the port tack and her bows are pointing at a spot somewhere ahead of D. As the mooring chain tightens once more, it will pull her round again. Now we should be in a position from which we can pass clear of B on the starboard tack and let go the moorings. In this way our boat will be both farther up to windward and farther from B, and, therefore, should be able to weather that vessel with no trouble. If, however, we are only just going to weather B, remember that when our boat's midships has passed her, we can put the helm to port to swing our stern clear.

Now that we have seen how useful a sternboard can be, let

us examine another way to use a sternboard to get us clear from a crowded anchorage. We are at A, and B, C, D, and E are four other yachts moored close all round us. We want to sail to star-

Problem C

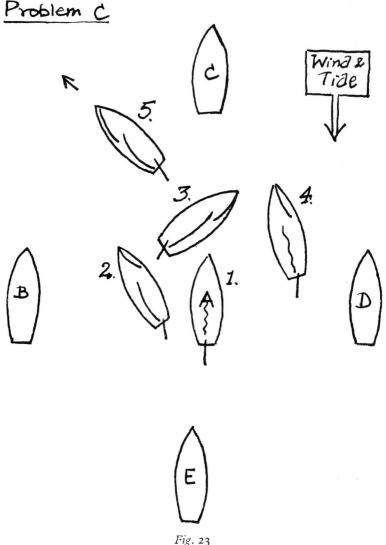

Fig. 23

board on the port tack and we can use our sternboard to enable us to pass astern of the yacht marked D in Fig. 16.

First hoist mainsail and jib. She will start, of course, to sheer from one tack to another but you must use the tiller to get her lying quietly head to wind; as soon as you have done this, let go moorings. She will now drift slowly astern. Use the helm, and if necessary the jib, to keep her on a straight course astern, and in this connection, remember that the rudder has the opposite effect when going astern to that when going ahead, or you will

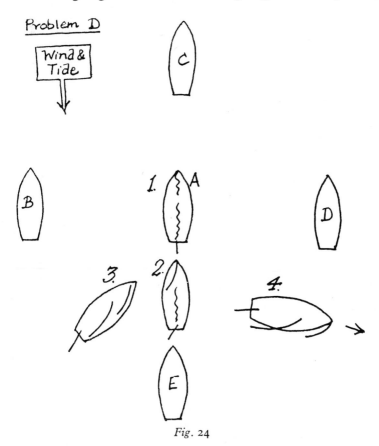

Fig. 24

find yourself in trouble. As soon as the boat has dropped far enough astern to pass clear of D's stern, helm hard-a-port and haul in the port jib sheet. The bows will now move starboard and her stern to port. When this has taken effect, steady the helm and sheet in the jib to starboard. The main sheet can now be properly trimmed for the course we are sailing and our vessel will pass easily under D's stern, steered by a skipper with perhaps a tiny, but justifiable, look of satisfaction on his face!

Now so far we have been considering what to do to get underway in cases where wind and tide are both in the same direction —(what is known as a lee-going tide)—let us progress to the opposite state of affairs (a weather-going tide). It is progressing, because the situation to be dealt with under these opposing conditions are more complicated. Now let's look at Fig. 25.

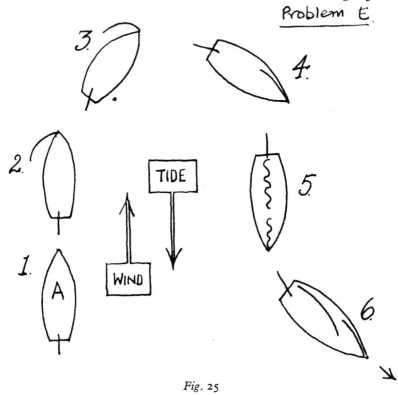

Fig. 25

Our yacht is at A in the figure. We wish to leave our moorings. There are no other craft near to worry about at this stage, but the yacht is tide ridden against the wind. The correct procedure is to prepare the mainsail for a quick hoist, drop the moorings and hoist the jib, sailing down to leeward under the jib until there is sufficient sea-room to luff up (bring the bows up into the wind) and hoist the mainsail. Now what would have happened if we hoisted the mainsail, as we have been accustomed when wind and tide were in the same direction? Simply this— the sail would wrap itself all round the shroud. If a gaffsail, the

gaff would swing broad off as far as it could while the boat itself would drive ahead as soon as the wind filled the sail, and
would sail out to the limit of her mooring chain, then swing
broadside on, sheer away and be carried up wind by the tide,
repeating the vicious circle and giving the helmsman an ulcer.

Now let us suppose that the yacht is tide ridden but that this
time the wind, instead of being against the tide, is across it.
Our actions now depend on the exact direction of the wind in
relation to the vessel. If the wind is abaft the beam, let go
moorings, hoist jib, and luff up immediately and set the mainsail. However, if the wind is on the beam or just before it, you
can usually hoist the mainsail before getting underway by spilling the wind out of it. If our boat is gaff-rigged, we can do this
by lowering the peak and topping up the boom. If the mainsail
is loose-footed mainsail, the tack can be triced up with a tricing
line as high as is necessary to keep the sail from affecting the
ship. In the case of a Bermudan mainsail the lee runner should
be slacked right off and the boom swung broad off. In this way
the sail will be presenting very little of its surface to the wind,
and most of the latter will spill out of it. As soon as the mainsail
has been hoisted, the jib can be hoisted and you can get
underway in the usual manner.

The important thing in all cases is to prevent the mainsail
from having any positive effect before the mooring has been
slipped, or, if you are lying to an anchor, until the latter has been
broken out of the ground and is being weighed by (if you are
lucky) your crew!

It is not quite so simple to get underway if your yacht is at
anchor, though the procedure is the same. The anchor must be
hove in either by a winch or by hand. It is very worth while fitting one of these winches if your yacht is of 5 tons or more.
Worth's chain pawl, fitted either on deck or on the fair-lead at
the stem head, is the best for small yachts up to 5 tons. A geared
winch is better for larger yachts. Take a sounding with the lead
line (see Fig. 30), and if the depth is 2 fathoms, heave in on the
anchor until there is about $2\frac{1}{2}$ fathoms of cable out. You can
then quickly weigh anchor when the time comes. If there is not
a good winch aboard, with a strong tide running, take alternate
tacks up to the anchor. Your crew will be able to get in a bit of

cable each time, and take a turn round a samson post or bollard on the fo'c'sle as she goes about. Should the anchor not break out of the ground easily, the above method of 'tacking up to it' will generally 'sail it out'. If you cannot sail it out, you have probably got a foul anchor—that is, your anchor has got caught in some old ground chain on the sea-bed. The remedy for this is dealt with in the following chapter. Now we may not be at anchor or even lying to a mooring. Very frequently, when cruising, one finds it either necessary or desirable to moor alongside a quay or wharf. To get underway from such a situation is not difficult, especially if there is little wind or a following or head wind, and obviously very easy if the wind is blowing directly off the quay. With a following wind, the mainsail should not be set and the yacht must be steered clear of the wharf under jib alone, using a boat-hook to cant the bows away from the wharf. The position is even simpler if you are lying head to wind. Set mainsail and jib, haul the yacht along the quay for a few feet to get steerage way, use the helm to cant the bow away from the jetty, and bear off with a boat-hook. Alternatively, haul the jib to weather to help push out the bows. As soon as the sails are full, let go the last rope and sail away. The various ropes by which you will be secured to the quay are dealt with also in the next chapter.

It is more difficult when the wind is setting onto the jetty. In this situation, run the kedge anchor out in the dinghy as far away as possible and at right angles to the jetty face. Return aboard and cast off mooring ropes from the quay, leaving one (or more) as a precaution until you are sure that the anchor will not drag. The rope left can be paid out as the yacht is hauled out to the kedge. Haul the vessel out to the kedge anchor. With the yacht lying to an anchor you can proceed in the usual way, remembering that the jetty is still near by.

The last ropes to let go are only those necessary to hold the yacht in a position from which she can best be got underway. If there is no one on the quay who will let go your line for you, it is usually simplest to have the last lines made fast inboard, taken ashore round a bollard, or through a ring-bolt, and back to the yacht, where they can be easily let go. In passing, it will be obvious from all this, that you should not only have plenty of mooring ropes aboard, but also that they should be of adequate length and in good condition.

Now that we have learned how to leave moorings or a quayside, let us go a step farther and learn to sail our boat on a variety of points of sailing. As we frequently find when leaving moorings that we are sailing to windward—that is to say, 'close-hauled'—let us start with this point of sailing, although it is, in some respects at all events, the hardest to learn to do properly and well. You will find, when sailing close-hauled, if your boat is well-rigged, that you can pin the sheets in and make her point about 3 points off the wind (that is $33\frac{3}{4}$ degrees) but she won't sail fast. She will sail along nicely if you 'free her' a point and sail about 45 degrees off the wind.

'Don't starve the ship' is the golden rule when sailing to windward. The sails should never be pinned in so hard in an effort to make her sail close to the wind that the boat becomes sluggish. If you do this the sails merely cease to drive the boat through the water. It is a common impression, and nearly always a wrong one, to think when sailing to windward in company with other yachts that they are pointing closer to the wind than you are. Though it is natural to try to get your boat to point as close to the wind as the other boats *seem* to be pointing, you must never do this, as your vessel will only lose speed. You should concentrate on sailing as close to the wind as possible without stopping your boat's way. That is the whole art of windward sailing, and let me here admit that it is not an easy art to master. Whereas you sail on a mark or by a compass when reaching, in this instance you sheet in the sails as flat as will go to make the boat give the best performance (some sails are trimmed flatter than others; experience will show you), and you fence with the wind by using the tiller. Thus, if the wind draws ahead, the luffs of the sails will shake (or lift) and your immediate reaction must be to put the tiller 'up' (to windward). This will turn the boat away from the wind and will in consequence bring the wind more on the beam until the sails fill again and the luffs cease to shake. You must watch the luff of the sail and the burgee or, as considered by some racing helmsmen to be the best method, you can sit down to leeward, and watch the leech of the jib. You are not sailing close enough if you find that the

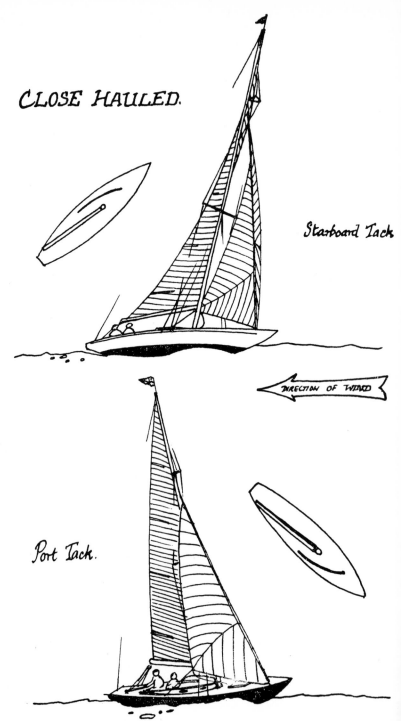

CLOSE HAULED.

Starboard Tack

DIRECTION OF WIND

Port Tack.

Fig. 26

burgee is making a broader angle with the boat than the sail. You must put the helm 'down' (away from the wind) and bring the bows up into the wind until the luff starts to shake. Then away just enough to quiet the luff again, and so on.

Constant attention is needed to get the most out of your boat when she is sailing close-hauled. The best practice for this is sailing a dinghy, because a dinghy's reactions are very quick. You learn to be alert, becoming accustomed to constant little changes of course, and making the boat always point as close to the wind as possible. You will find that the more windward sailing you do, the less will you be gazing at the angle of the burgee. In the end one seems to acquire a sixth sense and, of course, the more you know your boat, the more easily and the better will you sail her.

Sheeting the sails to sail to windward is mainly a question of knowing your yacht. As a general rule, when starting, trim the main sheet so that the end of the boom is just over the lee quarter, that is, the lee corner of the stern. Trim the jib sheet not quite as hard in as you can get it. The stronger the wind, the tighter you can pin in the sheets, but you will only succeed in stopping your boat altogether by pinning in the sheets very hard in light airs.

There is certain to be some lee-way, that is to say, loss of ground down to leeward, when you are sailing close-hauled. However, there is a way to make the yacht 'eat out' to windward and help to cancel out the lee-way: you must take advantage of the slightest puff of the wind to get back a little to windward. When the puff comes and the yacht heels to it, gently ease the helm down, and let the boat sail closer to the wind. As the puff dies away, the luff of the mainsail and the leech of the jib will start their tell-tale shaking, and you must then bear away again to 'put them to sleep', as the correct expression goes. Although windward sailing may appear to be the most dangerout course, as a yacht always heels more sharply when sailing to windward than on any other point of sailing, this is something of an illusion. With a quick movement of the tiller down wind, you can always point the boat's bow up into the wind (luff up) and in so doing allow the wind to blow on both sides of the sail at the same time. The sails flutter out, doing no work, and the boat will right herself and cannot be knocked down. But remember to keep way on her, otherwise you will lose control of her!

The wind may strike you so suddenly in very squally weather that your yacht will not act quickly enough to be safe. In this instance, a far quicker safety valve than luffing up is starting the sheet. This has an immediate effect, whereas the boat takes a second or two to react to the helm when luffing. However, as I said, for safety you must keep the boat moving. It is, therefore, better to luff than to start the sheet. When you luff, you kill the boat's headway, and you must sail away from the wind again, before headway is lost. Starting the sheet, in the same way, will immediately kill the boat's headway, and you must quickly trim the sheet in again before losing steerage way. Remember, a vessel which is stopped is at the mercy of the elements! If you want to progress in a direction which is dead into the wind, you can only make headway by sailing a zigzag course known as tacking. You first sail on one tack, then the other. You are sailing on the starboard tack when the wind is coming over the starboard side; and vice versa, on the port tack.

The origin of the expression 'tacking' dates from the days of the square riggers. Each of the two lower corners or clews of the sails had a sheet leading aft, and a tack leading forward. If the wind was forward of the beam, the weather tack was hauled aboard, making the sail take up an angle with the wind like that of your yacht's mainsail when reaching. Then, with the wind blowing over the starboard side, the starboard tacks were hauled aboard. This was said to be sailing 'on the starboard tack'.

It is not difficult to go from one tack to the other. If you think that the objective can be reached in two tacks, stay on the first until the objective is well away on the weather quarter, or well over 90 degrees from your present course. Although your next course will point approximately 90 degrees from your present one, the leeway will have a surprising effect. Try to have the objective well on the lee bow after you have tacked. Your yacht must have plenty of way on her to go from one tack to the other. Before reaching the end of a tack or board, warn everyone on board by calling out 'Ready about!' and call out

'Lee oh!' when quite ready to turn. Move the helm down and the yacht will rapidly turn up into the wind. When the wind comes on the other bow, the jib will be 'taken aback' and help to push the boat's bows round to the new tack. As the bows of the boat swings past centre towards her new course, you let fly the jib. The mainsail will fill on the new tack, and the boom will smartly swing over. Sheet the jib for the new tack and steady the helm. You will have to ease the *new* lee runner and set up the *new* weather runner. Always set up the new weather runner *before* the strain comes on it. If this is not done, the mast will not be properly stayed against the pull of the sails. If the sea is rough you must take care to have plenty of way on when tacking. Try to choose a (relatively) calm patch and have as much way on the boat as possible when coming about, because the action of the waves when sailing in heavy weather tends to make a boat sluggish.

When going about, you should ease the boat round, and, while she has steerage way, push the helm down hard enough to bring her onto the new tack. You will lose no time and really make some gain in that you have moved the boat some way into the wind. This movement ahead while actually going about is known as 'fore-reaching', and is one of the hall-marks of a good windward helmsman.

To jam the helm suddenly down, and spin the boat round so far onto the other tack that you cannot luff readily, is quite obviously wrong. You must not carry the boat right off the wind and have to bring her back onto her course. However, a word of warning! You may get 'caught in stays' if you don't put the helm over enough. This is when the boat points directly into the wind, and the wind blows on both sides of the sails. The danger here is that you have little or no headway and are not able to finish the tack. There is but one answer to this problem. Assuming you are on the port tack, you come to the end of a 'board' and begin to go about. You cry 'Ready about!' and then 'Lee oh!' and put the helm down. You did not have enough way on the boat, and she goes up into the wind, hangs there, and then begins to slowly drift backwards.

Immediately this happens put the helm to port—not to starboard, and sheet the jib to starboard. You very soon swing past the dead centre of the wind and get the wind over the starboard bow, and this is where you want it. Now, put the tiller to starboard and in a moment you will have steerage way and can try again.

The reason you put the helm to port in this instance I have quoted is because the yacht was not moving ahead while you were hanging in stays. With the boat moving, it would have been possible to swing past the dead centre onto the starboard tack. However, the boat had started to drift backwards, and when this happens, as we have learned, the action of the rudder is reversed. Remember when sailing against the wind that the moment your boat is not going ahead, it will start to go astern. The water flows from the aft end of the rudder towards the forward end. Therefore, to make the bow turn to port, push the tiller to port, bringing the rudder to starboard. In the same way, by trimming the jib sheet and keeping the boom amidships or slightly to starboard, you give the wind a chance to drive the bow round to port.

We have so far been discussing a boat with a single headsail but the same principles apply to cutters, that is, craft which carry a staysail as well as a jib, and to any two or more headsail craft. There is, however, a species of headsail which is now so commonly found that mention of it should be made here. It is a large jib, overlapping the mainsail by about one-third of its width, known as the Genoa jib. Efficient handling of a Genoa jib is entirely a matter of practice. It can be carried on a reach and is very effective on that point of sailing, but it is used mainly for going to windward. The Genoa jib is a great nuisance when going about, and, therefore, primarily a racing sail. If tacking in a large boat, the lee sheet must be cast off and a 'hand' must go forward to carry the jib round the windward shrouds, the mast, and the leeward shrouds. In a small racing yacht, the Genoa is eased round the mast and shrouds by the sheet. Sometimes a line from about midway along the foot of the sail, called a tacking line, is used.

The Genoa will pay dividends when holding a course for any length of time. It is remarkably efficient—at times you can point closer with it than with any other headsail and it has tremendous driving power. It must be sheeted in hard to get it properly set. This places a great strain on the mast and the hull. You should only put a Genoa on a boat with a strongly built hull, and the stay on which the sail is set and the corresponding back-stay must be strong. It is often set on the fore-stay, however, more often today, especially in ocean-racing craft, the tendency is to set it either on the foretopmast-stay, or, in a better position, on a stay running from the stem head to a point a short distance below the mast head. One often sees paintings and even photographs of yachts at such an angle of heel that the cross-trees almost seem to be touching the waves. Some yachts are safe with the water running along the lee scuppers, but most do not sail at their best this way. When sailing close-hauled with the wind forceful enough to make the boat heel well over and become sluggish, it is time to reef. There is a critical point, known as the 'critical angle of heel', when it is easier for a vessel to remain turning over than to return to an even keel. This critical angle of heel is most noticeable in shoal-draught centreboard boats, with flattish bottoms. They are very stable, or 'stiff', as it is called, and they need a great deal of wind to make them heel over much. However, after the critical point has been reached, they are no longer 'stiff' at all and will go all the way over! A keel boat presents no such resistance in the shape of a hard bilge, and will heel over far more easily, but after reaching a certain point, she won't heel any farther and it will take a hurricane to knock her down. There is usually more wind at the top of the mast than near the surface of the water, and all the time the boat is heeling her sail area is brought lower down and catches less wind. The iron keel acts as a pendulum, and the farther the boat heels, the greater the leverage of the keel. So it is clear that a keel boat has a great margin of safety.

But whether sailing a shoal-draught centreboard boat or a keel boat, you should reef before the situation becomes dangerous. If, for some reason, you cannot reef, you can sail quite safely and efficiently in the following way: trim the jib sheet in flat; ease off the main sheet until the sail starts lifting. Continue until about a third of the sail is lifting. You will be amazed how well and at the same time how safely you can sail in this way.

When sailing close-hauled, it is only by taking advantage of every little puff and reacting to every shift of wind that you will 'get there'. Until you become really expert, close-hauled sailing is definitely a whole-time job, demanding continual and hard concentration, if you are to do it well.

There are few more exciting and satisfying feelings than when you have learnt how to make your boat go to windward well. And now let us consider the point of sailing known as reaching.

Reaching is the fastest point of sailing. While reaching, the yacht makes less lee-way than when close-hauled. A reach can be defined as any course that is not directly before the wind, when the sails are not sheeted in hard.

To trim the sails properly for a reach, once the boat is on her correct course, ease out the main sheet and head sheets until the luffs of the sails are starting to shake. Now haul in on the sheets until they stop shaking. Then haul in a fraction more to get the best trim, and belay the sheets. You should always study the wind's direction and trim your sheets accordingly, to get the best out of your vessel when on a reach. You can tell when the wind draws ahead or aft by watching the burgee, the sails, and the direction of the waves, and when you have had more experience, by the feel of the ship. If the wind draws ahead, the luffs of the sails will begin to shake. To trim the sheets correctly for the course you are sailing, you must haul them in until the luffs cease to shake. However, if the wind draws farther aft, the boat will heel over more, she will feel laboured, and you will lose speed. The burgee will point farther ahead and the feel of the wind on your face will be less. In order to trim the sheets correctly for this change of wind, ease them until the sail is making about the same angle with the ship's centre-line as the burgee. The burgee is always a good guide to the trim of the sails.

If you pin the sheets in too hard when reaching, you will waste wind and increase lee-way, and the boat will heel over with water pouring along the lee rail. But, as we saw when the wind shifted aft while we were reaching, speed is lost, because of the wastage of wind by incorrect trimming of the sails, and because of the extra friction caused by the immersion of the ship's top strake and rail in the water. The only time when this state of affairs may be permitted is when your boat is about to be photographed and you want a dramatic picture!

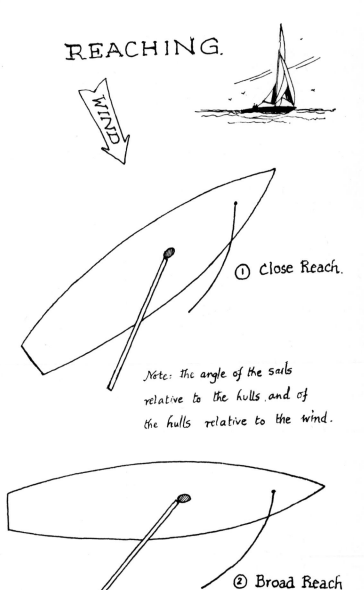

REACHING.

WIND

① Close Reach.

Note: the angle of the sails relative to the hulls, and of the hulls relative to the wind.

② Broad Reach

Fig. 27

When the sails are trimmed fairly flat and the boat is almost close-hauled, the boat is said to be on a close-reach. With the wind abaft the beam, and the sheets eased off a bit, she is said to be on a broad reach. (See Fig. 27.)

Most yachts are designed to carry what is called weather helm, that is, when you have to hold the tiller very slightly 'up' or towards the wind. Yachts are designed in this way because it is easier to steer a yacht to windward if she has a little pressure on the tiller, and also because the hydrodynamic efficiency of the hull is increased. With the rudder at a slight angle to leeward, the combination of the boat's keel and rudder becomes a more effective hydrofoil (like an airofoil or aeroplane wing).

If you find that you have to hold the tiller well up to windward to get her to keep on her course, your boat has too much weather helm. But this is probably no fault of the hull design. It is far more likely because the main sheet has been hauled in too hard. Your yacht pivots about a central point, which for the sake of illustration we will say is somewhere near the mast. If there is too much pressure on the mainsail, as it is sheeted in too hard, you will see that the yacht's stern will tend to swing away from the wind and the bows to swing into the wind. It will be clear that to stop this excess of weather helm you just ease the main sheet. Of course, if the jib is sheeted in too hard the boat's bows will tend to swing away to leeward, but partly because of its shape and the shape of the boat's hull, the effect is not nearly so pronounced as it is in the case of the mainsail. One effect that a jib being sheeted in too hard relative to the mainsail is that it 'backwinds' the mainsail and destroys the essential smooth curved shape of that sail, and the mainsail will be 'lifting' along its luff. To cure this, ease out the jib sheet until it is taking up about the same curve as the mainsail.

So much, then, for reaching. Finally, sailing before the wind. (See Fig. 28.) The oldest, easiest, and in some respects most dangerous form of sailing. The last remark may come as a surprise. But a boat sailing to windward is a boat under great control. A movement of tiller or sheet (or both) acts as a quick safety-valve. With the wind astern it is difficult to reef. A heavy sea can sometimes come aboard and 'poop' you, filling the cockpit with water. To steer a vessel before a heavy following sea

WHEN THE WIND IS RIGHT AFT
The yacht is said to be RUNNING.

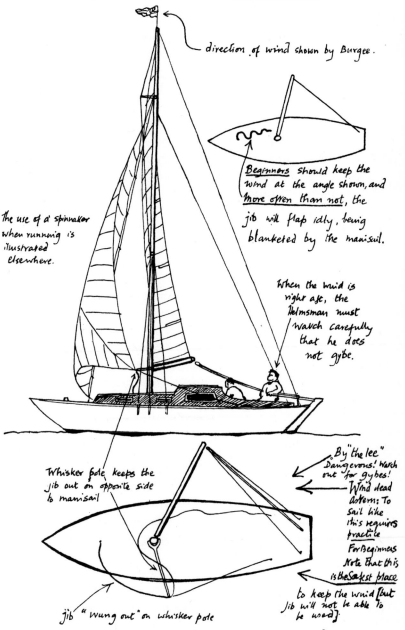

direction of wind shown by Burgee.

Beginners should keep the wind at the angle shown, and more often than not, the jib will flap idly, being blanketed by the mainsail.

The use of a spinnaker when running is illustrated elsewhere.

When the wind is right aft, the helmsman must watch carefully that he does not gybe.

Whisker pole keeps the jib out on opposite side to mainsail

By "the lee" Dangerous! Watch out for gybes!

Wind dead astern: To sail like this requires practice

For Beginners Note that this is the safest place

to keep the wind [but jib will not be able to be used]

jib "wung out" on whisker pole

Most yachts tend to "roll" when sailing down-wind.

Fig. 28

requires skill and sometimes courage. But it must also be said that down-wind sailing is the least exciting point of sailing. The wind, blowing in the same direction as the ship is sailing, deprives the yachtsman of the thrill of the sensation of speed which comes with windward sailing. As a matter of fact, a boat sailing down-wind does not travel at her fastest, because her own speed to some extent negatives that of the wind, since both wind and sail are travelling in the same direction.

The technique of sailing before the wind is simple. Pay out the main sheet until the mainsail is more or less at right angles to the fore-and-aft line of the ship. The boom will be at an angle of about 80 degrees to the fore-and-aft line. The top half of the mainsail will be at 90 degrees because it will sag forward ahead of the boom under the wind's pressure. If the course you wish to steer lies dead before the wind, the mainsail can be paid out either to port or starboard, but here a warning. It is much safer to have the wind definitely over one quarter or the other. This is because of the risk of an involuntary gybe when the ship rolls and the wind temporarily catching the fore side of the mainsail swings it and the main boom across with a crash often, in high winds, doing damage. It is difficult when sailing before a moderately large running sea, to steer a completely steady course. Large waves running under and ahead of the ship tend to swing her to port and starboard of her course. If the wind is dead aft the ship may easily swing in this way so that the wind is blowing from the same side of the ship as the mainsail is out. This is called sailing 'by the lee'. Sometimes, occasionally, it has to be done, to weather some rocks, say, or in some such emergency. But it is a state of sailing to be avoided, especially by the beginner.

The fact that an involuntary gybe spells danger, does not mean, however, that a ship cannot alter course by means of a controlled gybe. This, although it should not be attempted by a beginner in strong winds, is in moderate weather a quick and easy method of going about. The method is as follows: call out 'Gybe-oh!' to warn your crew that you intend to gybe and to watch for the swinging main boom and to prepare to work the sheets and runners. If you have been running with the boom out to starboard, the port runner will be the 'weather' runner, and will be taking the strain. The starboard runner will be the 'lee' runner and will be eased right off. The jib will be sheeted to starboard, but there will probably be no wind in it as it will be blanketed by the mainsail. Now put the helm up, that is, into the wind, in this case to port, and the bows will begin to turn to starboard. As the yacht turns, haul in the main sheet until the wind has passed the stern of the yacht and she is sailing 'by the lee'. As the wind comes onto the new quarter the boom will swing over. Just before this happens the slack runner (the old 'lee' runner) must be set up and the taut runner (the old 'weather' runner) eased right off. The starboard jib sheet must be let go. Now, as the wind fills the mainsail on the new quarter, ease out the main sheet and trim main and jib sheets for the new course.

Sometimes, when running with the wind almost right aft, and when the jib is completely blanketed by the mainsail, the jib can be spread out to catch the wind on the opposite side of the mast to the mainsail, by the use of what is called a 'whisker pole'. This is a light spar with jaws on one end that fits round the mast, and a spike on the other, the spike being pushed through the clew of the jib. With a little ingenuity an ordinary boat-book may be improvised as a whisker pole, lashing the inboard end to the mast. In this way the jib acts as a sort of spinnaker; which brings us to that sail. Now the spinnaker is a large, baggy, triangular sail. It is made of nylon or Terylene and occasionally of silk. It is set (like the whisker pole) on the opposite side of the mast to the mainsail. It is secured by its three corners, the head, the clew, and the tack, and is not attached to any spar or stay along any of its edges like most sails. The tack is made fast to the outer end of a light spar which is itself secured to the mast near the mast band. This light spar is called the spinnaker boom. The spinnaker boom has attached to it a line called the guy which leads from the outer end of the boom to a point in, or alongside, the cockpit. The clew has a line secured to it also which leads round the other side of the mast under the main boom, to a point in, or alongside, the cockpit.

Let us now take a look at the method of hoisting and use of the spinnaker. The spinnaker is a rather difficult sail to handle and it is wisest to use it only after you have become experienced at running. The first thing we must do is to clear the spinnaker of any twists. Then one member of our crew goes forward and fastens the head of the spinnaker to the spinnaker halliard, which is usually kept cleated to the mast ready for use. There should be a swivel-shackle and a snap hook attached to the spinnaker halliard so that it can be snapped into the loop at the head of the sail. Now, we must see that the spinnaker boom should be placed on the weather deck with the outboard end forward, and the tack of the spinnaker secured to the outboard end of the boom. The sheet which is made fast to the clew of the sail is held by one hand aft, and the hand forward passes the boom guy (secured to the outer end of the boom) around outside the shrouds and back to the cockpit. The helmsman now belays the guy to a cleat. A member of the crew up forward can now start to hoist the sail by hauling on the spinnaker halliard. At the same time he should push the boom out over the bows, making sure its inboard end is secured to the mast. This is done either by means of a conical socket device or a small gooseneck. If, on the other hand, the boom has jaws, they are simply rested against the mast. The spinnaker then goes up, and, when sufficiently high, the hand hoisting makes fast to the nearest cleat. At the same time, the hand whose job is to control the guy is hauling on it and so hauling the boom itself aft. In the case of sailing dead before the wind, the boom is hauled aft until it is at right angles to the boat. It must be remembered that with a heavy wind a hard strain will come on the guy when the boom is hauled aft, and it may even be necessary to use a winch. Now, when the boom is at right angles to the boat, our sail is drawing and we can belay the guy to a cleat. The sheet hand continues to keep the sail drawing. If the luff of the sail starts to flap, he pulls in the sheet until the sail is once again drawing. In this event, the hand on the guy in the meantime would ease away. The sheet can then be eased and the boom hauled aft again. Attention and adjustment in this way will keep the spinnaker full and drawing.

Now, supposing we have a quartering as opposed to a following sea. We cannot now guy the boom at right angles to the boat. The reason for this is that the wind would then tend to blow on the forward side of the sail and it would collapse. The answer is to allow the boom to be at an angle a good distance forward of the beam. It is a good idea to try and trim the sails so that the spent wind of one is spilt into another. In order to assist the mainsail in spilling its wind into the spinnaker, we top up the boom with the topping lift. When using the spinnaker, we can leave the jib hoisted, and then, if correctly trimmed, the mainsail should spill into the spinnaker and the spinnaker into the jib.

A forward guy, as well as an after guy, is particularly useful in a quartering wind. It is led forward from the outboard end of the spinnaker boom through a block shackled to the deck, a little abaft the stemhead and so aft to the cockpit. It can be hauled on or eased along with the guy and sheet, and gives an added measure of control.

Now, when we want to take in the spinnaker, we simply reverse the method of hoisting it. First of all, a member of the crew goes forward, and another eases off the guy, so that the boom moves forward, spilling the wind out of the sail. Then, the hand forward unships the inboard end of the boom and brings it inboard. Once the boom is inboard, the clew and the tack can be cast off. The sheet hand gathers in the foot of the sail in the lee of the mainsail. The forward hand then lets go the halliard, and as the sail is lowered, he lashes the two ends of the halliard to their proper cleat and coils down the guy. The sail is then bagged and placed in the sail locker, probably through the fore-hatch.

To increase the efficiency of the spinnaker, some boats have a small topping lift and a downhaul attached to the spinnaker boom. This is definitely worth while, even though it will, of course, increase the amount of gear on the fo'c'sle. When sailing in very light airs, the topping lift will help to keep the sail drawing; in a strong breeze the downhaul can be used to check the tendency of the spinnaker boom to fly up into the air. In some larger ocean cruising, or racing type of craft, the setting of the spinnaker can be made somewhat easier by reeving an outhaul through a sheave on the outboard end of the spinnaker boom. When the boom has been secured inboard it is pushed out at right angles to the mast and held in position by the guy and the topping lift and downhaul. Then when the spinnaker has been hoisted, it lies in the lee of the mainsail, and when required may be spread by hauling on the boom outhaul, and so hauling the sail out to the end of the boom, which is already in position.

When it is required to lower the sail, the procedure is simply reversed.

In larger craft, spinnakers are frequently set in stops. To do this, lay the spinnaker on deck with the luff and the leech alongside one another. Next, the centre part should be tightly rolled up, so that the luff and leech lie together on the outside and the clew and tack together at the bottom. Now take some cotton thread and tie the rolled-up sail with a single thread at intervals of about 2 feet. The sail is now stopped and may be hoisted by means of the spinnaker halliard so that it lies like a long, thin white sausage up and down the mast. When it is required, the sheet is made fast to a cleat and the tack to the outboard end of the boom in the usual way. Then, when the boom is guyed aft, the stops will go as the wind fills the sail.

When we first came to discuss down-wind sailing, I said that it was to some extent a dangerous point of sailing, and in this connection, a short warning about rolling and broaching-to would seem appropriate here. Rolling may cause a yacht to get her boom in the water with obvious unpleasant results. If your vessel has a centreboard, the latter should always be well down when running, as this will, to some extent, guard against rolling. But the best precaution against getting the boom caught in the water is to haul in the main sheet a little and top up the boom with the topping lift. If your boat is of broad beam, she will roll far more easily than a narrow boat when running.

The other danger, broaching-to, is most likely to take place in a seaway. You can be happily sailing along when the yacht suddenly starts coming around into the wind with the boom broad off. Since the yacht is heeled over, the boom will dip into the water, and the rudder becomes useless and there is a very real possibility of the boat being pulled over. There need be no danger of this happening if you watch your steering carefully, as in the case of gybing. At the first sign of your yacht broaching-to, check her with the rudder. If she continues to show a tendency to broach-to, it is a sign that you should take in a reef.

If she is gaff-rigged, you can ease her by lowering the peak of the mainsail.

The danger of broaching-to is most apparent when sailing with a quartering wind. This point of sailing is very like sailing before the wind, except there is no danger of the accidental gybe or of rolling. Broaching-to can be avoided by alert steering, as before. When sailing with a quartering wind, the mainsail should be trimmed a bit slower and the jib will draw rather than flap in the lee of the mainsail. If our boat still shows a definite tendency to broach-to, we can reef or, in a gaffsail 'scandalise' the mainsail, that is, lower the peak of the gaff, as we did when running. We must remember that when our course is altered to sail to windward, the peak must first be hoisted. Now, usually, dropping the peak of a gaffsail is a sufficient guard against broaching-to, but the following can be done to complete the scandalising of the mainsail and further reduce the sail area without reefing. First of all, pass a line through the highest reef cringle in the luff of the sail that you can reach, or else over one of the mast hoops. Untie the tack lashing or undo the shackle or other fitting and trice the fore part of the foot of the sail up to the cringle. This is only really worth doing in the case of a loose-footed sail. If the sail is secured to the boom it is impracticable. Generally speaking, this method of 'scandalising', as it is called, is not necessary, dropping the peak of a gaffsail is enough. In the case of a Bermudan sail, if it is not desired to reef, the topping lift may be used to top up the boom and spill a little wind out of the sail, if necessary easing the main sheet a bit. In such circumstances, experience of the sea and knowledge of your boat are the only sure guides.

The continual changes in the condition of the sea, and the strength and direction of the wind, create for the sailorman an ever-varying challenge to his ingenuity and seamanship. A book on sailing can only hope to give the merest outline. A book on how to court a beautiful woman can perhaps start a man off, but once he has begun his courtship he will be amazed and delighted at the infinite variety of moods and whims with which he has to contend. And courting the sea, in a small ship, is a remarkably similar experience. One starts with a measure of caution, gains confidence, and confidence brings increasing affection, and let it be admitted, even in this irreverent age, an increasing respect!

In conclusion of this chapter I would like to discuss briefly the question of balance and trim, with a word about the gentle art of helmsmanship. It takes time for any helmsman to develop the feel of his ship—to be able to sense immediately if she is properly balanced and trimmed. After a fair amount of experience, he will know right away whether she is going well or whether she is being impeded by too much canvas or by too little. Do not be too eager to make continual adjustments, of course. It often pays to let the boat do the sailing. If your yacht is well-balanced, she can frequently sail better herself than you can sail her. There is something definitely wrong with your boat if she has heavy 'weather' helm, that is, if she tries to turn up too much into the wind, just as there is something wrong with a boat whose behaviour is the opposite and which denotes 'lee' helm. A study of the relationship between the sail-plan of a boat and her hull will help us to understand how to counteract lee or weather helm. There is a point called the centre of lateral resistance in the centre of every hull's profile. If a rope was fastened to the centre of lateral resistance and then pulled sideways, the vessel should move bodily without turning. We are going to examine the relationship between the C.L.R. and the C.E., that is, the centre of effort, which is the point in the centre of the sail-plan, and which may be determined as follows:

Imagine a drawing of a Bermudan sloop (see Fig. 29). First take the mainsail, and draw a line from the head of the sail to the centre of the foot. Now draw another line from the clew to the centre of the luff. Where these two lines cut is your C.E. of the mainsail. Follow the same procedure for the jib. Then join the two centres, a and b. Raise a perpendicular from a, and drop a perpendicular from b. The two extremities of these perpendiculars, we will call c and d. The proportion of ca to bd should be in exact ratio of the proportion of the area of mainsail to the jib. Next join cd. Now where cd meets ab we have the C.E. of the whole sail-plan. If you have a yacht with two head-sails, obtain the C.E. of the fore-triangle by using the same method and then carry on as above. If, on the other hand, she is gaff-rigged, divide the mainsail into two triangles and first locate their combined C.E. Fig. 29 shows that by dropping a perpendicular from the C.E. of the sail-plan to the L.W.L., we can compare its position on the L.W.L. in relation to the C.L.R.

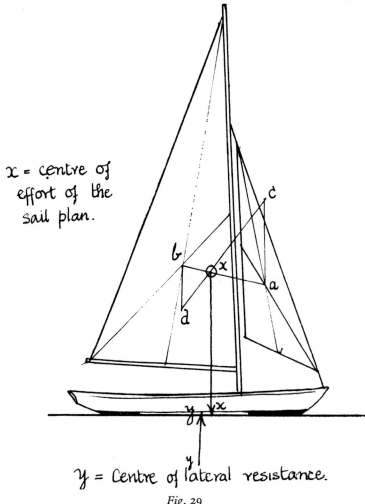

x = centre of effort of the sail plan.

y = Centre of lateral resistance.

Fig. 29

Now this is where we can determine the balance of our ship. The centre of effort should be positioned in front of the centre of lateral resistance. Anything that upsets this relationship will be reflected in the helm. It would seem, however, that if the C.E. is in front of the C.L.R., there would be *lee* helm. But this is not so, because once the yacht is heeled over, the C.E. is outside the C.L.R., resulting in a swinging 'moment' towards the wind's direction which gives heavy weather helm. So as to lessen the weather helm, designers put the C.E. in front of the C.L.R., by an amount which can be arranged to suit each yacht.

As an illustration: supposing we have a crankily rigged yacht with a small mainsail and an enormous jib, the centre of effort would then move forward, the bow of the boat would tend to be pushed in the opposite direction to the wind, and she would therefore be carrying lee helm. But supposing our yacht has a large mainsail and a very small jib, the reverse would occur, and we would be carrying weather helm. For these theoretical illustrations we must assume that our imaginary yacht is upright and not heeled. We will get lee helm, furthermore, if the jib is sheeted in much harder than the mainsail so that the jib will be offering too much resistance to the wind. On the other hand, when the jib is sheeted too loosely and not offering enough resistance to the wind, we will then get weather helm.

Now if a competent craftsman has designed your yacht and if you trim your sails properly, you can count on her being well-balanced. Where you must take care is when you have to reef, that is, reduce the boat's mainsail when the wind is blowing too hard. You will carry at least one small spare jib, designed to accompany the mainsail when the area of the latter is reduced by reefing. Let us assume now that you are sailing with the smaller jib and have taken two reefs in the mainsail. Then the wind eases, so you shake out both reefs in the mainsail but neglect to replace the small jib with the working jib. The result is that the C.E. is far astern of the C.L.R. and the boat will carry a heavy weather helm. To solve this problem, you must set the large jib.

Now, supposing you have double-reefed your mainsail, but still have the large jib hoisted, the C.E. will then be well forward of the C.L.R., and you will be carrying a lee helm. In this case, you must hoist the smaller jib. As I said earlier, however, if the boat is well heeled the lee helm may not become apparent. In this instance, although weather helm seems to operate quite naturally, many boats are a law unto themselves when it comes to lee helm.

Let us now consider the question of ballast. Proper ballast can greatly improve the performance of any yacht. There are two types of ballast, inside and outside. Inside ballast is composed of pieces of lead or iron of a size and weight that can be lifted by one man. These are stowed in the yacht so that the timbers bear the weight instead of the planking. Although a new boat will have her ballast properly stowed when she is laid up, the ballast is usually removed and very often put back the next season in not quite the same position. You should take a careful note of the positioning of your ballast and keep a plan. However, it is quite possible that, by moving the interior ballast, a great deal of good, as well as harm, can be done to a boat's performance. For instance, to give an obvious example, if a vessel seems to sink too deep in the water and is slow and sluggish, then it is very likely that there is too much ballast. If, however, your yacht is very 'tender', that is to say, she heels over very readily, and tends to put her deck under water and if you find that you must reef unduly, then your ballast is insufficient.

When stowing ballast, always place it as close to the yacht's fore-and-aft line as possible, and as far down in the hull as possible. You must choose between spreading the ballast out to the ends of the boat or grouping it amidships. If you decide to bunch the ballast all amidships, the boat will respond quickly to the helm. She will come about easily. If, on the other hand, you decide to spread the ballast out to the ends of the boat, she will be less lively in response to the helm, but she will not pound or slam when punching into a heavy sea. However, since the spray that does come aboard will travel the whole length of her, she will be a wet ship. Although the ship with the ballast bunched all amidships may pound more, she will toss off the spray on either side.

You may have to experiment a great deal before your boat is ballasted correctly, but it is well worth the effort. This question of trim and ballasting is of great importance in the performance of your boat. Ballast can quickly become rusty, and, to guard against this, you should have all your iron ballast red-leaded or painted with black varnish. Outside ballast is very simple and very effective. It consists of a ballast keel, or shaped piece of lead or iron built into the keel of the boat and secured by a number of long keel bolts. The proportion of ballast to the displacement of a yacht is a little less than half. Boats with their ballast all outside tend to be jerky in a seaway and less comfortable than those with interior ballast, but an outside ballast keel enables a yacht to 'stand up to her canvas' as the saying has it.

In the case of sailing dinghies, the ballast is provided by the helmsman and crew, who lean outboard to counteract the heeling to leeward of the boat when reaching or sailing to windward. Simple, effective, good for the stomach muscles and the reflexes. On which hopeful note, let us close this chapter.

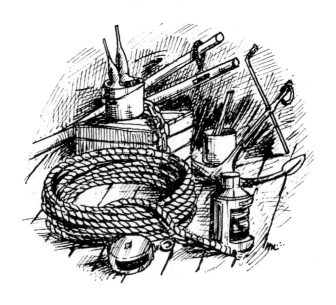

CHAPTER V

ANCHORING, PICKING UP MOORINGS, AND STOWING SHIPS

IN the last two chapters we learned to get underway from various situations and to sail our ship on all points of sailing. Now the time has come to anchor.

We will assume that you have been for a short cruise and have arrived at your chosen harbour. If it is your first time of entering this harbour (and even if it is not!), look carefully at the chart (see chapter on charts) for the general lay-out of the harbour. If there are other vessels at anchor, this will be a rough guide for you regarding depth of water. The anchor should be ready. If it is unstocked (the stock may be lying alongside the shank rather than at right angles to it), push the stock in position and drive home the pin provided. Lay out (range) a fathom or more of cable on deck and see that the cable can easily run through the chain pipe (sometimes called the navel pipe). You will have noticed the depth of water on the chart (see Tides, Chapter VI). Supposing that there are 4 fathoms where you plan to anchor, you will have to veer at least 12 fathoms. The length of cable that you veer should be three or four times the depth of water at high tide. If there is a strong wind, you will have to veer more. You have now decided to bring up in 4 fathoms of water, at high tide in a place not far from shore, quite sheltered, and with sufficient space to swing round with the tide or to move a little with the wind without endangering the other yachts near you in the harbour. You have observed from the chart the direction of the tidal stream. The cable should be marked so that you know how much of it you veer. This may be done at one, or more, fathom intervals. The cable should be led through the bow fair-lead and back inboard so that you have only to throw the anchor over the side. But before you do this you must consider how you are going to approach the anchorage and the tactics to be used in doing so. It is a help if one can memorise certain rules for anchoring. Try and commit to memory the following:

Rule (1). When there is no tide:

(*a*) Luff head to wind.
(*b*) Lower headsails.
(*c*) Wait till the yacht gathers sternway.
(*d*) Let go the anchor.

Rule (2). When the wind and tide are in the same direction:
(Yacht is *close-hauled.*)

Same as for (1).

Rule (3). When wind is against tide:
(Yacht is *running.*)

(*a*) Lower mainsail and approach your chosen anchorage under headsails.
(*b*) Just before reaching anchorage lower headsails.
(*c*) Wait till yacht gathers sternway.
(*d*) Let go the anchor.

Rule (4). When wind and tide are in same direction:
(Yacht is *running.*)

(*a*) Lower mainsail and approach the chosen anchorage under headsails.
(*b*) Lower headsails a little way from the anchorage.
(*c*) Let go the anchor.
(*d*) Snub the cable and allow the boat to swing to the tide.

Now let us put into practice one of these examples; say, Rule (2). Here the wind and tide are in the same direction. We are sailing towards our chosen anchorage. Arriving, we luff up head to wind. Next we lower the jib. The boat now moves ahead, slowly losing way and shortly comes to a dead stop. Soon, she slowly starts to move astern. As soon as this happens, we throw over the anchor. It is important to have sternway on the boat before letting go, because if we were to let go when the boat was stopped, the cable would all fall on top of the anchor. A coil could easily get caught round one of the flukes and cause the anchor to drag. An anchor winch helps one to control the

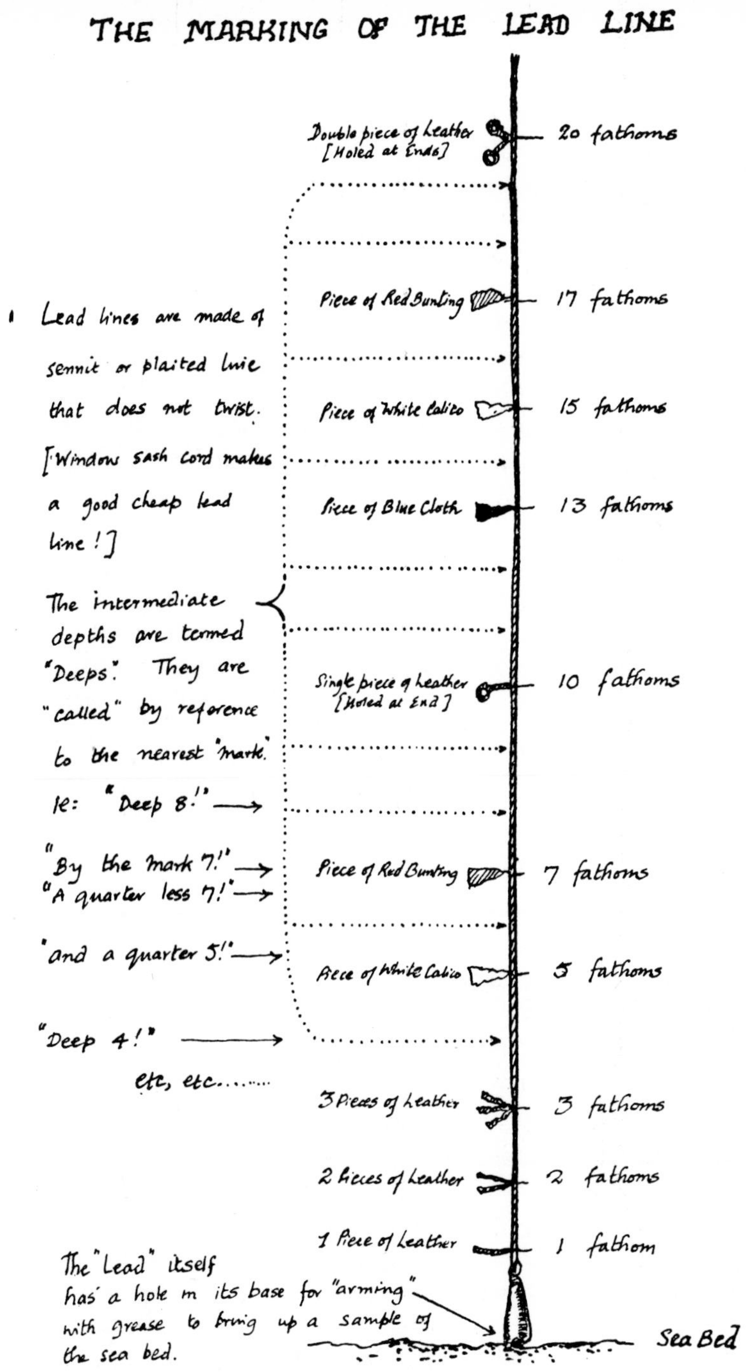

THE MARKING OF THE LEAD LINE

Double piece of Leather [Holed at Ends] — 20 fathoms

1. Lead lines are made of sennit or plaited line that does not twist. ['Window sash cord makes a good cheap lead line!']

Piece of Red Bunting — 17 fathoms

Piece of White Calico — 15 fathoms

Piece of Blue Cloth — 13 fathoms

The intermediate depths are termed "Deeps". They are "called" by reference to the nearest "mark".

Single piece of Leather [Holed at End] — 10 fathoms

ie: "Deep 8!" →

"By the mark 7!" →
"A quarter less 7!" →

Piece of Red Bunting — 7 fathoms

"and a quarter 5!" →

Piece of White Calico — 5 fathoms

"Deep 4!" →

etc, etc.......

3 Pieces of Leather — 3 fathoms

2 Pieces of Leather — 2 fathoms

1 Piece of Leather — 1 fathom

The "Lead" itself has a hole in its base for "arming" with grease to bring up a sample of the sea bed.

Sea Bed

Fig. 30

amount of cable veered; otherwise, it can be controlled quite simply by standing on it. We let out the cable gradually, not all at once, noticing as we do so white marks painted at fathom intervals on the cable, and we count the number of fathoms veered. When we started we were not quite sure of the water depth, so we took a sounding with the lead line, a piece of gear that should always be on board. It should be made of sennit or plaited line that does not twist. For the way in which it is marked to show various depths see Fig. 30. To sound with the line we took hold of the lead with about 3 or 4 foot of line in hand, making certain the line was able to run easily over the side, and we threw the lead far ahead of the boat. The line ran through our hands and as it straightened out, we felt it touch the bottom. The mark on the line closest to the water's surface gave us the depth. When using the lead line, if the depth and any of the marks on the line correspond, this is called 'by the mark 5', 'by the mark 7', etc. If the depth corresponds with one of the deeps, it is 'deep 6', 'deep 8', etc. If a half or a quarter more than a mark or deep, it is known as 'and a quarter 7', 'and a quarter 8', etc. If less than a mark or deep, 'a quarter less 7', etc. (see Fig. 30).

If you plan to remain long at anchor, to prevent your anchor dragging, you should moor with the kedge or small anchor. A yacht at single anchor when the tide turns will ride over her anchor and foul it. Then, with any wind, she will drag. Before mooring with the kedge, bend one end of a long rope of coir or grass line preferably, called the kedge warp, on to the ring of the kedge anchor with a round turn and two half-hitches or a bowline. Veer the needed length of cable and fasten one end of the kedge warp to a samson post or cleat on the fo'c'sle. Put the coil of the warp into the dinghy near the transom, with the anchor in the stern. Capsize (or overturn) the coil so when you row away from the boat the warp will pay out freely astern. Then put the anchor over the dinghy's stern and hold it there with a short piece of line passing through the ring of the anchor and fastened to the thwart with a slippery hitch (see Fig. 31). Now row astern of the yacht. When all the warp is out and quite taut, slip the small line on the thwart and let go the kedge. Then row back to the boat and bend any slack in the warp you have hauled in onto the cable with a rolling hitch (see Chapter XI). To place the kedge well below the yacht, you now veer at least a fathom of cable. The main (or bower) anchor and the kedge should both lie in line with the tide. The former, being larger and carrying heavy cable as opposed to rope, should lie in the direction from which will come the most pressure. Assuming

Sketch showing "Slippery" hitch on the

thwart of a dinghy.

Fig. 31

you were anchoring in a river with a strong ebb, the main anchor would be up river. Should you be anchoring in a creek open to the sea, the main anchor should be in the direction of the mouth of the creek. If you anchor over-night in an open anchorage like this, before turning in, see that everything is ready for weighing anchor. If a strong wind should come on to blow during the night you can then quickly get underway and out of danger. Always, if possible, choose an anchorage that is shielded from the prevailing wind. It is not a very happy experience to drag your anchor onto a lee shore. If you are approaching an anchorage, and wish to moor with two anchors, it is not necessary to use the dinghy at all. Assuming the wind and tide are in the same direction, you luff head to wind. Then let go the main anchor and drop astern, veering cable as you do so. You let out twice the amount of cable normally required for the depth of water. That is, in 3 fathoms, veer 18 and not 9. Let go the kedge and haul back on the main anchor's cable. At the same time easing out the kedge warp until your bows lie about midway between the two. Bend the kedge warp to the cable with a rolling hitch and let out the cable so that the place where the two join is far enough under the yacht, enabling her to swing with the tide without hindrance. When the wind is against the tide, let go the main (or bower) anchor, and easing it out, sail on against the tide under jib for twice the length of cable required. Then let go the kedge. Lower the jib and drift back on the tide, pulling in the cable and paying out the kedge warp until the boat is middled between the two. Using a rolling hitch, bend the warp to the cable as soon as the yacht is middled. Then veer more cable so that the rolling hitch is below the yacht's keel and then the yacht can swing with ease as the tide turns.

It is wise to avoid anchoring near a lot of mooring buoys in a strange harbour. Where moorings have long been laid for yachts, the whole sea-bed will be full of old moorings, rusty ground chain, unmarked ground chain of new moorings, and so forth. A new-comer in such waters is very likely to get his anchor entangled in all this chain, a state of affairs aptly termed a foul anchor. The best prevention for this is to ask permission to buoy the anchor with a small buoy. The buoy rope should be strong enough to weigh the anchor and rather longer than the distance from the surface to the bottom at high water. Use a clove-hitch (see Chapter XI) to bend the lower end to the *crown* of the anchor and the upper end to the strop of a small buoy. If you find it difficult to free the anchor when weighing, try one good tug at the buoy. Should you be unfortunate enough to have to ditch anchor and cable, later salvagers will be able to use the buoy as a guide. Prevention is, of course, better than cure, but the cure must be known, and it is as follows:

Heave in on the anchor chain as much as you can, so that you lift off the bottom the chain in which the anchor is caught. When you have heaved it as high as you can, secure the cable, and try to reach the offending ground chain with the boat hook. However, even if you can reach the chain it may well be far too heavy for you to hold it with the boat hook. A better method, although difficult, is to try and drop the lead on your lead line ahead of the mooring chain, and, using the boat hook, pick it up the other side. Next bend a stout warp to the lead line. Haul it taut under the mooring chain and back inboard and make fast. Now veer the cable until the warp is taking the weight of the mooring chain. Continue easing the cable until the anchor drops clear of the mooring chain. Now the anchor can be cleared, and, when ready to set sail, you have only to slip the warp. It would be unwise, however, to regard the 'ground chain-warp' mooring as anything but very temporary, however secure it may seem at the time!

An anchored yacht rides to the weight of cable rather than to the anchor itself. However, if the wind becomes very strong and the tide rises, she will stretch her cable as she drifts to leeward and pull it taut as she pitches in the sea. This is called snubbing and puts a strain on the cable. There is a way, however, to help the yacht's motion and at the same time ease the strain on the cable when this happens. Attach a pig of lead or iron ballast to the cable by using a large shackle. Bend a light line to the shackle or the pig so that the latter can be lowered a good distance down the cable. Acting as a buffer, it will then take the strain off the cable, because before the cable can be brought up taut it must bear the weight of the ballast, and before it can do that, the wave will have passed, and again the weight will cause the cable to sag. The pig becomes an elementary shock-absorber.

A boat should always have two anchors aboard, and a large boat three. If your yacht is a 5-tonner, the minimum weight of your anchor should be 35 lb., and the kedge anchor should weigh about three-quarters as much as the bower anchor. The weight should go up about 10 lb. for every 2 tons. For example, an 8-tonner's main anchor should weigh about 45 lb., a 10-tonner's main anchor about 55, etc. A yacht should veer about three times the amount of cable as the depth at high water. Generally the amount of cable carried in a 5-ton yacht is 30 fathoms. This means that the greatest depth she could bring up in really safely would be 10 fathoms. Dragging anchors is an expensive business, so it is best to follow the rule whenever possible, although in practice you will often anchor in deeper water probably quite safely.

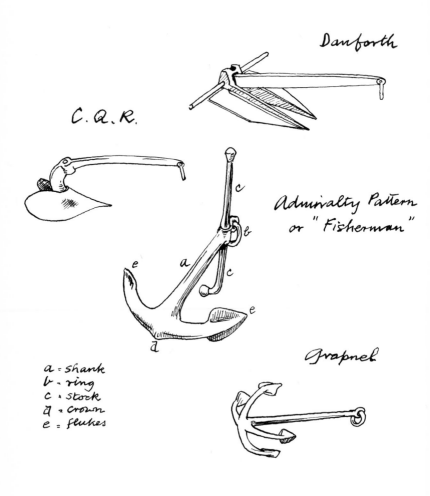

a = shank
b = ring
c = stock
d = crown
e = flukes

Fig. 32 Anchors in Common Use

To be able to estimate how much cable you are veering, paint a white mark at regular intervals on the cable. Some choose every fathom, others prefer every 5 fathoms. Personally I prefer the former interval—painted in white and every 5-fathom interval painted in red or yellow.

Up to this point when we have considered anchors, we have been speaking of the ordinary fisherman's anchor (see Fig. 32); however, the C.Q.R. form of anchor is nowadays very much in favour. It has much to commend it. It need be only half the weight of the fisherman-type anchor, because it is said to have twice the holding power. (See Fig. 32.) The C.Q.R. type of anchor makes use of the ploughshare principle for its holding power.

The usual way in which a vessel fouls her anchor is by riding up over it on the tide and by getting the cable caught round one of the flukes of the anchor. She will then swing with the tide, and if it blows, the cable can easily pull up the anchor. Unless you are on board and are aware of the situation, you stand a very good chance of losing your ship!

Although the cruising yacht will frequently have to anchor, a yacht in her home port will have a mooring of her own. The technique of coming up to, and picking up, a mooring requires study and practice. Before we examine this in detail, let us for a moment consider this question of moorings.

Let us assume that we have bought a yacht and she will soon be launched and we must decide where to moor her. We can choose one of several courses open to us. We can ask the harbour master for a mooring to be laid for us in a suitable area. We can inquire at a shipyard having moorings on its frontage which can be rented by the week or by the month. Another course is by putting down moorings of our own, though this is not recommended for beginners. Furthermore, it is usually worth the expense of having your mooring laid for you. The local people know all the important factors, such as the strength and direction of the tide, the direction of the prevailing winds, the nature of the bottom, etc.

When choosing an anchorage, there are certain points to be considered. Your anchorage should be in a place well shielded from storms and sheltered from the prevailing wind. Have your mooring at a safe distance from the other boats, so that when they swing with the tide and wind, there will be no risk of your boat hitting them.

The type of mooring you use will depend on the sea bottom. An anchor that will hold well in sand will pull through a mud bottom, or an anchor that will hold well in a mud bottom will drag along on the top of sand. The size of the mooring depends mainly on the depth of water and on the exposure of your position.

A commonly found type of mooring consists of two or more anchors, each having a length of ground chain, which meet at a point to which is attached another length of chain known as the riding scope. The riding scope should be twice the depth of the water at high-water springs; that is, the greatest depth. The anchors should be twice the weight of an ordinary anchor, and the ground chain should be proportionately heavy. A good, heavy chain will last much longer than a light chain and will make quite a good mooring in itself, and take a great deal of the strain. It will often remain safe even when rusted. Concrete blocks are sometimes used in place of anchors. A single block for a 4-tonner should weigh approximately $1\frac{3}{4}$ cwt.

Generally the procedure in attaching the mooring chain to a buoy is by shackling the riding scope to a mooring line, to which in turn is attached a cork or wooden buoy. As to the weight of the mooring line, if you have a 4-tonner, a 2-inch grass line would be perfectly suitable. The buoy should be painted in one or more bright colours and should have on top of it a wire or rope loop so that it can be easily picked up. Where the mooring line is lashed to the riding scope, the rope should be spliced round a galvanised iron thimble to protect the splice. A piece of rubber hose on the part of the riding scope which touches the bow of the ship will prevent the cable from spoiling the paintwork. Sometimes steel wire rope is used for a mooring line, often ending in a spliced loop which can be slipped over a king post or cleat on deck. In this case the rubber hose protection is even more essential to protect your bows.

However, wire loop or rope to moor securely the mooring chain itself must be hauled aboard through the bow fair-lead, until you have enough to take two turns round the samson post in the fo'c'sle. It is important that this post is well built into the boat rather than merely screwed to the deck. Having taken two turns pass the chain under itself and over the top of the post, and there you are.

Now let us consider the actual technique of approaching our mooring buoy and picking it up. Let us assume we are beating to windward with a fair tide. We sail right past the mooring, lower the mainsail, and sail back to the buoy under jib. Furl the jib just before reaching the buoy. The boat will lose way just as she comes up to the buoy, if our judgment has been correct. If the wind is on the beam, the tide is fair, we would follow the same procedure. However, before lowering the mainsail we must get to windward of the buoy, so that we can get back easily under the jib.

If we were beating against a foul tide, we should sail up to the buoy, luff onto it, and lower the headsail. Again, if we were reaching against a foul tide, we would lower the jib and luff onto the buoy. As soon as the buoy is aboard, the main sheet should be eased right off to keep the wind out of the mainsail, so that the latter will not move the boat.

Running with a fair tide provides rather more of a test. The vessel must be 'rounded' up to the buoy, and to do this we must judge the strength of the tide and set it against the amount of way our boat carries. This requires knowledge of the boat and experience in being able to estimate the tide's strength accurately. Practise this as often as you can. Experience and skill in rounding up alongside an object in the water like a buoy perhaps one day will enable you to save the life of a man fallen overboard!

While on this unfortunate subject, if somebody should fall overboard, throw them a lifebuoy, and then no matter on what point of sailing you are on, *gybe*. The boat must come alongside the person in the water when she has little or no way on her, and she must be head to wind and under full control. It is essential, therefore, to approach from leeward, and the fastest way to get the boat in this position is to gybe.

When cruising, there will no doubt be numerous occasions when you will have to moor alongside another yacht or a quay. As you approach, you should have everything all ready; a warp coiled down for'ard and another warp coiled down aft, and all fenders handy on deck. Come alongside the other yacht against the tide when possible, having as little way on as you can. Get the bow warp ashore or on the other yacht as rapidly as you

can. When this is secured aboard the other yacht, let your craft
drift back on the tide while the stern warp is made fast. When
mooring alongside another yacht, the rise and fall of the tide
will not disturb you. If you moor alongside a jetty, however,
the longer the headrope and sternrope and the farther they are
apart on the shore, the better, because the closer together they
are the more effect the rise and fall of the tide will have. Where
there is no tide, it will be sufficient to back up the head and
stern warps by shorter lines. But if there is any tide at all, you
must put out 'springs'. (See Fig. 33.) To do this, you lead a

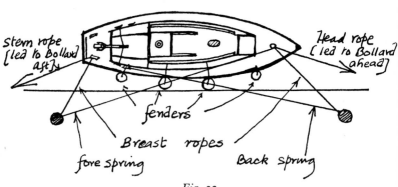

Fig. 33

warp from the inboard bow to a cleat or bollard ashore far aft
of the beam, and another warp from the inboard quarter to a
cleat well for'ard. You can then, however strong the tide, keep
the yacht in a firm position by adjusting the strain on these
springs. In Chapter IV we discussed how to leave a jetty and it
will be clear that one of these springs can be used to 'spring'
out either the stern or bow of the ship when doing this.

You will find it extremely difficult to keep your fenders in
position if you find, as is woefully often the case, that you are
alongside a quay with a great ridge of timber jutting out from
the quay wall. To prevent your fenders slipping out of place,
heave a spare spar (like a sweep, boat-hook, or spinnaker boom)
over the side outside the fenders and leaning against them. The
spar will act as a buffer and the fenders will keep the spar from
damaging the side of your yacht.

If you have to come alongside a quay when the wind is blowing directly off the quay, the best way of approach is on a close-reach. Time it so that the yacht will be heading into the wind when she is to leeward of the quay-side. Then, trimming the sheets, put down the helm, luff into the wind and run directly up wind towards the quay. The boat will stop before she reaches the quay if your timing has been accurate, but even if you have a little too much way on, you can fend off from the bows with a boat-hook. As the boat stops, throw a heaving line (or your warp if it is not too large), or if there is no one on the quay to assist you, one of your crew can jump ashore. It is, of course, easier if there is someone on the quay to pick up your heaving line or warp, and make it fast to a near-by cleat. You can then lower sail, haul the yacht to the quay, and bring her alongside with the stern warp. Don't panic if the first line you throw misses the quay and you begin drifting astern. If the yacht is only drifting slowly, there will probably be time for a second shot. If not, it is best to hoist sail, sail away from the quay, and start again. Although the boat will behave quietly at the quay with her sails set as long as she is pointing head to wind, remember that you must lower sail before turning the boat's stern round with the stern warp.

Now, supposing that the wind, instead of blowing directly off the quay, is blowing directly on to the quay face. Here, a good method of approach is to sail as near to the quay as possible, luff into the wind and anchor. Then lower sail and gradually ease out on the cable, until the boat's stern is nearly touching the quay. You can then get your warps ashore and safely bring the yacht alongside.

If you have any choice in the matter, it is always best, if possible, to moor on the *lee* side of a quay, because you will lie much more quietly. Otherwise, no matter how many fenders you put out, if it blows hard the boat will bump about in an unpleasant way and the fenders are likely to wear out, and it is really surprising how much fenders cost!

It is only through experience that you will learn the technique of coming alongside or leaving a quay. Only attempt it in a boat when you know how far she will 'shoot'. By shooting is meant bringing the boat up into the wind from a given direction so that she will lose all headway and come to a stop just when you want her to.

Always bear in mind the effect of any tidal stream that may be running. With wind and tide in the same direction you must shoot up harder into the wind to prevent the tide killing the boat's way. On the other hand, if wind and tide are of about equal force in opposite directions, stop the ship at a short distance from the quay, because otherwise the tide will carry her on to it. As always in sailing—experience alone brings mastery.

Finally, having secured to our buoy and made fast alongside we must 'stow ship'. First ease down the boom on the topping-lift so that it rests in its crutch. Take in the slack of the main sheet to hold down the boom. Now we stow the mainsail. Haul the sail across the boom until it all lies on one side. Now get hold of the leech and take it forward along the boom, letting a little, say, a foot or two, overlap. Stretching over the boom, pick up the belly of the sail evenly and push it down inside itself. Continue doing this, each time getting a new hold on the sail farther down than the last until all the sail has been smoothed into a tight roll. Secure this roll to the boom with gaskets or tiers (narrow strips of canvas). There is a canvas 'coat' on most boats which laces under the boom and covers the mainsail. This should now be rigged. Next you stow the headsail (or head-sails). You must *not* furl or bag the mainsail and headsails if they are wet. If it is not raining, hoist them and let them dry; but should it be raining, stow them, without covering the mainsail. At the first opportunity, hoist them and let them dry in the wind and sun. They will do so very quickly. This precaution is necessary with all canvas sails. Terylene (Dacron) and other synthetic fibres, being less susceptible to mildew, do not require such careful nursing. Now that we have stowed the sails, we must turn our attention to the halliards which should be secured round their proper cleats and the ends coiled down. If it should come on to blow they will beat against the mast so it is wise to attach them to the main shrouds with a piece of marline or light line, or twist one of them round the mast and secure it to its cleat. Haul down the ensign and burgee at sunset and, if at anchor or the outboard boat of a group, hoist an anchor light on the fore-stay. Use an ordinary 'D' shackle and shackle the handle of the lamp to the fore-stay. Shackle the jib halliard to the same handle and the lamp can be hoisted up the fore-stay as high as necessary by means of the halliard. In disturbed water you can hold the lamp firm by leading one lanyard from each side of the bottom of the lamp down to the fo'c'sle.

CHAPTER VI

PILOTAGE AND NAVIGATION

THE definition of navigation has been given as 'the art of conducting a ship in safety from one point to another on the surface of the Earth'. This requires a knowledge of the position of the two places on the earth, the point of departure and the final destination, and also a knowledge of some method of connecting the two, *i.e.* some way of indicating the direction of one in relation to the other.

A knowledge of navigation and pilotage will make all the difference to both the yachtsman's endeavours and enjoyment. The ability to navigate and pilot a yacht can benefit a man in many ways. It will add to his self-respect, make him of more use to his country in critical times, and, far from least importance, increase his own pleasure. Everyone who has navigated a small yacht taking day and night and weather conditions in his stride is bound to experience a feeling of accomplishment and that particular feeling of freedom and adventure known only to the seaman.

Now look at Fig. 34 which shows the earth represented by a circle. We will put two imaginary points on this circle, A and B. We must then draw in some datum lines to which the position of the points will be relative and can be defined as such. First, from north to south draw in the diameter of the globe. Now draw in the circumference, a line midway between the two poles, which represents the equator. We then draw in the Greenwich meridian, which is a half-circle from one Pole to the other, passing through Greenwich Observatory. By glancing at Fig. 34, having drawn in these datum lines, we can state any position as to its distance north or south of the equator. We can also define any position as to so much east or west of Greenwich. The first measurement is called latitude and the second, longitude. We can consider every position on the surface of the earth as having its own parallel of latitude and its own meridian of longitude and can express any point by this means. A great circle is any circle round the earth which bisects the earth. To determine the distance a ship must sail to go from

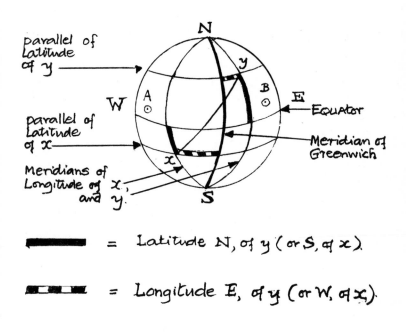

= Latitude N, of y (or S, of x).

= Longitude E, of y (or W, of x).

Fig. 34

one point to the other, we will go back to our original two points and join them by means of an arc of a great circle, and this arc will express the shortest distance between them. This distance is measured in terms of a sea mile, which is an angular measurement, being the length of one minute of arc measured through the plane along the meridian. We know that the earth is flattened a little at both the Poles, and not a perfect sphere. This fact would cause quite a problem in calculation, as it tends to make a difference in the length of each minute of arc along any particular meridian. Therefore, a standard length of 6080 feet, the length at the latitude 48 degrees, has been decided upon internationally. A knot is the term used for the rate of speed of one nautical mile per hour.

Let us study Fig. 34 which shows two positions, x and y. Assuming that we are situated at x and wish to travel to y, we must first discover the direction of y from x. We notice from the illustration that the direction of point y from point x is shown by the angle between the meridian of x and the arc of the great circle passing through these two points. (The line xy looks curved in the figure, but for a short distance it is more practical to treat it as if it were straight.) The measurement of the angle is arrived at by working clockwise from the meridian of the observer. It will be measured from true north, since all meridians run from the North Pole to the South Pole. We now know the positions of x and y, the distance xy, and the angle which xy makes with true north. We are, therefore, ready to start sailing from x to y, keeping our ship on the necessary angle for the requisite number of nautical miles. When actually sailing from x to y, we are certain to come across occasional stretches of land obstructing our direct course, and we will have to change our route to sail round them.

Now let us consider the Magnetic Compass. Iron ore and other substances have the useful property of magnetism, that is, attracting and repelling one another. There are several ways to induce magnetism. You can rub the article you want to magnetise with another magnet, hammer it in a magnetic field, or pass an electric current through it. A compass needle is an example of an artificial magnet, suspended in such a way that it remains nearly horizontal. One end of it points towards magnetic north, which is located in the area to the northwest of Hudson's Bay, and is situated far down in the earth. The nearer one travels to the magnetic pole, the more the compass needle will 'Dip' (become deflected) downwards, until at the pole itself it points vertically down. Consequently, in areas near the pole, where a great deal of the magnetic force is used to pull the compass needle downwards, the magnetic compass is not a very dependable indicator of the bearing of magnetic north. 'Red End' is the term used for the north-seeking end of the compass.

The south-seeking end of the compass points in a similar way to the South Pole and is called the 'Blue End'. As the South Pole, situated in the northern part of South Victoria Land, is also deep down in the earth, the 'Dip' principle operates again.

The fundamental law of magnetism is that unlike poles attract and like poles repel. Therefore, when a magnet is placed near the compass needle, the blue pole of the magnet immediately attracts the red pole of the compass needle, and vice versa. The earth may be considered as a magnet with the north magnetic pole being the blue pole and the south magnetic pole the red pole. Therefore, a compass needle will have its blue end pointing to the south, and its red end to the north. But it is not really all that simple, because the magnetic poles are constantly changing their position at the rate of a few miles every year. There is, therefore, a continually changing difference between magnetic north and south and true north and south (the actual physical poles). Variation is the term used for the difference between true north and magnetic north. This, of course, will not be the same in all parts of the globe. The variation increases or decreases depending on the relative position of the two poles, and since these magnetic poles are shifting, the variation will not only differ from place to place but from year to year. When calculating magnetic bearings, this difference must be allowed for by the amount stated along the east/west axis of the magnetic rose. If, for example, the date of the chart is 1960 and the variation is 10° west, decreasing 5′ annually, then 9° 10′ will be the variation in 1970.

When sailing a small yacht, you may use the magnetic compass rose exactly as it is, if you have made certain that the date of the chart you are using is quite recent or if there has been only little change in the variation. However, you will most likely have to make a correction for deviation. A normally correct compass may, when placed in a ship, point several degrees to the east or west of magnetic north. Also, this deviation from magnetic north will change according to the direction in which the vessel's head is pointing. The ship's own magnetism causes this deviation. The compass will be greatly affected by a metal ship having a magnetic field of her own. A professional compass adjuster can compensate for this influence by placing certain small bar magnets under the compass. The deviation is much less in the normal wooden yacht, and generally no compensating magnets are used. However, the nearness of the compass to such things as the engine and its fittings, will, in all probability, cause some deviation. This deviation must be accounted for when using the compass, and therefore a deviation table must be made. Later in this chapter the method of making this table is illustrated.

We have now learned that variation is the amount by which north on the face of a magnetic compass (in other words the north-seeking end of the magnetic needle) points away from true north, and that deviation is the amount by which the same needle is farther deflected from the correct magnetic bearing by the ship's own magnetism. And so we get this definition: Variation is the difference between a true and a magnetic bearing, and Deviation is the difference between a magnetic bearing and a compass bearing.

Now supposing that from a chart we have worked out that the course we wish to follow is true south. We must then apply the two corrections of variation and deviation which will produce a new course for us. The course on the chart is called the course to make good; and the course acquired by applying variation and deviation is called the course to steer. Conversely, a course steered must be corrected before it becomes a course made good and can be plotted on the chart.

All magnetic boat compasses are made on the same principle. The compass bowl is fitted into a portable binnacle with a gimbal ring. An electric or oil lamp is fitted on one side of the binnacle to illuminate the compass card during the night. A cruising yacht should have her compass placed where it is possible to take all-round bearings, otherwise she should carry a secondary compass for taking bearings. It is generally not possible for a yacht to have her steering compass in such a position, as first of all the helmsman must have good sight of the steering compass on either tack, which means that the compass is quite low down in the ship. If a yacht carries a secondary compass, both compasses should be tested for deviation and also against each other. A deviation table can be made for the steering compass by comparison with the secondary compass, provided that the latter is situated for the purpose at least 6 feet from the nearest iron or steel. Hand-bearing compasses are very good instruments and need not be expensive. When you use a hand-bearing compass, make sure that you hold it away from any wire rigging or other metals which can influence it.

However, the compass should not be too brightly illuminated in a yacht, where the helmsman must watch the sails carefully and must also be on the look-out. It follows, then, that courses are given in points, unlike the case in large steamers where the compass is brightly illuminated and courses are given in degrees. In Fig. 35 we see a compass card marked in degrees as well as in points.

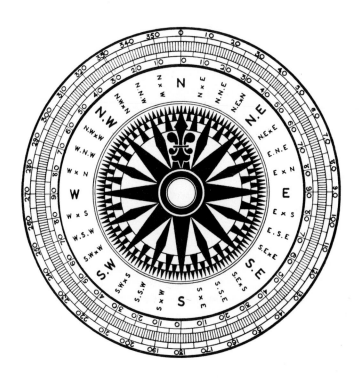

Fig. 35

Now let us consider the other tools of the navigator's trade. Leaving out the sextant, which is dealt with in the next chapter, these consist of charts, nautical almanack (various other publications like tidal atlases need not be mentioned here at this juncture), parallel rules, a pair of dividers, a protractor, a soft rubber, and three or four hard, sharp pencils. If possible, get hexagonal pencils, as they will not roll off the chart table when the ship rolls. A rubber is necessary to erase the work on the chart and leave it ready for the next time. The dividers should work easily and still stay open at the desired angle.

There are generally two kinds of parallel rules, rolling or sliding, and both have definite snags. On a very small chart table, the rolling type is useless. If the sliding type warp, get bent, or work stiffly they can well-nigh cause apoplexy. On most parallel rules, there are degrees shown along one edge and points along the other. Among the number of makes of parallel rules on the market, Captain Field's is an excellent make of simple sliding-rule. There is a good type of rule designed by Commander Luard, R.N., and manufactured by Holt Marine Factors Ltd., which combines a number of relatively modern features and is extremely easy to move across the chart. If you cannot get parallel rules, you can use transparent set squares, which are even preferred by some navigators.

Now to consider our charts. There are three main types of charts: Passage Charts which may show the whole plan of the voyage; Coastal Charts which are on a much bigger scale; and Harbour Plans. Choose your charts carefully. The Admiralty annual catalogue of charts will be of much assistance to you, as it indicates the areas covered by each chart and you will be able to familiarise yourself with the scale of a chart. Charts are rather expensive, and although it is better to have too many than too few, a wise choice can save you money. You are most likely to require a small-scale passage chart (or several, depending on your ambition), a set of coastal charts covering the area (each one slightly overlapping the other), and also a set of harbour plans of the anchorages and harbours which you may wish to visit. By studying the passage chart carefully you can tell which harbour plans you might need in an emergency. Admiralty charts are clear and extremely informative and may be obtained from recognised Admiralty chart agents and most yacht chandlers. However, their size creates a problem for the small yacht, and for this reason there are several charts of much smaller size on the market. Such charts are the Stanford Charts and the Imray Laurie, Norie and Wilson Charts; both of them coloured and with a reputation for excellence. Such charts can be used on small chart tables, saloon tables, cabin soles, and even cockpit floors. The examples given are of Admiralty charts, and all chart work references are to them.

Every chart has a 'title', which gives the name of the chart, several abbreviations and signs used in it, and any pertinent warnings or danger areas. It will further inform you as to whether the soundings showing the depths of water are in feet or fathoms.

Each chart has a number which is shown in the right-hand bottom corner and on the label on the back of the chart. At the bottom of every chart is shown the date of the latest edition of that chart, and references to the date are made in the bottom left-hand corner. Here also may be found references to the source of any corrections, known as 'small corrections', which have been made since the chart was published. The new chart you buy will be corrected to the present date. The date of printing is given in the top right-hand corner, and the date of publication is shown outside the bottom margin of a chart in the middle. The date of a new edition is to the right of the date of publication. Admiralty charts, and indeed most charts, are drawn on what is called Mercator's projection. The principle of this is that straight lines are used to represent all rhumb lines. In Fig. 36 we see that a rhumb line is a line on the surface of the earth which cuts every meridian at the same angle. If a ship steers along a rhumb line which joins two places on the earth's surface, her course will stay the same during the whole voyage. A chart drawn on Mercator's projection will show:

(a) The equator as a straight line.

(b) The course between two places as a straight line.

(c) The meridians which appear on the chart will be shown as parallel straight lines perpendicular to the equator.

To give you a very good idea of the principle of Mercator's projection, without making too extensive a study—first, imagine

RHUMB LINE AND GREAT CIRCLE COURSES.

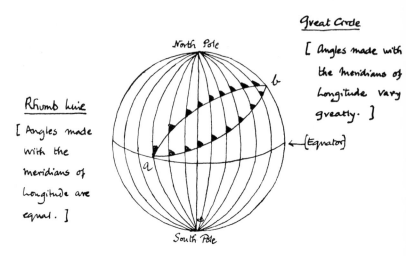

Great Circle

[Angles made with the Meridians of Longitude vary greatly.]

Rhumb Line

[Angles made with the meridians of Longitude are equal.]

A RHUMB LINE COURSE

ON A MERCATOR PROJECTION. [Note the equal angles the Course line makes with the meridians of Longitude]

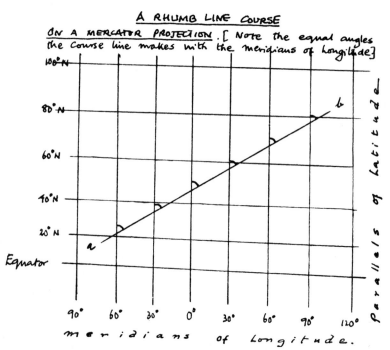

Fig. 36

a transparent globe which shows the world and meridians and parallels of latitude. An electric light bulb is inside the globe and placed round the globe is a sheet of white paper which is as wide as the circumference of the globe and twice the length. All the data on the globe's surface are now projected as shadows onto the paper. You will see that the shadows of the meridians of latitude are projected onto the paper as straight parallel lines, and not converging at the poles. Notice that the parallels of latitude are also straight lines parallel to the equator and that the farther they are from the equator, the greater becomes the distance between each successive parallel of latitude. To obtain our projection, we trace the shadows with a pencil, and then unroll the paper. Mercator's projection is never used for high latitudes, as you will see when you extend the paper for very high latitudes near the poles, the magnification becomes too great to be of use.

It is very important that you use the area of the latitude scale as nearly as possible opposite the section of the chart where you are studying. As we have learned, the latitude scale varies by increasing towards the poles. Measure the distance on a Mercator chart along the vertical edges of the chart, never the horizontal edges. The shortest distance between any two places on the earth is represented by the arc of the great circle passing through those places. This would be shown as a slightly curved line on a Mercator chart. Although a rhumb line is not the very shortest distance, it appears on the chart as a straight line. For distances of up to four or five hundred miles, there is only a slight difference in distance. When working on the chart, it is, of course, far more simple to use straight lines.

And so we can see that navigation is very much simplified by means of the Mercator projection and an unchanging direction rhumb line course between two points. Courses and bearings are indicated by simple straight lines on a scale plan of the waters.

What is called the gnomonic projection is used for areas in very high latitudes, where the Mercator method is useless. The average yachtsman is not likely to be sailing in such areas.

A gnomonic chart is drawn on a flat surface, touching the earth at one point (generally the centre of the chart), called the tangent point. From the centre of the earth, lines are drawn through points on the surface of the earth until they reach the flat surface of the chart. The gnomonic projection is, therefore, a true geometrical projection, which the Mercator projection is not. In a gnomonic projection: parallels of latitude are shown as curves; meridians are shown as straight lines converging to the pole; and great circles appear as straight lines. A certain type of gnomonic projection is used to draw harbour plans. The small section of the earth you are working on is treated as flat.

In Fig. 37 is seen an example of what is called a compass rose. These compass roses appear at various places on coastal charts. They consist of two concentric circles. The outer circle is graduated clockwise in degrees starting from o degrees at true north; the inner either in a quadrant rotation starting at north and south and graduated from o degrees to 90 degrees east and west but more usually from o degrees to 359 degrees on modern charts, as in Fig. 37. The amount of local variation will cause magnetic north (north/south axis of the magnetic rose) to point to the east or west of true north (the north/south axis of the true rose). This will be exact in a brand-new chart, whereas in an old chart you will have to apply the correction shown along the horizontal or east/west axis of the magnetic rose (see Fig. 37).

It is quite simple to lay off a course on a chart. Place the edge of the parallel ruler on the required course on the compass rose and bring the ruler across the chart until the edge touches the spot representing the yacht's position, and then using a sharp, hard pencil lightly draw in the course.

Now the conduct of a vessel from A to B would be very much simplified if there were no such thing as a tidal stream. Tides have been defined in the *Admiralty Navigation Manual* as 'Periodic vertical movements of the water on the Earth's surface'. The cause of tides is the gravitational attraction of the moon and the sun. The earth and moon have the same centre of gravity and revolve round it in equilibrium once a month. Since the gravitational force which draws the earth and the moon together is counterbalanced by the centrifugal force which pulls them apart, this revolving motion is steady. These two opposing forces are equal and opposite at the centre of the earth, but everywhere else on the earth exists a force moving either towards or away from the moon. This force is known as the 'lunar' tide-generating force, which causes a high water on the earth's surface on the side closest to the moon,

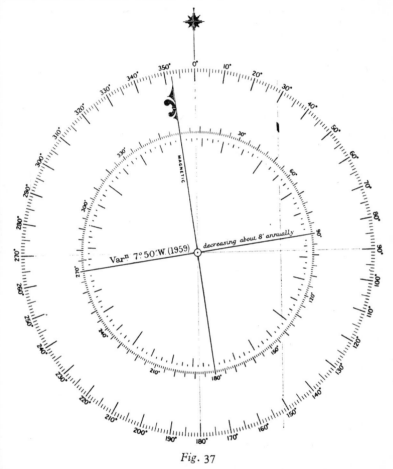

Fig. 37

and another high water on the side of the earth opposite to it. (See Fig. 38.) It will be seen by the illustration that we are assuming, for the purposes of our theory, that water covers the whole of the globe's surface and that the two high waters are balanced by two low waters in between them. Considering the relative distance of the earth and the moon from the sun, and their relative sizes, the force of the sun's attraction is about three-sevenths that of the moon (the moon being a great deal nearer). However, it takes about 29 days for the moon to revolve completely round the earth, and 365 days for the earth to revolve round the sun. The moon, therefore, passes between the sun and the earth just once in every 29 days, consequently causing a high tide. The earth will be between the sun and the moon every 14½ days, or half that time. These two tides are called spring tides and the highest high water and the lowest low water occur at these times. Now twice during the lunar month the sun and moon have their high tide effect at right angles, and therefore, to some degree, opposing that of the sun, there will still be a high water opposite the moon and a low water opposite the sun. However, the high water will be to some extent low and the low water to some extent high, since the two bodies are working in opposition to another this time. These tides are known as neap tides (see Fig. 38). Between these two extremes, the water level varies regularly between the levels of spring and neap tides. It would be quite simple to calculate the variations of level if the whole of the earth's surface were covered with water, but tidal waters are, of course, affected by the land masses of the surface of the earth, which cause high and low water to arrive at successive places at quite different times. Detailed observations must be made in order to foretell the height of the tide at any particular place. From an analysis of these one can determine the length of delay, which is stated as being so many hours and minutes after the moon's meridian passage over the area. For instance, at times when there is a full moon or change of moon, it may be said that the next high tide at Dover will occur 8 hours and 10 minutes after the moon's meridian passage over Dover. It is expressed on paper as: Dover, H.W.F. & C. VIII hrs. 10 mins. (High Water, Full and Change, Eight hours, 10 minutes). This is known as the 'establishment of a port'.

The task of working out the tides is greatly simplified for the navigator by certain formulated tide tables which indicate the times of high and low water, as well as the heights of the tide. *Reed's Nautical Almanack* published by Thomas Reed Publications is excellent for tidal information of all kinds. From it you can find (1) the time of high water at any port. (2) The time of low water at any port. (3) The depth of water at a particular place at a given time; and (4) the time at which there will be a stated depth at a particular place. You can also find from the *Almanack* (1) which way the tidal stream is running at any given time, and (2) at what rate. The tidal section of the *Almanack* is

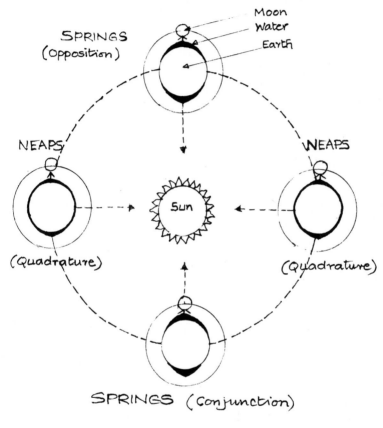

Fig. 38

arranged so that all the local information is given together. For example, information for the 'Secondary port' of Margate is shown as related by so many hours and minutes to the Standard port of Sheerness.

To obtain information you use the most suitable port predictions near your vessel's position. The tidal section is divided into Standard ports and Secondary ports. Twice-daily predictions

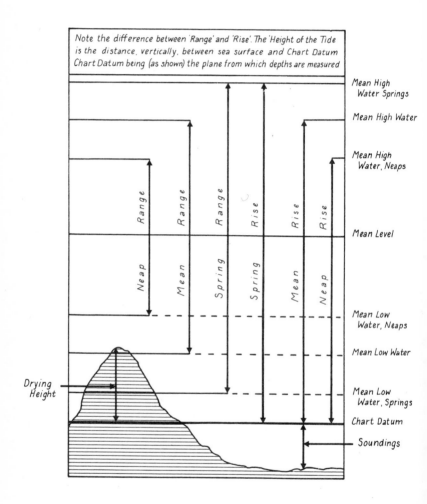

Fig. 39 Diagrammatic illustration of Tidal Definitions

are given of the time (to the nearest minute) and height (to a decimal of a metre) throughout the year for the standard ports.

All ports not standard are called secondary, and tidal differences (to find the time and height of the tide) are given, on adjacent pages—to be applied to a standard port in the same locality. Secondary ports are not necessarily based on the nearest standard port but on the nearest one where the tides are most similar in character.

As well as the standard port section giving you the height and time, there is also information showing the page number where the secondary port data based on that particular standard port may be found.

Fig. 39 illustrates the principles used in correcting for rise of tide. On British charts, chart datum is usually near or somewhat below the level of mean low water springs.

The height of high water above this datum is the rise of the tide. The *mean level* of the water at a place higher than the datum can be said to be about half the spring rise at that particular place. The usual spring tide will rise above this mean level by half the spring range, and to the same degree will fall below the mean level. Every tide will vary the same amount on either side of the mean level, with the result that the range of a neap tide is less than the neap rise by the difference between spring and neap rise. The soundings shown on the chart indicate, more or less, the height of the tide at low water springs. The soundings at high water springs will be greater by the amount of spring rise. They will be greater at low water neaps by the amount of the difference between spring and neap rise. At high water neaps they will be greater by the amount of the neap rise.

Certain gradual changes in level take place in any regular tide. During the first hour after either high or low water, one-sixteenth of a change in level takes place; during the second hour, three-sixteenths; during the third and fourth hour, one-quarter; during the fifth, three-sixteenths of a change; and during the sixth, completing the cycle, one-sixteenth.

Returning to Fig. 39, then, we see that the difference in level between high water and chart datum is the rise of a tide. We also see that the range of the tide is the difference in level be-

tween any high water and the following low water. The amount
a spring tide rises above chart datum is the spring rise or the
spring range. The neap rise is the amount the neap tide rises
above chart datum, but since the low water level at neaps is
higher than the level of chart datum, the neap range is not the
same. Therefore, the neap range is the amount the neap tide
rises from low water neaps.

The information given in *Reed's Nautical Almanack* is adequate
for all the practical purposes of yacht navigation. Now the
movement of the tide which we have been discussing is responsible for tidal streams. The vertical undulation which we call
the tide, meets the resistance of shoaling water, which causes
horizontal advancing and retreating movements, known as a
tidal stream. The chart or a tidal atlas will show tidal stream
predictions, which, again, is the result of a great many observations. You can obtain the speed (rate) and hourly direction (set)
of the tidal streams, with reference to the time of high water at
Dover. A detailed account of tidal atlases is unnecessary, as
they are more or less self-explanatory, so let us consider for a
moment the tidal information shown on an Admiralty chart.
Capital letters enclosed in squares or diamonds indicate positions of the various tidal streams. They are scattered about the
chart at intervals because in different parts of the sea the tidal
streams vary very much. Each of these figures refers to data at
the side of the chart denoting the set and rate of the tide for
each marked area for every hour of the day. Admiralty charts
give all the directions in true bearings, and converting these
directions into a magnetic bearing is easily done, as both true
and magnetic compass roses are given on the chart (unless the
chart is not up to date and you must correct for variation).

An example of what you might find on the chart is: 5 hours
after H.W. Dover, 150 degrees, 3 knots (springs); 2 knots
(neaps). In other words, if H.W. Dover is at 8 A.M., then at
1 P.M. the tide will be setting you 150 degrees at a rate of 3
knots at spring tides, 2 knots at neaps, and at proportional
speeds in between. As I have already mentioned, much information concerning tidal streams may also be gleaned from *Reed's
Almanack*. There are numerous (over 100) tidal chartlets.

Now let us examine how we can use the navigational instruments we have so far discussed to plot a course for our ship. A ship at sea must know where she is. From the moment she leaves harbour, her navigator must be able to see at any given moment where his vessel is on the chart. At the offset of the voyage all the navigator knows is that he wishes to sail from A to B. This all sounds simple enough, but there are a number of factors which make it considerably more complicated. First of all, the navigator must take into consideration the tide. Then he must also consider the amount by which a yacht may be set off her course down to leeward (away from the wind). Given a course to steer, a yacht sailing to windward will 'sag' away to leeward. Actually, the modern yacht makes comparatively little lee-way. Each yacht owner, or for that matter, yacht helmsman, should make himself familiar with the amount of lee-way his own yacht makes under given conditions. This amount will differ with each yacht, according to hull form, draught, etc., and, of course, increases considerably as the weather deteriorates. One way of determining lee-way is to watch over the stern the angle your wake is making with the course you are steering. This might be, say, 6 degrees, and, if so, you may compensate for lee-way by steering 6 degrees up to windward.

A good navigator will also, when the yacht is sailing to windward, make an allowance for 'helm error'. Practically all helmsmen, many of them without knowing it, tend to steer either slightly leeward or slightly to windward, of their course; generally the latter. Of course, for the navigator to be able to compensate for this necessitates knowing his helmsman pretty well, and in the absence of this, it is probably best to assume that the course to steer is, in fact, being steered. What other things set the ship off her appointed course? After the wind has been blowing strongly in a given direction, there will be surface drift which may well set the yacht a quarter of a point or so off her course down to leeward. Although the two principal factors which must be taken into consideration by the navigator are the effect of tidal streams and lee-way, there are two other vital factors with which the navigator is concerned, which we have mentioned briefly before but which require further study; variation and deviation.

We know that when a compass is placed in a yacht, it will

most likely deviate from the magnetic meridian due to the ship's own magnetic effect. We have also learned that because of the difference in the positions of true and magnetic north we must correct for variation when we take our course from the true compass rose on the chart. Let us assume that your chart is a new one, and therefore the variation indicated on the true or magnetic rose is correct.

But we are still left with deviation. If our yacht is small and built of wood and her compass has been well placed, we should find only little deviation. It is therefore not likely that we will want to insert correcting magnets. Furthermore, we will be using a small type of compass which is not generally fitted for correction magnets. In a larger yacht, however, where the deviation is greater, it is likely that we would want to install correction magnets. This is a job which requires expert knowledge and should be done by a compass adjuster. He steps aboard, and, while remaining in the same position, he turns the ship through all the points of the compass and notes the bearing by the ship's compass of a certain object on shore, the right bearing of which is known to him. It is then easy for him to see the difference between the bearing by the ship's compass and the correct bearing, and accordingly inserts his small correction magnets.

It is not the fact that your compass has deviation that matters, but that you *know* the deviation on each bearing. If we then make for ourselves a deviation table, we can always know the deviation for any given course. To do this we first of all choose two objects in a sheltered anchorage which, when brought into line, will give a bearing of, let us assume, south 20° west. When two such objects are brought into line and give a definite bearing, they are known as transits, and well-known or obvious transits are indicated on most charts. Now start gradually turning the boat round with the engine, keeping the two landmarks in line. If you have no engine, ask someone to tow her round with a launch, or, failing that, to row her round with the dinghy. Hold her steady for a minute on each of the cardinal and intercardinal points, beginning at North. Each time, write down the bearing of the transit from the boat's compass, and you will find yourself with a table resembling this:

Yacht 'Kay'—Deviation Table, 27th May 1978

Ship's head by compass	Compass bearing of landmark	Magnetic bearing of landmark by transit	Deviation
North	S. 19° W.	S. 20° W.	1° E.
NNE.	S. 18° W.	S. 20° W.	2° E.
NE.	S. 17½° W.	S. 20° W.	2½° E.
ENE.	S. 17½° W.	S. 20° W.	2½° E.
East	S. 18° W.	S. 20° W.	2° E.
ESE.	S. 19° W.	S. 20° W.	1° E.
SE.	S. 20° W.	S. 20° W.	Nil
SSE.	S. 21° W.	S. 20° W.	1° W.
South	S. 22° W.	S. 20° W.	2° W.
SSW.	S. 22½° W.	S. 20° W.	2½° W.
SW.	S. 22¾° W.	S. 20° W.	2¾° W.
WSW.	S. 22½° W.	S. 20° W.	2½° W.
West	S. 22° W.	S. 20° W.	2° W.
WNW.	S. 21½° W.	S. 20° W.	1½° W.
NW.	S. 21° W.	S. 20° W.	1° W.
NNW.	S. 20° W.	S. 20° W.	Nil

The graph for the above deviation table would appear as shown in Figure 40. Generally, these notations should be adequate, because if the yacht's head is pointing in a direction not shown on the deviation table, for example, NEXN, you would interpolate between 2½° E. and 2° E. and say the deviation was 2¼° E. However, for a more accurate deviation you can refer to the deviation curve, which is prepared by sketching a graph from your deviation table. This graph will prove slightly more helpful than the deviation table in that the deviation for any intermediate direction of the ship's head can be found at a quick glance.

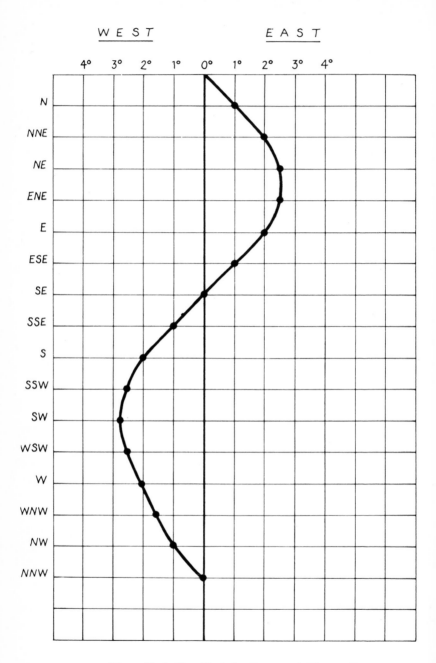

Fig. 40 *Yacht* Kay, *Deviation Curve, 27th May,* 1978

Now we find from our table or our graph that when the boat's head is pointing east, the deviation is 2° E., and the course we plan to steer is east. But before we can work out what course we should steer by our ship's compass to make us sail east, we must consider the three things we have been discussing: tidal stream, lee-way, and deviation. We want a course to steer the boat *through the water* to make us steer east (that is, east magnetic) *over the ground*. The first is known as 'the course to steer', and the second, 'the course to make good'.

Let us now assume we are sailing in a given direction on a broad reach. We have observed from the *Nautical Almanack* that the time of high water Dover today is 09.00. The time at present is 11.00. Now let us look up the tidal stream (either in the *Nautical Almanack* or in the tidal atlas, or on the chart itself) and check on what the tide is doing and will be doing in the next hour of our passage. For the sake of this example, let us say that the direction of the tide for the next hour is south and the rate is 3 knots (the speed of the tidal stream in knots is called the 'rate'). Now, if the current had been running in the same direction as we wished to sail, obviously no allowance of tide would be required. This is known as sailing with a 'fair' tide. Similarly, if the current is setting dead against our course, no allowance need be made. This is termed a 'foul' tide. However, in our example, the tide is setting across our course pushing us to the south of the direction in which we wish to go. The problem is, therefore, the same as that of lee-way. In other words, we must steer to the north of our course by the same amount as the tide is going to set us to the southward of it. In this instance, we found that the cross current was setting us south at 3 knots. Now what is our own yacht's speed? This we will have to estimate, which, if we know our ship fairly well, is not nearly as difficult a feat as might at first be imagined. There is, however, a more accurate way still of ascertaining the speed of a yacht through the water. This is by using an instrument called a patent log. The log has a dial marked in nautical miles which is indicated by a revolving arm like a speedometer —only with this difference, it does not indicate the speed of the ship, but the distance the ship has travelled through the water. The dial part of the log is clamped to the covering board or the transom or to some suitable place right aft. From its after end, a line of about 75 feet streams behind the ship when the ship is moving through the water. At the end of the line is a metal rotator, like an elongated propeller, which turns the line at varying speeds as the ship moves through the water—the distance that the ship moves being recorded in nautical miles on the dial of the log. A new log may have an error and should be tested over a known distance before being relied upon for navigational use. To find the speed of your ship, you simply take two readings of the log, one at any given time, and the second an hour later—the additional number of miles shown gives the number of knots your ship has logged in an hour and, consequently, the ship's speed *through the water* in knots. Incidentally, the reason that this useful piece of machinery is called a log dates from the old days when a ship's speed was calculated by heaving a weighted wooden board, usually of a triangular shape, over the side. The wooden board was called a log ship and to it was attached a long line with a knot every 48 feet. As the log was heaved over the side, a member of the crew timed, by means of a sand-glass, 14 seconds for fast speeds and 28 seconds for slow. That member of the crew who was paying with the log line would be simultaneously counting the knots as they ran through his hands. A more sophisticated modern method is the use of an electronic distance run and speed indicator worked by a submerged impellor. (More expensive but very useful!) But let us get back to our private navigational problem. We can now assume that a speed has been found from the patent log of 4½ knots, and we will go on to plot our magnetic course of east on the chart.

Working from Fig. 41, at any point along the line take a point C. Since the current is setting south, from point C draw a line pointing magnetic *north* (the direction opposite to the current). The rate of the tide (found from the chart) is 3 knots, so using the dividers, we measure along the latitude scale, that is the vertical edge, of the chart. When we measure the latitude scale, we should see that the middle of the dividers come just about over the latitude of the mid-point in the magnetic course to be laid off, and we thereby average out any difference due to the irregularities of a Mercator projection.

We now have our dividers measuring 3 miles, so we will lay off this distance along the current line from C. Where the dividers cut this line we will call B. Now with our dividers we

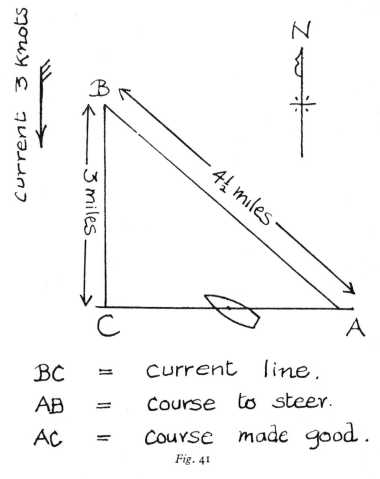

BC = current line.
AB = course to steer.
AC = course made good.

Fig. 41

measure off the ship's speed, 4½ knots. We do this by placing one point of the dividers on B and cutting off 4½ miles on the course line away from the direction in which we are heading. This point will be called A. Now join AB, and note that we have a triangle ABC. Put one edge of the parallel rule along AB and run it over to the nearest magnetic rose on the chart. Now read off the course which we must steer in order to proceed in the direction we wish to make good. If we follow the course AB, the current will be forcing us towards BC, so that actually we shall 'crab' along line AC while our nose points along AB, and at any particular time during our passage, we will be at some point along the line AC.

There are several things we can learn from this simple triangle. AB represents the course to steer and the distance we will travel through the *water*. AC represents the course along which we wish to travel, and also the distance we will travel over the *ground*. AC is shorter than AB, because a proportion of the distance we have travelled through the water has gone to offset

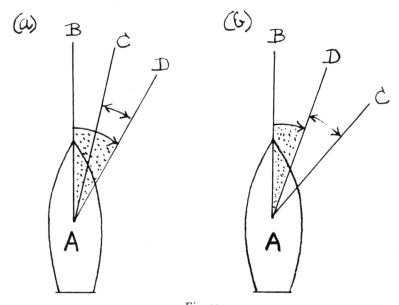

Fig. 42

the force of the current. Conversely, when the tide is fair the distance travelled over the ground would be greater than the distance covered through the water.

We have so far learned to lay off a course allowing for tide, and we know now to apply the deviation of which we spoke earlier. Although we have worked out a course which will take into consideration the tidal effect, we must make allowance for deviation before we can give that course to the helmsman to steer. From the deviation graph, we see that the deviation for our new course, that is to say the course we wish to steer, is

2° E. Now in Fig. 42, AB is the direction of our vessel's head. The angle DAB can represent the compass course, and the angle CAB, the magnetic course. Now easterly deviation we will call plus, and westerly deviation we will call minus, to denote that we will either add or subtract them from the compass course measured as an angle clockwise between 0 degree and 360 degrees. Now to Figure 42 (a). Here the magnetic course is seen to be less than the compass course by the amount of the westerly deviation. It is, therefore, clear that to find the magnetic course, we must subtract the westerly deviation from the compass course. In Fig. 42 (b) the magnetic course is greater than the compass by the amount of the easterly deviation. So by the same token, we must add the easterly deviation to the compass course in order to arrive at the magnetic course. It will be clear from these two examples that, when the deviation is easterly, the compass needle is deflected clockwise, and that with westerly deviation the compass needle is deflected counterclockwise. This brings us to a rule which can be used when applying deviation: to convert a magnetic course to compass course, apply westerly deviation clockwise and easterly deviation counter-clockwise. That is to say, if the course on the chart is north and there is 2 degrees of westerly deviation, if we apply the rule 'magnetic to compass—westerly clockwise', the course to steer (the compass course) will now be not north, but N. 2° E. Furthermore, to convert a compass course, that is a course taken from the compass into a magnetic course, that is, a course to be plotted on the chart, the same rule gives us 'westerly deviation counter-clockwise, easterly deviation clockwise'.

I have so far deliberately omitted the variation of which we spoke earlier in this book. This is because, in practice, you will find you can take most of your courses and bearings from the inner (magnetic) rose on the chart. Your chart, unless it is extremely old, will be corrected quite accurately enough for variation for a small yacht. However, exactly the same principle as for deviation applies when converting a magnetic course into a true course. In this case the variation is applied to the magnetic course by the same rule, clockwise for easterly and counterclockwise for westerly. Similarly, when converting a true course or bearing, plotted from the true rose on the chart into a magnetic course or bearing, variation should be applied clockwise for westerly and counter-clockwise for easterly. As I have said, however, the conversion on a modern chart of a course from true to magnetic, may, for the purposes of a small yacht sailing in coastal waters, be done on the compass rose on the chart itself.

Now that we can allow for lee-way, deviation, and tidal currents in laying off a course, all we have to do is occasionally check up on our position by keeping what is known as a 'reckoning'.

It is very unlikely that you will have a fair wind for the whole of your voyage. Our climate being what it is, you will have to beat to windward at some point during the passage. The navigator must note down all the alterations of course, convert these into magnetic courses, and plot them on the chart. If circumstances prevent him from doing this at the time, he must jot down the times of the alteration of courses, the magnetic course and also the distance covered as indicated on the patent log. Then he can 'work up his reckoning' at a convenient moment. If he is plotting every alteration as it occurs, generally the procedure is to lay off the current at the final point working from when he started. The final position obtained is called the Dead Reckoning Position (D.R.Pn.), which is his estimated position at the end of the run. The course as plotted is known as the Dead Reckoning (D.R.). The D.R. position should not vary much from your actual position, even after a long journey, if you have carefully allowed for currents and lee-way. However, the most careful recordings of the navigator can be thrown off by such things as: tides, fluky winds, surface drift, etc. Since all tidal calculations are approximate and tidal currents are affected by the weather, there is a possibility of error here. Fluky winds will, of course, alter the lee-way and speed of the ship. The effect of surface drift will decrease very obviously as the draught of a vessel increases. Consequently, after a voyage of 60 miles you are very likely to find a difference of several miles between the D.R. position and the true position. This would not be a difficult situation if your anchorage is in good visibility, but should the visibility be poor, it is most necessary to be sure of your position. This is only one reason why it is important that from time to time you should check up on the actual position of your ship. If you find the two positions differ, you must start your D.R. again from the new, and certain, position. Any position estimated from the dead reckoning that is the most accurate available, though not completely certain, is known as an Estimated Position (E.P.). This position is shown by a dot with a triangle round it and the time written alongside. A dot surrounded by a circle and also with the time alongside denotes an observed position, which is termed a fix. This position can be arrived at either by two or more cross bearings, radio bearings, or by the observation of heavenly bodies. All fixes, E.P.s, position lines, and bearings are quite useless unless they have the time when they were taken written alongside them. There is no need to worry if your fixes stay reasonably near the course line; but if there is much difference between the two positions, then the D.R. position should be discarded and the dead reckoning started again from the new fix.

In Fig. 43 we see how the reckoning is worked up. Our ship starts from A at 09.00 hours and, as her course is to windward, she proceeds in a series of tacks. The time is jotted down whenever she changes course. Let us say that at 11.25 hours, 2 hours and 25 minutes after our first fix at 09.00, we want to find our dead reckoning position on the chart. If there had been no tide at 11.25, we should be at B, but since the tide has been driving against us constantly in different directions, we must allow for it. We then plot back from B the distance and direction of the tide for each of the 2 hours and 30 minutes we have travelled. Notice that we are now at a position much farther south and that this position has the same time alongside it as position B. This is our D.R. position at 11.25.

Let us now suppose that on shore we can sight two definite landmarks. We take a bearing of each, first taking the bearing on the bow, and secondly the beam bearing, since this changes more rapidly as we sail past it. We can plot the bearings as observed on the chart, since our deviation card shows that there is no deviation for the course we are steering. Where the two bearings cross we have our fix. We encircle the fix, write the time alongside it, and compare it with the dead reckoning position. Let us suppose that it is far to the eastward of the D.R. position. We must, therefore, discard the D.R. position, and from the new fix once again start plotting our reckoning.

Perhaps our tidal allowance was wrong, or it may have been that the helmsman was steering to leeward of the correct course while sailing on the port tack.

Generally the method the navigator will use to fix his ship's

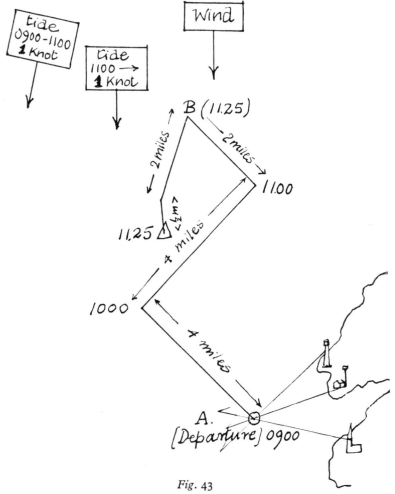

Fig. 43

position is that of cross bearings (or position lines), which is the method we have just applied. The chances of error are much less if three position lines can be obtained instead of two. It is best, of course, if the lines all meet in the same place, but often they will make a small triangle. In this triangle (called a 'cocked hat'), you should make your fix the nearest point to danger.

However, if there is no danger near, place your fix in the centre of the triangle. The cross-bearing method of necessity requires two or more shore objects, but there may be only one shore object which you can identify. To solve this problem you can choose one of three methods. In Fig. 44 we see the first, which is called the 'four point bearing' method. When your landmark is 45 degrees on the bow, note the time and the reading of the patent log. Then sail on, holding a steady course, and as steady a

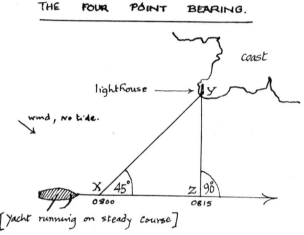

THE FOUR POINT BEARING.

Coast

lighthouse ⟶ Y

wind, no tide.

X 45° Z 90
0800   0815

[Yacht running on steady course]

Bearing of lighthouse Y taken first at X when Y is 45° on
the Port Bow, and second at Z, when Y is 90° to the
Yacht's fore-and-aft line. XZ ∴ = distance run
in ¼ hour. XZ = ZY = Distance of yacht from the
lighthouse at 0815.

Fig. 44

speed as possible, until the object on shore is abeam. Again note the time and the reading of the patent log. Compare the difference between the log readings or the time interval with the ship's speed, and you will have the distance sailed between the two bearings. Now it is unlikely that the course you have steered is the course you have actually made good over the ground. The effect of the tide must be considered, since the course with which the two bearings make an angle will be the course made good. Let us suppose you are steering north and the tide is eastwardly setting across your course, then the course made good will be not north, but somewhere to the east of north.

This first method deals with the angle which the object's bearing makes with the 'course made good'. Therefore, when there is any tide to consider, you must work from the course made good. Let us suppose that you were steering your ship south by compass, but you found from the chart that her course made good was 190°, due to the tidal effect. The first position line then for the 4-point bearing of a given object to starboard must be taken when the object bears 4 points off the course made good. In this case, when the object bears 235°, and not

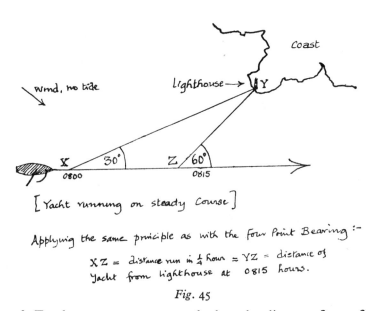

DOUBLING   THE   ANGLE   ON   THE   BOW.

Fig. 45

225°. Furthermore, you must calculate the distance factor from the speed made good and not the speed through the water.

The principle of the second method is the same as that of the 4-point bearing method. This method is known as 'doubling the angle on the bow'. You take a bearing, say 30 degrees on the bow, of a given object on the shore. Then run on, maintaining a steady course until the object is bearing 60 degrees on the bow (that is, double the first one). Remember, to obtain an accurate fix, you must make allowance for the tide. Follow the same procedure as with the 4-point bearing, noting the time and log reading of both bearings. The distance covered will be the same as the distance from the object on shore when the latter bears 60 degrees.

If it is not possible to get a bearing just at the right time to double the bow angle, and if there is only one shore object, we must use what is known as a 'running fix'. Using this method, we take a bearing and note the time and the reading on the patent log. Then run on a steady course for about half an hour and take another bearing, noting the time and reading on the patent log. Now lay off these two bearings on the chart, and, if necessary, make corrections for deviation and variation. The ship was on some point along that position line when both the first and second bearings were taken, and has held a steady course between the two bearings. So if we can now find a line equal to the *distance made good* (in other words, including the tide's influence) and which points in the same direction as the *course made good*, our ship's fixed position will be defined by the points at the ends of this line, that is, where it meets the two position lines.

We see in Fig. 46 that our ship is sailing on a course of east magnetic at a steady speed of 4 knots, which we have calculated from the patent log. Visibility is only fair, but we can see a lighthouse to the northward of us. We take our first bearing at 09.00, and the log reads 22 miles. We take another bearing at 09.30, and the log reads 24 miles. We will call these two bearings CA and CB. We are being driven by the tide in a north-easterly direction at 2 knots. We will now take a point L on CA and from it draw a line eastwards. We measure off 2 miles along the line and call this point N. LN represents the course steered, and the course and distance run through the water. Now draw a line northeastwards from N, and measure off 1 mile, since we have been sailing just a half-hour between bearings. This gives us NM and indicates the tidal set. If we join LM, we have the course and distance *made good*. Next, place the parallel ruler on CA, run it over to CB, just touching the point M, and this will give us a new line, PQ. Where this cuts CB will be the actual position of the ship at 09.30. If we wish to check this, we put the parallel ruler along LM, move it up until it touches CB at the ship's new position, and the distance between the two new points (where it cuts CA and CB) will be exactly the same as LM.

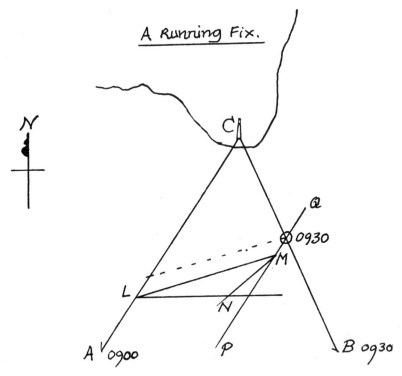

A Running Fix.

LM = Co and distance made good.

NM = current from 0900 to 0930

PQ = 1ˢᵗ bearing transferred

⊙ 0930 = Vessel's position at 0930.

Fig. 46

Now, supposing you are sailing due east and have been able to get a first bearing of a certain light and then fog sets in and you are unable to get your second bearing. You continue on your course, logging a steady 4 knots. You manage to get a quick bearing of another light in between fog patches, but this will suffice. You will still be able to fix the ship by using a method called the transferred position line.

Transferred Position Line.

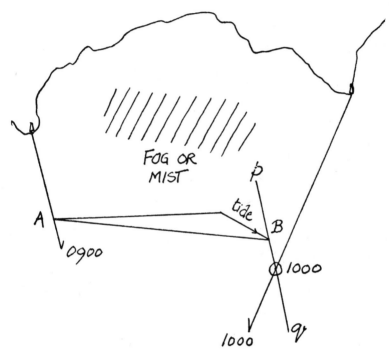

AB = Co and distance made good.

pq = transferred position line.

⊙ 1000 = ship's position at 1000 hrs.

Fig. 47

The two bearings we have taken will give us two position lines. What we will do is transfer the first of these lines over to cut the second. Although where they cut will not give us an absolute fix, we will have something more accurate than a dead reckoning position estimated by calculations of tide, and the ship's course and speed.

Looking at Fig. 47, we will first draw in the two bearings on the chart and mark the times alongside them. We then take any point on the first position line and call it A. Now we plot the course made good, the same as we did for our running fix. We will call this line AB on the chart, and placing the parallel ruler on the first position line, we transfer the latter until it reaches the point B. We will call this new line *pq*, and where it cuts the second position line we have our estimated position, which is the position the ship is most likely to be in at the time of the second bearing (10.00). It will be obvious that we must know the course and distance made good quite accurately to make either of these two methods of any avail.

We have now learned five different methods by which we can fix our ship's position, and these should be adequate for the beginner: cross bearings, 4-point bearings, doubling the angle on the bow, the running fix, and the transferred position line.

However, I must make some mention here about aids to navigation. Nowadays the yachtsman has many such aids. There are numerous radio aids, which may be listed as follows: (1) Radio Direction Finding by marine Radio Beacons. (2) Radio Ship Position finding systems. (*a*) Loran, (*b*) Decca and (*c*) Consol. (3) Radar. This is certainly not the place to embark upon a lengthy description of how these various aids work. They are all basically position-finding systems—some much more expensive to instal than others! Information concerning them can be obtained from any reasonably large yacht chandlers and from yacht builders. There is, however, one point I would like to make. Radio navigational aids are what the name implies—aids! They do not take the place of the older methods of finding the vessel's position by bearings, sights and soundings. They will, of course, improve as each year goes by, but it must be remembered that each has certain limitations and furthermore, most need a good deal of experience and practice to get really accurate data from them. If a navigator's fix is confirmed by radio aid he is relieved of anxiety. If the radio fix disagrees with his workings out he should 'work it out again'! These wonderful scienti-

fic advances must be used, in other words, for what they are—
navigational "aids".

We have now studied several methods by which we can fix
our ship's position, and can realise the importance of correcting
the Dead Reckoning course and position as soon as it is possible
to fix the ship. At the end of a rather long passage you may
often find a difference of several miles between the fixed
position and the E.P. This will most likely be the case if you
are inexperienced in making tide allowances, lee-way, etc.; but
don't be discouraged by this. Until you improve with experience, be thankful that you can obtain your fix and accordingly
correct your position.

You will most always find that you must alter course when
correcting your position in this way. Whenever your fixed
position differs from your D.R. position, you will have to lay
off a new course from the new position.

If you are reaching the end of a voyage, though not yet in
sight of land, shortly you will make your landfall. During the
day, you will have to distinguish between all the pieces of coast-
line which look so much alike, but at night it will be easier as
you have only to recognise flashing lights, each having its own
distinctive characteristic. If your passage has been a long one,
there are many factors likely to prevent you from finding the
harbour mouth dead ahead on the bow. You may not have
allowed enough for lee-way; or the patent log may not have
been properly registering the distance run; or the tide may not
have been behaving in the expected manner.

But never mind, we have arrived safely and with reasonable
accuracy and now we must lay a course for the harbour entrance.
We fix the ship by means of objects on shore, or, if it is dark,
by means of the various lights which we identify from the chart.
Now as a competent navigator, we will have studied the harbour
chart and are prepared for any dangers, such as sandbanks,
fast-running currents, outlying rocks, etc., which may be
indicated. We will have familiarised ourselves with the landmarks, buoyage, port rules, and regulations of the new harbour.
If the harbour entrance is not clearly visible, there are two
different methods of entering which are frequently very helpful.
The first is by running along a bearing of a given object on

shore. Note a definite landmark on the chart and rule a line from it that will steer the vessel away from all dangers. Looking at Fig. 48, we see that if the line ruled is southwest, we then try to position the ship so that this particular object bears northeast, and as long as the ship holds the object on that bearing, she can safely enter the harbour. The second and, it must be admitted, ideal method of entry is to choose two prominent landmarks, and by keeping them in line, the ship can be easily steered on a true course with no chance of deviation errors.

Fig. 48

The importance of the navigator knowing the buoyage system and also the rule of the road at sea cannot be over stressed, and so I conclude this chapter with certain vitally important articles from the International Regulations for Preventing Collisions at sea, and with a short description of the buoyage system.

NEW COLLISION REGULATIONS

The following are taken from the International Regulations for Preventing Collisions at Sea, 1972. I have included those most likely to affect yacht owners. The full text may be obtained anywhere where charts, etc., are sold and is also included in full in Reed's Nautical Almanac.

INTERNATIONAL REGULATIONS FOR PREVENTING COLLISIONS AT SEA, 1972

PART A—GENERAL

Rule 1 *Application*

(a) These Rules shall apply to all vessels upon the high seas and in all waters connected therewith navigable by seagoing vessels.
(b) Nothing in these Rules shall interfere with the operation of special rules made by an appropriate authority for roadsteads, harbours, rivers, lakes or inland waterways connected with the high seas and navigable by seagoing vessels. Such special rules shall conform as closely as possible to these rules.

Rule 2 *Responsibility*

(a) Nothing in these Rules shall exonerate any vessel, or the owner, master or crew thereof, from the consequences of any neglect to comply with these Rules or of the neglect of any precaution which may be required by the ordinary practice of seamen, or by the special circumstances of the case.
(b) In construing and complying with these Rules due regard shall be had to all dangers of navigation and collision and to any special circumstances, including the limitations of the vessels involved, which may make a departure from these Rules necessary to avoid immediate danger.

Rule 3 *General Definitions*

For the purpose of these Rules, except where the context otherwise requires:

(a) The word "vessel" includes every description of water craft, including non-displacement craft and seaplanes, used or capable of being used as a means of transportation on water.

(b) The term "power-driven vessel" means any vessel propelled by machinery.

(c) The term "sailing vessel" means any vessel under sail provided that propelling machinery, if fitted, is not being used.

(d) The term "vessel engaged in fishing" means any vessel fishing with nets, lines, trawls or other fishing apparatus which restrict manoeuvrability, but does not include a vessel fishing with trolling lines or other fishing apparatus which do not restrict manoeuvrability.

(e) The word "seaplane" includes any aircraft designed to manoeuvre on the water.

(f) The term "vessel not under command" means a vessel which through some exceptional circumstance is unable to manoeuvre as required by these Rules and is therefore unable to keep out of the way of another vessel.

(g) The term "vessel restricted in her ability to manoeuvre" means a vessel which from the nature of her work is restricted in her ability to manoeuvre as required by these Rules and is therefore unable to keep out of the way of another vessel.

(h) The term "vessel constrained by her draught" means a power-driven vessel which because of her draught in relation to the available depth of water is severely restricted in her ability to deviate from the course she is following.

(i) The word "underway" means that a vessel is not at anchor, or made fast to the shore, or aground.

(j) The words "length" and "breadth" of a vessel mean her length overall and greatest breadth.

(k) Vessels shall be deemed to be in sight of one another only when one can be observed visually from the other.

(l) The term "restricted visibility" means any condition in which visibility is restricted by fog, mist, falling snow, heavy rainstorms, sandstorms or any other similar causes.

PART B—STEERING AND SAILING RULES

SECTION 1—CONDUCT OF VESSELS IN ANY CONDITION OF VISIBILITY

Rule 4 *Application*

Rules in this Section apply in any condition of visibility.

Rule 7   *Risk of Collision*

(a) Every vessel shall use all available means appropriate to the prevailing circumstances and conditions to determine if risk of collision exists. If there is any doubt such risk shall be deemed to exist.

(d) In determining if risk of collision exists the following considerations shall be among those taken into account:

> (i) such risk shall be deemed to exist if the compass bearing of an approaching vessel does not appreciably change;
>
> (ii) such risk may sometimes exist even when an appreciable bearing change is evident, particularly when approaching a very large vessel or a tow or when approaching a vessel at close range.

Rule 8   *Action to avoid Collision*

(a) Any action taken to avoid collision shall, if the circumstances of the case admit, be positive, made in ample time and with due regard to the observance of good seamanship.

(b) Any alteration of course and/or speed to avoid collision shall, if the circumstances of the case admit, be large enough to be readily apparent to another vessel observing visually or by radar; a succession of small alterations of course and/or speed should be avoided.

Rule 9   *Narrow Channels*

(a) A vessel proceeding along the course of a narrow channel or fairway shall keep as near to the outer limit of the channel or fairway which lies on her starboard side as is safe and practicable.

(b) A vessel of less than 20 metres in length or a sailing vessel shall not impede the passage of a vessel which can safely navigate only within a narrow channel or fairway.

Rule 10   *Traffic Separation Schemes*

(j) A vessel of less than 20 metres in length or a sailing vessel shall not impede the safe passage of a power-driven vessel following a traffic lane.

SECTION II—CONDUCT OF VESSELS IN SIGHT OF ONE ANOTHER

Rule 11   *Application*

Rules in this Section apply to vessels in sight of one another.

Rule 12 *Sailing Vessels*

(a) when two sailing vessels are approaching one another, so as to involve risk of collision, one of them shall keep out of the way of the other as follows:

> (i) when each has the wind on a different side, the vessel which has the wind on the port side shall keep out of the way of the other;

> (ii) when both have the wind on the same side, the vessel which is to windward shall keep out of the way of the vessel which is to leeward;

> (iii) if a vessel with the wind on the port side sees a vessel to windward and cannot determine with certainty whether the other vessel has the wind on the port or on the starboard side, she shall keep out of the way of the other.

(b) For the purposes of this Rule the windward side shall be deemed to be the side opposite to that on which the mainsail is carried or, in the case of a square-rigged vessel, the side opposite to that on which the largest fore-and-aft sail is carried.

Rule 13 *Overtaking*

(a) Notwithstanding anything contained in the Rules of this Section any vessel overtaking any other shall keep out of the way of the vessel being overtaken.

(b) A vessel shall be deemed to be overtaking when coming up with another vessel from a direction more than 22.5 degrees abaft her beam, that is, in such a position with reference to the vessel she is overtaking, that at night she would be able to see only the sternlight of that vessel but neither of her sidelights.

(c) When a vessel is in any doubt as to whether she is overtaking another, she shall assume that this is the case and act accordingly.

(d) Any subsequent alteration of the bearing between the two vessels shall not make the overtaking vessel a crossing vessel within the meaning of these Rules or relieve her of the duty of keeping clear of the overtaken vessel until she is finally past and clear.

Rule 14 *Head-on Situation*

(a) When two power-driven vessels are meeting on reciprocal or nearly reciprocal courses so as to involve risk of collision each shall alter her course to starboard so that each shall pass on the port side of the other.

(b) Such a situation shall be deemed to exist when a vessel sees the other ahead or nearly ahead and by night she could see the masthead lights of the other in a line or nearly in a line and/or both sidelights and by day she observes the corresponding aspect of the other vessel.
(c) When a vessel is in any doubt as to whether such a situation exists she shall assume that it does exist and act accordingly.

Rule 15   *Crossing Situation*

When two power-driven vessels are crossing so as to involve risk of collision, the vessel which has the other on her own starboard side shall keep out of the way and shall, if the circumstances of the case admit, avoid crossing ahead of the other vessel.

Rule 16   *Action by Give-way Vessel*

Every vessel which is directed to keep out of the way of another vessel shall, so far as possible, take early and substantial action to keep well clear.

Rule 17   *Action by Stand-on Vessel*

(a)   (i) Where one of two vessels is to keep out of the way the other shall keep her course and speed.
(ii) The latter vessel may however take action to avoid collision by her manoeuvre alone, as soon as it becomes apparent to her that the vessel required to keep out of the way is not taking appropriate action in compliance with these Rules.
(b) When, from any cause, the vessel required to keep her course and speed finds herself so close that collision cannot be avoided by the action of the give-way vessel alone, she shall take such action as will best aid to avoid collision.
(c) A power-driven vessel which takes action in a crossing situation in accordance with sub-paragraph (a)(ii) of this Rule to avoid collision with another power-driven vessel shall, if the circumstances of the case admit, not alter course to port for a vessel on her own port side.
(d) This Rule does not relieve the give-way vessel of her obligation to keep out of the way.

Rule 18   *Responsibilities between Vessels*

Except where Rules 9, 10 and 13 otherwise require:

(a) A power-driven vessel underway shall keep out of the way of:
    (i) a vessel not under command;
    (ii) a vessel restricted in her ability to manoeuvre;
    (iii) a vessel engaged in fishing;
    (iv) a sailing vessel.

(b) A sailing vessel underway shall keep out of the way of:
    (i) a vessel not under command;
    (ii) a vessel restricted in her ability to manoeuvre;
    (iii) a vessel engaged in fishing.

(c) A vessel engaged in fishing when underway shall, so far as possible, keep out of the way of:
    (i) a vessel not under command;
    (ii) a vessel restricted in her ability to manoeuvre.

(d) (i) Any vessel other than a vessel not under command or a vessel restricted in her ability to manoeuvre shall, if the circumstances of the case admit, avoid impeding the safe passage of a vessel constrained by her draught, exhibiting the signals in Rule 28.

(ii) A vessel constrained by her draught shall navigate with particular caution having full regard to her special condition.

SECTION III—CONDUCT OF VESSELS IN RESTRICTED VISIBILITY

Rule 19 *Conduct of Vessels in Restricted Visibility*

(a) This Rule applies to vessels not in sight of one another when navigating in or near an area of restricted visibility.

(b) Every vessel shall proceed at a safe speed adapted to the prevailing circumstances and conditions of restricted visibility. A power-driven vessel shall have her engines ready for immediate manoeuvre.

(c) Every vessel shall have due regard to the prevailing circumstances and conditions of restricted visibility when complying with the Rules of Section 1 of this Part.

(e) Except where it has been determined that a risk of collision does not exist, every vessel which hears apparently forward of her beam the fog signal of another vessel, or which cannot avoid a close-quarters situation with another vessel forward of her beam, shall reduce her speed to the minimum at which she can be kept on her course. She shall if necessary take all her way off and in any event navigate with extreme caution until danger of collision is over.

PART C—LIGHTS AND SHAPES

Rule 20 *Application*

(a) Rules in this Part shall be complied with in all weathers.

(b) The Rules concerning lights shall be complied with from sunset to sunrise, and during such times no other lights shall be exhibited, except such lights as cannot be mistaken for the lights specified in these Rules or do not impair their visibility or distinctive character, or interfere with the keeping of a proper lookout.

(c) The lights prescribed by these Rules shall, if carried, also be exhibited from sunrise to sunset in restricted visibility and may be exhibited in all other circumstances when it is deemed necessary.

(d) The Rules concerning shapes shall be complied with by day.

(e) The lights and shapes specified in these Rules shall comply with the provisions of Annex I to these Regulations.

Rule 21 *Definitions*

(a) "Masthead light" means a white light placed over the fore and aft centreline of the vessel showing an unbroken light over an arc of the horizon of 225 degrees and so fixed as to show the light from right ahead to 22.5 degrees abaft the beam on either side of the vessel.

(b) "Sidelights" means a green light on the starboard side and a red light on the port side each showing an unbroken light over an arc of the horizon of 112.5 degrees and so fixed as to show the light from right ahead to 22.5 degrees abaft the beam on its respective side. In a vessel of less than 20 metres in length the sidelights may be combined in one lantern carried on the fore and aft centreline of the vessel.

(c) "Sternlight" means a white light placed as nearly as practicable at the stern showing an unbroken light over an arc of the horizon of 135 degrees and so fixed as to show the light 67.5 degrees from right aft on each side of the vessel.

(d) "Towing light" means a yellow light having the same characteristics as the "sternlight" defined in paragraph (c) of this Rule.

(e) "All-round light" means a light showing an unbroken light over an arc of the horizon of 360 degrees.

(f) "Flashing light" means a light flashing at regular intervals at a frequency of 120 flashes or more per minute.

Rule 22 *Visibility of Lights*

The lights prescribed in these Rules shall have an intensity as specified in Section 8 of Annex I to these Regulations so as to be visible at the following minimum ranges:

(b) In vessels of 12 metres or more in length but less than 50 metres in length;

—a masthead light, 5 miles; except that where the length of the vessel is less than 20 metres, 3 miles;
—a sidelight, 2 miles;
—a sternlight, 2 miles;
—a towing light, 2 miles;
—a white, red, green or yellow all-round light, 2 miles.

(c) In vessels of less than 12 metres in length:

—a masthead light, 2 miles;
—a sidelight, 1 mile;
—a sternlight, 2 miles;
—a towing light, 2 miles;
—a white, red, green or yellow all-round light, 2 miles.

Rule 23   *Power-driven Vessels underway*

(a) A power-driven vessel underway shall exhibit:

(i) a masthead light forward;
(ii) a second masthead light abaft of and higher than the forward one; except that a vessel of less than 50 metres in length shall not be obliged to exhibit such light but may do so;
(iii) sidelights;
(iv) a sternlight.

(b) An air-cushion vessel when operating in the non-displacement mode shall, in addition to the lights prescribed in paragraph (a) of this Rule, exhibit an all-round flashing yellow light.

(c) A power-driven vessel of less than 7 metres in length and whose maximum speed does not exceed 7 knots may, in lieu of the lights prescribed in paragraph (a) of this Rule, exhibit an all-round white light. Such vessel shall, if practicable, also exhibit sidelights.

Rule 24   *Towing and Pushing*

(a) A power-driven vessel when towing shall exhibit:

(i) instead of the light prescribed in Rule 23(a)(i), two masthead lights forward in a vertical line. When the length of the tow, measuring from the stern of the towing vessel to the after end of the tow exceeds 200 metres, three such lights in a vertical line;

(ii) sidelights;

(iii) a sternlight;

(iv) a towing light in a vertical line above the sternlight;

(v) when the length of the tow exceeds 200 metres, a diamond shape where it can best be seen.

(b) When a pushing vessel and a vessel being pushed ahead are rigidly connected in a composite unit they shall be regarded as a power-driven vessel and exhibit the lights prescribed in Rule 23.

(c) A power-driven vessel when pushing ahead or towing alongside, except in the case of a composite unit, shall exhibit:

(i) instead of the light prescribed in Rule 23(a)(i), two masthead lights forward in a vertical line;

(ii) sidelights;

(iii) a sternlight.

(d) A power-driven vessel to which paragraphs (a) and (c) of this Rule apply shall also comply with Rule 23(a)(ii).

(e) A vessel or object being towed shall exhibit:

(i) sidelights;

(ii) a sternlight;

(iii) when the length of the tow exceeds 200 metres, a diamond shape where it can best be seen.

Rule 25 *Sailing Vessels underway and Vessels under Oars*

(a) A sailing vessel underway shall exhibit:

(i) sidelights;

(ii) a sternlight.

(b) In a sailing vessel of less than 12 metres in length the lights prescribed in paragraph (a) of this Rule may be combined in one lantern carried at or near the top of the mast where it can best be seen.

(c) A sailing vessel underway may, in addition to the lights prescribed in paragraph (a) of this Rule, exhibit at or near the top of the mast, where they can best be seen, two all-round lights in a vertical line, the upper being red and the lower green, but these lights shall not be exhibited in conjunction with the combined lantern permitted by paragraph (b) of this Rule.

(d) (i) A sailing vessel of less than 7 metres in length shall, if practicable, exhibit the lights prescribed in paragraph (a) or (b) of this Rule, but if she does not, she shall have ready at hand an electric torch or lighted lantern showing a white light which shall be exhibited in sufficient time to prevent collision.

(ii) A vessel under oars may exhibit the lights prescribed in this

Rule for sailing vessels, but if she does not, she shall have ready at hand an electric torch or lighted lantern showing a white light which shall be exhibited in sufficient time to prevent collision.

(e) A vessel proceeding under sail when also being propelled by machinery shall exhibit forward where it can best be seen a conical shape, apex downwards.

Rule 28   *Vessels constrained by their Draught*

A vessel constrained by her draught may, in addition to the lights prescribed for power-driven vessels in Rule 23, exhibit where they can best be seen three all-round red lights in a vertical line, or a cylinder.

Rule 30   *Anchored Vessels and Vessels aground*

(a) A vessel at anchor shall exhibit where it can best be seen:
    (i) in the fore part, an all-round white light or one ball;
    (ii) at or near the stern and at a lower level than the light prescribed in sub-paragraph (i), an all-round white light.

(b) A vessel of less than 50 metres in length may exhibit an all-round white light where it can best be seen instead of the lights prescribed in paragraph (a) of this Rule.

(c) A vessel at anchor may, and a vessel of 100 metres and more in length shall, also use the available working or equivalent lights to illuminate her decks.

(d) A vessel aground shall exhibit the lights prescribed in paragraph (a) or (b) of this Rule and in addition, where they can best be seen:
    (i) two all-round red lights in a vertical line;
    (ii) three balls in a vertical line.

(e) A vessel of less than 7 metres in length, when at anchor or aground not in or near a narrow channel, fairway or anchorage, or where other vessels normally navigate, shall not be required to exhibit the lights or shapes prescribed in paragraph (a), (b) or (d) of this Rule.

PART D—SOUND AND LIGHT SIGNALS

Rule 32   *Definitions*

(a) The word "whistle" means any sound signalling appliance capable of producing the prescribed blasts and which complies with the specifications in Annex III to these Regulations.

(b) The term "short blast" means a blast of about one second's duration.

(c) The term "prolonged blast" means a blast of from four to six seconds' duration.

Rule 33 *Equipment for Sound Signals*

(a) A vessel of 12 metres or more in length shall be provided with a whistle and a bell and a vessel of 100 metres or more in length shall, in addition, be provided with a gong, the tone and sound of which cannot be confused with that of the bell. The whistle, bell and gong shall comply with the specifications in Annex III to these Regulations. The bell or gong or both may be replaced by other equipment having the same respective sound characteristics, provided that manual sounding of the required signals shall always be possible.

(b) A vessel of less than 12 metres in length shall not be obliged to carry the sound signalling appliances prescribed in paragraph (a) of this Rule but if she does not, she shall be provided with some other means of making an efficient sound signal.

Rule 34 *Manoeuvring and Warning Signals*

(a) When vessels are in sight of one another, a power-driven vessel underway, when manoeuvring as authorised or required by these Rules, shall indicate that manoeuvre by the following signals on her whistle:

　—one short blast to mean "I am altering my course to starboard";

　—two short blasts to mean "I am altering my course to port";

　—three short blasts to mean "I am operating astern propulsion".

(b) Any vessel may supplement the whistle signals prescribed in paragraph (a) of this Rule by light signals, repeated as appropriate, whilst the manoeuvre is being carried out:

(i) these light signals shall have the following significance:

　—one flash to mean "I am altering my course to starboard";

　—two flashes to mean "I am altering my course to port";

　—three flashes to mean "I am operating astern propulsion";

(ii) the duration of each flash shall be about one second, the interval between flashes shall be about one second, and the interval between successive signals shall be not less than ten seconds;

(iii) the light used for this signal shall, if fitted, be an all-round white light, visible at a minimum range of 5 miles, and shall comply with the provisions of Annex I.

(c) When in sight of one another in a narrow channel or fairway:

(i) a vessel intending to overtake another shall in compliance with Rule 9(e)(i) indicate her intention by the following signals on her whistle:

—two prolonged blasts followed by one short blast to mean "I intend to overtake you on your starboard side";

—two prolonged blasts followed by two short blasts to mean "I intend to overtake you on your port side";

(ii) the vessel about to be overtaken when acting in accordance with Rule 9(e)(i) shall indicate her agreement by the following signal on her whistle:

—one prolonged, one short, one prolonged and one short blast, in that order.

(d) When vessels in sight of one another are approaching each other and from any cause either vessel fails to understand the intentions or actions of the other, or is in doubt whether sufficient action is being taken by the other to avoid collision, the vessel in doubt shall immediately indicate such doubt by giving at least five short and rapid blasts on the whistle. Such signal may be supplemented by a light signal of at least five short and rapid flashes.

(e) A vessel nearing a bend or an area of a channel or fairway where other vessels may be obscured by an intervening obstruction shall sound one prolonged blast. Such signal shall be answered with a prolonged blast by any approaching vessel that may be within hearing around the bend or behind the intervening obstruction.

(f) If whistles are fitted on a vessel at a distance apart of more than 100 metres, one whistle only shall be used for giving manoeuvring and warning signals.

Rule 35 *Sound Signals in restricted Visibility*

In or near an area of restricted visibility, whether by day or night, the signals prescribed in this Rule shall be used as follows:

(a) A power-driven vessel making way through the water shall sound at intervals of not more than 2 minutes one prolonged blast.

(b) A power-driven vessel underway but stopped and making no way through the water shall sound at intervals of not more than 2 minutes two prolonged blasts in succession with an interval of about 2 seconds between them.

(c) A vessel not under command, a vessel restricted in her ability to manoeuvre, a vessel constrained by her draught, a sailing vessel, a vessel engaged in fishing and a vessel engaged in towing or pushing another vessel shall, instead of the signals prescribed in paragraphs (a) or (b) of this Rule, sound at intervals of not more than 2 minutes three blasts in succession, namely one prolonged followed by two short blasts.

(d) A vessel towed or if more than one vessel is towed the last vessel of the tow, if manned, shall at intervals of not more than 2 minutes sound four blasts in succession, namely one prolonged followed by three short blasts. When practicable, this signal shall be made immediately after the signal made by the towing vessel.

(e) When a pushing vessel and a vessel being pushed ahead are rigidly connected in a composite unit they shall be regarded as a power-driven vessel and shall give the signals prescribed in paragraphs (a) or (b) of this Rule.

(f) A vessel at anchor shall at intervals of not more than one minute ring the bell rapidly for about 5 seconds. In a vessel of 100 metres or more in length the bell shall be sounded in the forepart of the vessel and immediately after the ringing of the bell the gong shall be sounded rapidly for about 5 seconds in the after part of the vessel. A vessel at anchor may in addition sound three blasts in succession, namely one short, one prolonged and one short blast, to give warning of her position and of the possibility of collision to an approaching vessel.

(g) A vessel aground shall give the bell signal and if required the gong signal prescribed in paragraph (f) of this Rule and shall, in addition, give three separate and distinct strokes on the bell immediately before and after the rapid ringing of the bell. A vessel aground may in addition sound an appropriate whistle signal.

(h) A vessel of less than 12 metres in length shall not be obliged to give the above-mentioned signals but, if she does not, shall make some other efficient sound signal at intervals of not more than 2 minutes.

(i) A pilot vessel when engaged on pilotage duty may in addition to the signals prescribed in paragraphs (a), (b) or (f) of this Rule sound an identity signal consisting of four short blasts.

PART E—EXEMPTIONS

Rule 38 *Exemptions*

Any vessel (or class of vessels) provided that she complies with the requirements of the International Regulations for Preventing Collisions at Sea, 1960, the keel of which is laid or which is at a corresponding stage of construction before the entry into force of these Regulations may be exempted from compliance therewith as follows:

(a) The installation of lights with ranges prescribed in Rule 22, until four years after the date of entry into force of these Regulations.

(b) The installation of lights with colour specifications as prescribed in Section 7 of Annex I to these Regulations, until four years after the date of entry into force of these Regulations.

(c) The repositioning of lights as a result of conversion from Imperial to metric units and rounding off measurements figures, permanent exemption.

(d) (i) The repositioning of masthead lights on vessels of less than 150 metres in length, resulting from the prescriptions of Section 3(a) of Annex I, permanent exemption.

(f) The repositioning of sidelights resulting from the prescriptions of Sections 2(g) and 3(b) of Annex I, until nine years after the date of entry into force of these Regulations.

(g) The requirements for sound signal appliances prescribed in Annex III, until nine years after the date of entry into force of these Regulations.

ANNEX I

POSITIONING AND TECHNICAL DETAILS OF LIGHTS AND SHAPES

1. Definition

The term "height above the hull" means height above the uppermost continuous deck.

2. Vertical positioning and spacing of lights

(c) The masthead light of a power-driven vessel of 12 metres but less than 20 metres in length shall be placed at a height above the gunwale of not less than 2.5 metres.

(d) A power-driven vessel of less than 12 metres in length may carry the uppermost light at a height of less than 2.5 metres above the gunwale. When however a masthead light is carried in addition to sidelights and a sternlight, then such masthead light shall be carried at least 1 metre higher than the sidelights.

(e) One of the two or three masthead lights prescribed for a power-driven vessel when engaged in towing or pushing another vessel shall be placed in the same position as the forward masthead light of a power-driven vessel.

(f) In all circumstances the masthead light or lights shall be so placed as to be above and clear of all other lights and obstructions.

(g) The sidelights of a power-driven vessel shall be placed at a height above the hull not greater than three quarters of that of the forward masthead light. They shall not be so low as to be interfered with by deck lights.

(h) The sidelights, if in a combined lantern and carried on a power-driven vessel of less than 20 metres in length, shall be placed not less than 1 metre below the masthead light.

(i) When the Rules prescribe two or three lights to be carried in a vertical line, they shall be spaced as follows:

(ii) on a vessel of less than 20 metres in length such lights shall be spaced not less than 1 metre apart and the lowest of these lights shall, except where a towing light is required, not be less than 2 metres above the gunwale;

(iii) when three lights are carried they shall be equally spaced.

5. Screens for sidelights

The sidelights shall be fitted with inboard screens painted matt black, and meeting the requirements of Section 9 of this Annex. With a combined lantern, using a single vertical filament and a very narrow division between the green and red sections, external screens need not be fitted.

6. Shapes

(a) Shapes shall be black and of the following sizes:

(i) a ball shall have a diameter of not less than 0.6 metre;

(ii) a cone shall have a base diameter of not less than 0.6 metre and a height equal to its diameter;

(iii) a cylinder shall have a diameter of at least 0.6 metre and a height of twice its diameter;

(iv) a diamond shape shall consist of two cones as defined in (ii) above having a common base.

(b) The vertical distance between shapes shall be at least 1.5 metres.

(c) In a vessel of less than 20 metres in length shapes of lesser dimensions but commensurate with the size of the vessel may be used and the distance apart may be correspondingly reduced.

12. Manoeuvring light

Notwithstanding the provisions of paragraph 2(f) of this Annex the manoeuvring light described in Rule 34(b) shall be placed in the same fore and aft vertical plane as the masthead light or lights and, where practicable, at a minimum height of 2 metres vertically above the forward masthead light, provided that it shall be carried not less than 2 metres vertically above or below the after masthead light. On a vessel where only one masthead light is carried the manoeuvring light, if fitted, shall be carried where it can best be seen, not less than 2 metres vertically apart from the masthead light.

13. Approval

The construction of lanterns and shapes and the installation of lanterns on board the vessel shall be to the satisfaction of the appropriate authority of the state where the vessel is registered.

It is important to understand the buoyage system. Buoys mark navigable channels, wrecks, sandbanks, rocks, etc., and are identified by shape and colour by day; and by colour and flashing intervals at night. At present the system round the United Kingdom is based on the principle that a Port hand buoy is left to Port and a Starboard hand buoy to Starboard when going with the *main flood tide stream* (and vice-versa). This system is illustrated in Fig. 49. *However,* it *will be phased out* over a period of approximately four years beginning on 18th April 1977. It will be replaced in United Kingdom waters by the I.A.L.A. system 'A' (see Fig. 50). You will see at once by comparing the two systems that the I.A.L.A. system 'A' uses not only lateral marks but cardinal marks as well, and also isolated danger marks, safe water marks and other special marks. While the new I.A.L.A. system 'A' is being introduced, the direction of buoyage, instead of being related to the main flood tide direction as previously, may be defined by either the general direction taken by the mariner *when approaching a harbour etc. from seaward* or in some cases by the appropriate authority. As a general rule it will follow a clockwise direction around the land masses. The Cardinal Marks will be used to indicate that the deepest water in that

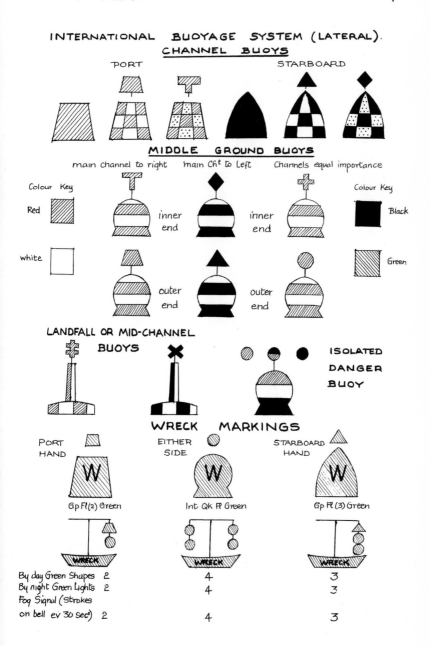

Fig. 49 The Lateral System of Buoyage

IALA BUOYAGE SYSTEM 'A'

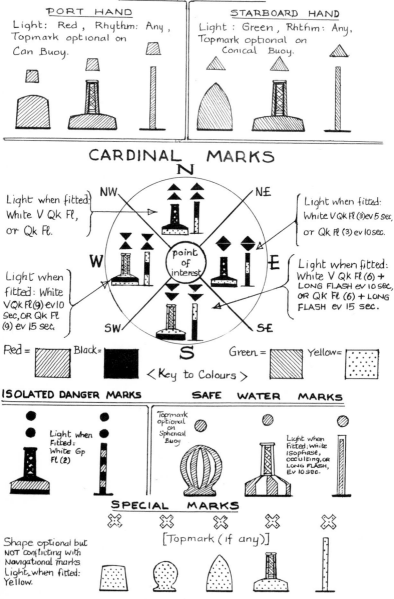

LATERAL MARKS

PORT HAND

Light: Red, Rhythm: Any, Topmark optional on Can Buoy.

STARBOARD HAND

Light: Green, Rhthm: Any, Topmark optional on Conical Buoy.

CARDINAL MARKS

Light when fitted: White V Qk Fl, or Qk Fl.

Light when fitted: White V Qk Fl (3) ev 5 sec, or Qk Fl (3) ev 10 sec.

Light when fitted: White V Qk Fl (9) ev 10 Sec, OR Qk Fl (9) ev 15 sec.

Light when fitted: White V Qk Fl (6) + LONG FLASH ev 10 sec, OR Qk Fl (6) + LONG FLASH ev 15 sec.

Red =   Black =   Green =   Yellow =

< Key to Colours >

ISOLATED DANGER MARKS

Light when Fitted: White Gp Fl (2)

SAFE WATER MARKS

Topmark optional on Spherical Buoy

Light when Fitted: white Isophase, OCCULTING, OR LONG FLASH, Ev 10 sec.

SPECIAL MARKS

[Topmark (if any)]

Shape optional but NOT conflicting with Navigational marks. Light, when fitted: Yellow.

Fig. 50 The new I.A.L.A. System 'A' of Buoyage

area lies on the named side of the mark; to indicate the safe side on which to pass a danger, and to call attention to such things as bends, junctions, the end of a shoal etc. With regard to lights for the lateral marks; Port hand (when fitted) will be Red (any rhythm) and Starboard hand Green (any rhythm).

This new buoyage system follows years of discussion. Two systems have finally resulted; system 'A' (suitable for Europe, Africa, India, Australia and some Asian waters) is now agreed. (System 'B' is still being prepared.) System 'A' uses a combination of two main types of mark; Lateral and Cardinal (see Fig. 50), as explained above. The main things for the sailor to remember are: Red = Port, or left; Green = Starboard, or right; the four buoys for North, South, East and West, and the marks for safe water, danger, direction and 'special'. The new system is being introduced in stages, starting at the Greenwich Meridian in the English Channel and gradually spreading through Europe. As soon as you are experienced enough to be making passages at sea I recommend a thorough study of the sections devoted to the buoyage system in an up-to-date copy of that invaluable book Reed's Nautical Almanac, where all the information required is set out in detail. When you come to cruise you will need a nautical almanac with its very full information about tides, lights, Collision Regulations and a hundred and one other things essential for the navigator. (Reed's Almanac also illustrates the limits of the areas where the new buoyage system will be phased in and the approximate dates of the changes.)

CHAPTER VII

INTRODUCTION TO CELESTIAL NAVIGATION AND THE USE OF THE SEXTANT

WE have learnt now how to work up the reckoning, how to allow for the effect of tidal streams and lee-way, and how to fix our position from objects observed on shore. When you become more ambitious (and experienced) you will, no doubt, wish to proceed out of sight of land and cross stretches of water when no land is visible for many hours or even days. For such passages observations on celestial bodies are by far the most valuable aids to navigation. These observations are made with an instrument known as the sextant. Before we look closely at this instrument, however, let us consider the theory of celestial navigation.

Navigating by heavenly bodies rests on the theory that for practical purposes the sun and the stars are stationary, while the earth and the moon (and the other planets) move in known orbits at calculable speeds. The revolutions of the earth are also calculable. It will be seen, therefore, that at any given moment the sun or any celestial body can only be in one place. If a line were drawn from such a celestial body to the centre of the earth, therefore, it would pierce the surface of the earth at one specific place. This would give a position on the earth of that celestial body and indeed it is termed that body's 'geographical position'. Now this geographical position can be located in terms of longitude and latitude like any other position on a chart. So we can now see that where lines from any celestial body to the earth's centre pierce the earth's surface, their G.P.s can be recorded or plotted upon a chart like any other position.

Now, two such lines to the centre of the earth will make an angle at the centre, and one such line will make an angle with a line drawn from it to any other spot on the earth's surface. These angles are fixed at any given time and are calculable. This task of calculation is done, fortunately for us, by astronomers who work out the positions of celestial bodies relative to the earth, and from their observations nautical tables are prepared mathematically. These tables show the positions of various celestial bodies in terms of two angles. First the angle they make with the North Pole (and the equator), and second the angle at the North Pole between their own meridians and the meridian of Greenwich. In other words, the first angles give latitude, the second longitude. Imagine that we have three geographical positions to reckon with. The North Pole, the geographical position of an observed heavenly body, and the position of an observer.

On the surface of the earth we now get a triangle. The three points of the triangle are the observer's position, the Pole, and the geographical position of our heavenly body. The sides of the triangle are slight curves, being great circles. Now look at Fig. 51. P. represents the Pole, C the earth's centre, S the geographical position of the heavenly body observed. We imagine a line from the centre of the earth through the position on the earth's surface of our observer. This line can be projected infinitely into space, just like the other lines, and so we get a position Z, being the zenith above our observer's head along the projected line from the earth's centre. So let us now picture our three spots, P, S, and Z, projected into space. You will notice that they form a larger triangle, a large triangle miles away in space. This large triangle is termed an Astronomical Triangle.

Now we know that the angle of one minute of arc at the centre of the earth subtends one nautical mile upon the earth's surface, so it follows that any angle at the centre of the earth between any two or three points, P, S, or Z, of our astronomical triangle, can be expressed in terms of nautical miles on the face of the earth.

The astronomical triangle is concerned in almost all celestial navigational problems. When an observer (the yachtsman) is taking a sight with his sextant, he is wanting to check his position. This position is a dead reckoning position and he wants to get a fix. He has two definite things with which to work; the distance PS, which, since P and S are known positions, he can get from his navigational tables, and the distance SZ, which he gets by subtracting the angle his sextant gives him (after certain corrections) from 90 degrees. Now, since S is a fixed point, his

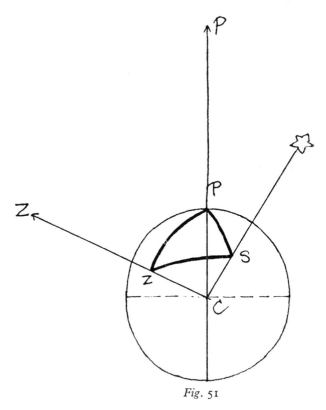

Fig. 51

position, and in consequence his yacht's position, will be somewhere on a circle drawn with centre S and radius SZ.

However, we spoke of corrections. A glance at Fig. 52 will show that sextant angle at the surface (Z) of the earth is not going to be the same as if the angle were measured at the centre of the earth, and it is from the centre of the earth that our angle must be measured. In relation to very distant stars the difference between the two angles is slight, but, in the case of the sun or moon, the difference becomes of material consequence and must be allowed for, by an allowance for what is called 'parallax'. This correction may be found from the tables. The sun and moon being large objects, a further correction must be made in the case of moon or sun sights. Observations of them are taken when the rim is shown as touching the horizon in the sextant mirror, and it is necessary to make an allowance for the 'semi-diameter' so as to get our bearing of the centre and not the edge. This allowance may be found in the tables. Furthermore, the moon is so near to the earth that the measurement of its semi-diameter varies because it is closer to the observer when

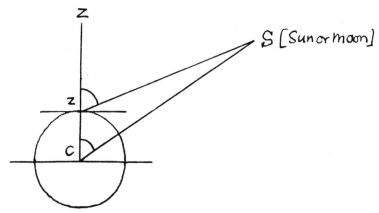

Fig. 52

overhead (and, therefore, the semi-diameter is larger) than when it is at right angles. This is also to be found in the tables. Now, in addition to these corrections, when taking sights, there are certain others which are concerned with the sextant itself. So the time has now come when we must take a look at the instrument, and learn how to work it.

The sextant is an instrument for measuring angles in either a horizontal, vertical, or diagonal plane. It is made of a frame carrying an arc which is divided to read to the nearest 10 minutes of arc. The arc is divided on silver, gold, or platinum. Pivoted in the middle of the arc is an arm, known as the index bar, to which is mounted perpendicularly, a mirror, called the index glass. It is mounted with small set-screws so that any adjustment can be made when required. A vernier scale giving the nearest 10 seconds of arc is set on the end of the arm, crossing the arc on the frame.

In the older type sextants, there was no thread cut on the

underside of the arc. A screw clamp was used to hold the arm in place, and the tangent screw was of the type shown in Fig. 53. But in the most recent type of sextant, the underneath part

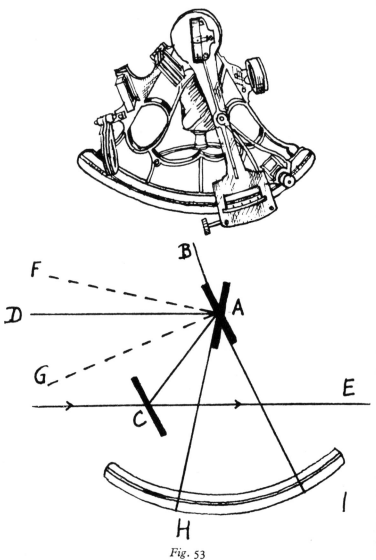

Fig. 53

of the arc forms a section of a worm wheel with a very thin thread. The tangent screw, or worm, which is used for any minute adjustment, is fastened to this segment. The worm can be unfastened by a spring clamp, thereby allowing the arm to be moved easily round the arc. Modern sextants have a micrometer head, which can be read far more quickly and easily than the vernier scale of the older type. The micrometer head carries a short, easily read vernier. The arm of vernier pattern sextants has a smaller swinging arm which carries a small microscope by which to read the scale, as well as an adjustable opaque glass screen.

The horizon glass is the other mirror of our sextant. It is perpendicularly attached to the plane of the instrument, and parallel to the index glass when the sextant is fixed at zero on the arc. The horizon glass is only half silvered, with the other half of clear glass. Two small set-screws allow the mirror to be adjusted in its mount.

Now, between the index and horizon glasses, we find four dark shades. The amount of light from the observed object will determine the choice of shade. When the horizon is too bright, there are three more shades beyond the horizon glass from which to choose. Finally, there is a telescope or sight tube screwed into a female thread which is attached to a metal collar. A handle is located on the underside of the frame. The instrument comes supplied with several different-powered telescopes and a sight tube without lenses. Since the ray of light from the subject being observed is reflected twice before it reaches our eye, the sextant is referred to as an instrument of double reflection.

Look again at Fig. 53, which illustrates the principle on which the sextant works. First of all, when the instrument is set at zero, the index glass, A, and the horizon glass, C, are parallel. The position I on the arc represents the index bar. Now, through the clear half of the horizon glass, C, a direct ray from the horizon passes to the observer's eye at E. Another ray reaches the index glass in the direction DA and is reflected along the line AC. From the silvered half of the horizon glass, this ray is reflected along the line CE to the observer's eye. We can now see that when the instrument is set at zero, the true and the reflected parts of the horizon appear as one straight line.

Now, let us take GA as the normal, that is, the perpendicular to the surface of the mirror at the point where the ray that is reflected strikes it. Since an optical rule is that the angle of incidence equals the angle of reflection, then we can say that ∠DAG equals ∠CAG, and therefore ∠CAD equals ∠DAG plus ∠CAG equals 2 ∠CAG.

Now, if position H on the arc represents the index bar, then the ray from a heavenly body B will be reflected from the index mirror at A, and along the line AC to C. It is reflected once more from C along the line CE to the observer's eye. Now, the mirror C is fixed, and the position of the pivot A about which the index mirror turns is fixed as well, so the angle ACE remains constant. If the index bar is moved and the mirror A is turned thereby until the body represented at B is seen by reflection from along the line CE, which meets the horizon when projected, then the object B will seem to be setting on the horizon. This is seen directly through the unsilvered part of the glass C. Since the horizon is at such a distance that DA and CE can be treated as parallel, then BAD equals the altitude of the object (the angular distance of the object B above the horizon).

Assuming that FA is the normal to the index mirror at A when the index bar is at the position H on the arc, then BAF equals CAF, and BAF plus CAF equals CAB; or, CAB equals twice CAF. But, referring to our formula above, CAD equals twice CAG, and so by subtraction, BAD equals twice FAG.

However, the angle between the normals, FAG, is the angle between the mirrors, equal to the angle IAH. We can therefore conclude that the index bar has been moved through an angle between the mirrors which is only half the angle between the objects. We see that although the arc of the sextant is only the sixth part of a circle, it is graduated in 120 degrees. Furthermore, allowance is made for readings a few degrees beyond 120 degrees, as well as a few degrees below the zero of the scale.

So far so good. Let us now learn the method of actually observing a heavenly body. Focus the telescope, screw it in, and set the sextant at zero. Point the telescope in the direction of the object, which will be observed by reflection, as well as directly in the horizon glass. Next, unclamp the index bar, and move the frame of the sextant forwards and downwards, keeping its plane perpendicular, and at the same time slide the index bar slowly away from you, along the arc. The horizon mirror

will show the object moving downwards. Hold it in view there
until it seems to be sitting on the surface of the horizon, which
can now be seen through the unsilvered half of the horizon
glass. Now, we can make the reflected image of the body
describe an arc approaching the horizon by simply giving the
instrument a slight swaying movement. This enables us to
make sure that the two edges, the body observed and the horizon itself, are not overlapping. Then, the index bar is clamped
and a tangent screw used to secure the adjustment. The observer
calls 'stop' once exact contact is made and the time by chrono-
meter or deck watch is noted down. In practice, a yachtsman
can use any really good watch as long as the time is accurate.

Now, although we are discussing celestial navigation, it should
be mentioned here that the sextant can be of great use in measuring horizontal angles of objects on shore. The way in which
to observe a horizontal or vertical sextant angle between two
shore objects is very similar to the way in which we observed
our heavenly body. To take the horizontal angle first. Hold the
sextant so that the plane is horizontal, with the mirrors on top.
The angle is then measured from the right-hand object, towards
the left-hand object. The sextant would have to be turned up-
side-down if the reflected image of the left-hand object were
brought towards the right-hand object. When measuring a
vertical angle, the first object should be the top and is observed
with the instrument set at zero. Next, its reflected image must
be brought down to coincide with the bottom object, most
likely the horizon, which is seen directly. Once the observation
is made, record the reading on the vernier. See that the particular setting is not changed when putting the sextant back in
its case. It can then be referred to should the reading be
questioned later.

Let us consider the sextant vernier in relation to the main
scale. The principle here is that 60 divisions on the vernier cover
119 divisions on the main scale, *i.e.*,

> 60 vernier equals 119 main scale
>
> I „   „ $\frac{119}{60}$ „   „   equals $1\frac{59}{60}$ main scale.

We can see that this is short of 2 by $\frac{1}{60}$th. So that one-
sixtieth of the smallest division on the main scale, or 10 minutes,

is the smallest amount that can be read with the vernier. The vernier reading to one-sixtieth of this shows the nearest 10 seconds of arc.

The first thing we do when reading the sextant is to look at the markings along the main scale. Then, just beneath the zero arrow mark on the vernier, we read the number of whole degrees, and between that number and the vernier zero mark, we find the number of minutes, which is the smallest division on the main scale. We read as much as is possible to read from the main scale, and a number of minutes less than 10, and tens of seconds over. We next read along the vernier scale until we reach the point where a mark on the vernier scale is exactly in line with a mark on the main scale, and read that mark on the vernier scale. The entire length of the vernier scale represents 10 minutes, with the smallest division 10 seconds. We will be reading the number of minutes on the vernier scale, plus tens of seconds, which is added to the reading we have obtained from the main scale.

Now, we may at times find that the zero mark of the vernier is below the zero mark on the main scale, in other words, 'Off the Arc'. Here we read from left to right the mark on the main scale next to the zero on the vernier, and between it and the zero on the main scale. The difference being that the 10 on the vernier is treated as zero and the zero as 10, as the vernier is read from left to right.

We now come to a subject we have touched on earlier, namely, the errors of the sextant. There are two types: errors which cannot be corrected by the observer, and those which the observer is able to detect and correct. A prismatic error, for example, is one which can only be corrected in a workshop. This error occurs when the mirrors are not plane. Another error which the observer is unable to correct is a centring error, which varies with the angle measured, and occurs when the pivot of the index glass is not at the centre of the arc. And still another, the shade error, which exists when the shades are not plane.

The certificate enclosed in the sextant box shows the centring error and all residual errors for various angles. These are noted and tabulated at the National Physical Laboratory. If the errors are greater than 2′, no certificate is issued. An 'A' certificate indicates that the errors are not more than 40″, tabulated for every 15° of the arc. A 'B' certificate also means that the errors are not greater than 2′, but are tabulated for every 30° of the arc.

Let us discuss those errors which are adjustable by the observer. An error in perpendicularity must always be corrected first. If the index glass is not perpendicular to the plane of the instrument, as it should be, first of all set the index bar near the centre of the arc. Then, while holding the instrument horizontally, look obliquely into the index glass, and you should now be able to see the reflected image of the arc in line with the arc itself. However, if this is not the case, the two can be made to appear in line by rotating a small screw in the middle of the frame of the index glass.

Here let us consider another error of the sextant which can be eliminated by the observer. This is the side error which exists when the horizon glass is not perpendicular to the plane of the instrument. In testing for this error, we first ship the inverting telescope. Then, with the sextant vertical, we look at some distinct object in the distance, and slide the index across the zero of the arc. We should now find that the reflected image passes over the direct image of the star. If, however, we find that there is an error here, we can correct it by means of a screw in the centre of the frame of the horizon glass.

When the axis of the telescope is shipped, it should be parallel to the plane of the instrument. If this is not so, then we are faced with a collimation error. Perpendicularity error and side error must be corrected first. The inverting telescope should be shipped with the wires parallel to the plane of the instrument. Next, we choose two heavenly bodies at least 90 degrees apart. These must be brought into correct contact on one wire of the telescope, and then the sextant is moved until these two bodies are on the other wire. If they are not still in contact, there is collimation error. In some sextants, this error can be taken out by two screws on the collar.

Then there is the index error which exists when the horizon glass is not parallel to the index glass when the index is at zero. One way in which to find index error is by observing a star. First, the index bar is set a few minutes one side or other of zero. Then, observe a star and bring the two images in contact in such a way that one cannot be distinguished from the other. Our reading will be the index error, plus (+) if 'off' the arc, and minus (−) if 'on' the arc. Now, if we look at Fig. 54, we can see that if the index is at C when the one image becomes indistinguishable from the other, BC will be the index error 'off' the arc and will therefore be plus (+).

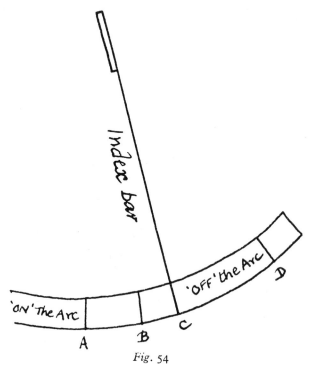

Fig. 54

Now, another method of finding index error is by observing the diameter of the sun 'on' and 'off' the arc. First of all, for clarity sake, let us look again at Fig. 54, where:

B is the zero graduated on the arc.

A is the position of the index when the suns are touching 'on' the arc.

D is the position of the index when the suns are touching 'off' the arc.

C is the point at which the arc should be graduated zero.

We can observe the diameter of the sun 'on' and 'off' the arc by first setting the sextant at about zero and moving the tangent screw to make the two images of the sun just come in contact with each other. We note the reading 'on' the arc, reverse the images, and then note the reading 'off' the arc. The index error will be half the difference of these readings. Referring once again to Fig. 54, we see that this is positive (+) if the greater reading is 'off' the arc, and negative (−) if the greater reading is 'on' the arc. With the index at A 'on' the arc, the reflected sun, which is shaded, is below the direct sun, which is not shaded. Then, the positions are reversed when the index is at D, 'off' the arc. In both cases, the angle we have measured is that which is subtended by the sun's diameter. This is due to the upper limb of one image being made to touch the lower limb of the other. Now, the index error is half the difference between two sextant readings of the sun's diameter. In this case, AB and BD are the sextant readings when the observations are made, and we can see that they differ by twice BC, the index error.

If we wish to make certain that our observations are correct, we can add together our sextant readings 'on' and 'off' the arc, divide this figure by four, and by referring to the *Nautical Almanack*, we should find that this is the semi-diameter of the sun given for the day. It is always best to find index error by means of observing a heavenly body. However, if there is no heavenly body available, index error can be found by observing the horizon in much the same way as we found the error by observing a star. Once we have corrected the index error, it is wise to make sure that any remaining index error is positive (+). This will avoid errors of subtraction and simplify the working of sights. Any small index error should be allowed for arithmetically in the working of the sight. In correcting a small index error of under 3', there is the risk of straining the horizon glass and making the adjusting screw become slack. If, however, the index error is over 3' and unwieldy, the small screw at the side of the base of the horizon glass should be used to correct it. Side error should be checked as well when making this adjustment.

There is another type of sextant which is worth our examination. It is called a bubble sextant. There are two types of bubble sextant. First, there is the type designed only for use with the bubble and used mainly for air navigation. There is, however, another type of sextant with a detachable bubble horizon. An example of this type is the *Gothic* sextant. Now, the bubble sextant has certain advantages and disadvantages. It is advantageous in that observations of heavenly bodies can be taken by day when the horizon is not visible. Also, observations of the moon and stars can be taken throughout the night. But it has the disadvantage that an error is caused, which at the time cannot be overcome, by bubble acceleration caused by the motion of the vessel. For this reason, observations taken in a lively ship cannot be expected to be accurate, and for this reason bubble sextants in very small yachts are of doubtful value.

If one is out of practice in using a sextant, or if working with a new one, sights should be taken with the ship moored in a known position, and thereby realise any personal error. A good point to remember in using the sextant is that of marking the different eye-pieces, so that they can be easily set to the correct focus, making it unnecessary to make an adjustment each time the instrument is used. Remember that the sextant should always be tested for perpendicularity, side error, and index error before taking sights. The first two errors should be corrected, and, as mentioned above, if the index error is small, it is best not to correct it and allow for it arithmetically in the working of a sight. Remember also that when measuring angles with a sextant, the objects should be observed in the centre of the field of the telescope. This will make the ray from each of the objects parallel to the plane of the instrument. When very small angles, such as vertical danger angles, are measured, they should be read both 'on' and 'off' the arc. This also applies to angles measured when the index error is checked by the sun. When a sextant which is not fitted with an endless tangent is not in use, see that the tangent screw is kept almost in the middle of its run.

Now, just a few final points on the use of the sextant. Remember that when the sextant is read, one should avoid holding it sideways to the light, but let the light come straight along the index bar to the vernier. It is often preferred to use a dark glass at the eye end of the telescope, rather than using the shades. You may find that the glasses become coated with moisture, particularly after sunset. The sextant should always be handled with the greatest of care, since only a slight blow is apt to throw all the adjustments out of gear. Never hold the instrument by the arc or by the index bar when lifting it, but always by the frame or handle. Also, care should be taken not to burr the threads when screwing a telescope into the collar. Sometimes it is necessary to make the graduations stand out more. This can be done by covering the arc with clock oil mixed with lamp-black and then lightly wiping it. Besides making the graduations more easily read, the arc will be cleaned as well.

If the sextant has been used in damp weather, remember to wipe away every bit of moisture, especially on the arc and mirrors. A chamois leather or clean silk handkerchief is best for this purpose. The sextant should never be left exposed to the sun's rays. And finally, when stowing the sextant, try to avoid placing it where there is any vibration and dampness. This latter direction varies, of course, in difficulty as to the size of your yacht. It may seem a counsel of perfection, but there is no harm in trying!

We have now learned how to look after and use a sextant and we have learned the basic principle of the astronomical triangle. There are several methods of solving the astronomical triangle necessitating only ordinary mathematics. There are, however, others somewhat more rapid, like special slide-rules or stereo-graphic scales. Opinions vary as to their accuracy and/or suitability for yachts. But whatever method you choose, a basic knowledge of celestial navigation is essential. There are on the market a very large number of books, many of them excellent on the subject. From them you can learn how to identify stars by means of star charts, how to work out the sight you have taken, and how to use the position lines obtained to give you a fix and determine your position. The subject is a large one, and will cause this book to be hopelessly unbalanced were I to attempt it here. It is, as the reader will have already realised, a complex subject and one not capable of many short-cuts if it is to be really understood. I, therefore, recommend to the yachts-man whose experience leads him well off-shore that he acquires one of the latter books of instruction that deal specifically with the fascinating subject of celestial navigation. But let it be remembered that the beginner must first learn pilotage and navigation of the sort we have here discussed in this book. They will get him far enough for some time! Indeed, the Board of Trade examination for the Yacht Master's Certificate of Competency (Coastal) does not require knowledge of celestial navigation, and anyone who has read (and observed the size!) of Mr. Frank Carr's most excellent *Yacht Master's Guide* will know how much there is to learn of boat-handling and seamanship and ordinary coastal navigation. So let us pass to the next chapter and stop theorising and get down to the planning and the making of a passage at sea!

CHAPTER VIII

PLANNING AND MAKING A PASSAGE AND LIVING ON BOARD

LET us assume that our boat is completely fitted out and we are looking forward to a holiday during which we plan to make a passage. We will consider our passage in advance so that we can be prepared for any eventuality. Now every skipper should visualise the different stages of a passage before he is actually underway; these stages fall into five definite sections: (1) preparation, (2) the start, (3) the passage itself, (4) landfall, and (5) making a harbour and berthing.

To take the first stage, preparation, we have decided on our destination and must now see that we have all the necessary charts and navigational books. These must be studied not only with regard to the planned cruise, but also with regard to all anchorages where one can shelter in the case of an emergency, a deviation from the planned cruise, etc.

Now it will most likely be the cook who will provision the ship. He can quite easily judge at what times and at what ports fresh provisions can be obtained. Groceries, such as sugar, flour, coffee, tea, etc., should be kept in either air-tight jars or tins, and labelled. If you have enough space on deck, it is a good plan to have some sort of meat safe in which to keep butter, meat, and other fresh food. If this is not possible, you may be able to fit in a food locker for fresh provisions near the galley, below decks, where fresh vegetables can be kept dry and sheltered from the sun. As well as the fresh provisions, it is wise to always carry tinned provisions for use in an emergency. Always try to get the unbreakable tins, avoiding anything in a glass jar. This will depend on your amount of stowage space, but generally in a small boat it is best to have as few breakable containers as possible. Tins should always be stowed in a dry place to prevent their rusting.

The cook will be looking after all the provisioning but the skipper must see to many things as well. He will be making a final check to see that all the sails are aboard and in good condition, also that there are sufficient life-jackets, fenders, heaving-lines, and spare lines. Is everything handy and stowed where it should be—the sea anchor, binoculars, matches, the anchor light, the navigation lights, Very pistol and sufficient distress flares, torch and enough spare batteries, fire extinguisher, tools for the engine, spare plugs, a fog-horn, the lead line, a boat-hook, the patent log, sail twine, palm, needles, oilskins, and sou-westers? Is there petrol aboard—oil—water—paraffin—first-aid gear—brandy—and gin? It is a good idea to make a list of the things which will be needed during the passage and check off each item. The skipper may be the navigator as well, in which case he can delegate some of the tasks of other provisioning to a bos'n.

We can now pass on to the second stage and make our start. The time at which one elects to start most often depends on the tide. It is generally wiser to start with a fair tide, since it is a good plan to make as much headway as possible in the first 5 or 6 hours of a cruise. In this case, to be sure of getting the most out of the fair tide, you should get underway half an hour to an hour before the tide turns. There are times, however, when it is better to start on a foul tide, for example, when it is possible to sail over the foul tide during the first part of the passage, but during a later stage in the passage, where there is a swifter current running, it is not only advantageous but essential to have a fair tide.

And now a word of advice. Even if the weather looks un-inviting, if you possibly can start, do so. Of course, if there is bad weather and a bad forecast, it would seem wisest to postpone your departure. However, there are several reasons why it is better to avoid doing so. First of all, one loses spirit and it is amazing how the passage continues to be postponed. Another reason is that you will be losing the available time for your passage. Also, if you do not get underway at the planned time, you may have missed a fair wind later on when it is most needed. It will most always be worth your while to go out of the harbour to have a look. You may find that the bad patch is only tempo-rary, and you are most concerned with the general weather conditions over the entire passage. Also, it is a good idea to have a look because sometimes the strength or even the direction of the wind cannot be judged properly when lying in harbour. You may find that the conditions are not nearly so bad once you have left the harbour and that you have a wind much more favourable than you expected.

Let us say, anyway, that we have braved the elements and have started. We now come to the third stage of the passage, the passage at sea itself. When we have passed clear of the land and know the direction and strength of the wind, we can set our course. The navigator sets the course from a point which is obtained by taking two, and if possible three, bearings of objects on shore which are clearly shown on his chart. These bearings, when drawn on the chart, will appear as three converging straight lines, and the position of the yacht will be defined by the point at which they all meet (see 'cocked hats' in the chapter on navigation). Taking the departure is the term given for this method of using shore objects to fix firmly the yacht's position at the start of a passage.

Now as we are to be at sea for a day or so we must set watches. It is a very good idea to have some definite watch system so that everyone aboard will get enough sleep. With no definite system, everyone is inclined to be on deck at the same time and then when the middle and first watches arrive, there is the risk of everybody being exhausted and unable to cope in the case of an emergency. The answer to this is that each member of the crew must know which are to be his watches on deck and which are to be his watches below and can then plan accordingly. The number of the crew will determine the number of people in each watch. Let us study the situation in your boat, which we will assume is a 5-tonner carrying a crew of three, including yourself.

The '4-hour' watches are as follows:

A.M.	12– 4	Middle Watch
	4– 8	Morning Watch
	8–12	Forenoon Watch
P.M.	12– 4	Afternoon Watch
	4– 6	First Dog Watch
	6– 8	Last Dog Watch
	8–12	First Watch.

Aboard a big ship the length of each watch is told by a bell which is struck every half-hour. These strokes are made in groups of two:

Middle Watch

0030	1 Bell
0100	2 Bells
0130	3 Bells
0200	4 Bells, Half Watch
0230	5 Bells
0300	6 Bells
0330	7 Bells
0400	8 Bells, Change Watch.

The Dog Watches are told as follows:

First Dog

1630	1 Bell
1700	2 Bells
1730	3 Bells
1800	4 Bells, Change Watch.

Last Dog

1830	1 Bell
1900	2 Bells
1930	3 Bells
2000	8 Bells, Change Watch.

If there are four in the crew, I think the best arrangement is to have 4-hour watches—each man working 2 hours at the helm. If there are three in the crew, 3-hour watches would seem to be the best, since 3 hours at the helm is usually enough for most people, particularly during the night.

The majority of cruising yachts have small crews, whereas ocean racing yachts will have considerably larger crews, and this system of watches can be altered to suit the requirements of each yacht. The skipper of an ocean racing yacht will require a large crew in order to have a reserve in the event of seasickness, etc., as well as to enable the helmsman to give his full attention to getting the ship through the water at the greatest possible speed. Such crowded conditions will not be favoured by the skipper of a cruising yacht. He will depend on a small crew to do the work competently.

Now that we have made our start and are well underway, we can concentrate on the sea routine of our passage. We shall have as much sail hoisted as is seamanlike during the daytime, and if we run into bad weather, we can reef. You can rely on the information given in the weather forecasts on the wireless, an invaluable part of every cruiser's equipment. These forecasts, along with your observations of the barometer, the sea, and the sky, will give you a good indication of the weather to expect. I will not go into detail in this question of forecasting the local weather conditions here, as this is dealt with, to some extent, in Chapter X.

If the weather becomes increasingly worse, you will have to decide whether to carry on or to find shelter. Seeking shelter is a seamanlike procedure but has its drawbacks. First of all, if you only have a certain amount of time available for your cruise, it will have a demoralising effect. There is so often some delay in getting underway again when once in harbour and you are apt to miss a favourable wind. The other and more serious snag is that even though the weather is beginning to make the passage uncomfortable, there are times when you will be taking a great risk in running for shelter. If you are not certain that you have within reach a good harbour with deep water at all phases of the tide, with no bar or shallow patch at its entrance, and that you can get there all right, then stay at sea. You can run into great difficulty if you are not very familiar with the area. More craft have been lost while running for shelter in bad weather than in any other way.

However, there will always be times when from every aspect it will be best to make harbour, if only to offer some rest for the crew. It is for these emergencies that you should always have a good supply of charts aboard. One can find shelter from certain winds at the various natural anchorages all round the coast, so it is not always necessary to go into harbour when seeking temporary shelter. Now if we do this, we must take certain precautions against the possibility of the wind shifting in another direction. We must first of all set an anchor watch. Then we must see that the sails are ready to hoist without a moment's delay. Now at the first sign of an unfavourable shift in the wind, so that you are caught shut in the bay on a lee shore, and the wind seems to be increasing, you will have to decide whether it is best to use your engine or sail the boat clear and either stand right out to sea or run for some other shelter. This is one of the advantages of having an engine. You can use it either to get you over a foul tide or to get into a position where you can anchor and wait for a fair tide or wind. Whenever you are becalmed in a foul tide, if it is at all possible to anchor, that is the thing to do. You should use the kedge anchor for this purpose. A heavy chain is not required for the kedge, as coir (grass line) is resistant to sea water and is very suitable for kedge warp. The best type of kedge warp is made from nylon, which is not only resistant to sea water, but has the advantage of not picking up mud from the sea-bed. I know one yachtsman who uses piano wire coiled ready for use on a drum!

When anchoring with the kedge, it is necessary to veer only twice the depth—even veering only one and a half times the depth can be sufficient. This is, of course, quite different from anchoring with the bower anchor when you must veer three times the depth at high water. When using the kedge to anchor, in order to keep the warp clear of the anchor fluke that is jutting out of the ground, the tiller should be lashed a little to port or starboard to give the ship a sheer in one direction or the other. If there is a strong tide running, this will also help to keep the vessel from yawing about from side to side. It is wise to take anchor bearings to see if the yacht is dragging her anchor. This is most important if there is a strong tide running.

Always proceed with great care in fog. The first thing you must do if you run into fog is study the chart and note your exact position. If you find you are in a shipping lane and can get clear of it and anchor in shallow water, then do so. Sail cautiously on dead reckoning from your last fixed position, taking careful soundings with the lead. You should always carry a good fog-horn aboard. Remember that you cannot often be certain of a yacht's position by merely listening to its hooter, as the direction of sound is extremely misleading in fog. Always bear in mind and obey Article 15, Sound Signals for Fog, etc., of the International Regulations for Preventing Collisions at Sea. If you are anchored in fog which prevents you from getting anchor bearings, you can quite simply detect whether or not the yacht is dragging by heaving the lead and letting it rest on the bottom. You will soon feel the lead bumping along the sea-bed if you are dragging.

The cruising yacht carries on when night falls, but it is a good principle to go carefully. A cruising yacht does not often carry a large crew, and during the night when the crew are in watches, there may be only one person on deck. Suppose the yacht is carrying a lot of canvas and suddenly the wind freshens and it is necessary to take in a reef. It will then be necessary to call out the watch below and cause them to lose out on their full amount of sleep. In order to avoid this, reduce to plain sail at sunset, which means ordinary working sails; in a sloop, mainsail and jib; in a cutter, mainsail, staysail, and jib, etc. Reduce sail even more if bad weather is expected.

When sailing at night, the man on deck should secure himself to the ship in some way. This will guard against the possibility of his falling overboard. To tie a bowline round your waist and make the standing part of the rope fast to some very strong fitting is the best way to anchor yourself to the ship.

There is always the possibility of meeting other ships while sailing at night and efficient navigation lights are a necessary safeguard against the possibility of collision. These should be lit at or just before sunset. It is a good idea to let the lamps burn for a minute or so before you put them in position, because the flame will increase as the lamp gets warm, and to prevent a smoky lens it is sometimes necessary to turn the wick down. Frequently it is very difficult for a steamer to see the navigation lights of a yacht, especially if there is a heavy sea and the yacht is heeled over. For this reason you should always have a good torch handy. You can attract the attention of the man of the steamer's bridge by shining a torch in the sails.

There should also be sufficient lighting in the saloon, in the galley, and over the chart table. There are many reasons why lights fail at sea; consequently, there should always be more than one lighting system aboard a ship. The three main ways of obtaining light aboard a yacht are: electricity, paraffin, and candle. The most reliable form of lighting is paraffin, although electricity is undoubtedly the most convenient. The paraffin system has the disadvantage of being messy and smelly and using up oxygen. Also, because it is easy to spill the paraffin, there is the risk of fire; and finally, oil lamps smoke if they are not looked after. Paraffin has many advantages, however. It is very cheap, and it does not burn extravagantly, so that a sufficient amount can be stowed for a reasonably long cruise. Oil lamps are very dependable and will operate when most other systems have failed. Paraffin is a very economical form for lights which have to burn all night, such as the riding light. (Candles will not burn brightly enough for navigation or riding lights.) If you run out of paraffin, you will find there are very few places where you cannot buy more.

Electricity is not as reliable a form of lighting as paraffin, though it is far more convenient. A portable battery can be used, and then taken ashore for charging. Alternatively, there can be a generator on the yacht's engine or a separate petrol-driven generator can be installed. On the other hand, this system has the disadvantage in that getting the batteries charged can present complications, and there is also often an uneasy feeling about wasting the battery. In addition, it may to some extent mar the ship's appearance, as much of the electric wiring as is possible should be kept in the open. Moisture can do great damage to any electric system, especially in dark, unventilated places.

Another means of lighting a yacht is by the use of acetylene. I have had no experience with this system, and I don't believe it is very commonly used. If Calor gas or butane is used for cooking, it is possible to use it both for heating and lighting as well. This, however, involves long lengths of piping which presents the great danger of leaks, and as far as I am concerned, the risk would be enough to rule this system out.

It is important that the interior lighting of a ship be arranged so that the helmsman will not be disturbed by any bright light shining into his eyes when the cabin doors are open. Great care should be taken in the lighting of the chart table and the compass. The chart table light should be screened so that it doesn't blind the navigator, and, at the same time, clearly light the chart. The compass light must be neither too bright nor too dull, as either effect will be a strain on the helmsman. Probably the best lighting here would be a small, low-powered electric light.

The normal paraffin light seems to get blown out in very rough weather. There should be a secondary method of lighting the compass, should the electric light fail, and paraffin would be best suited for this purpose.

Now returning to our passage, and nearing the fourth stage, we prepare to make our landfall. The best time to make a landfall is a debatable point. If entering a harbour at night, you can quite easily judge your position by the various flashing lights, although there are obviously some disadvantages in approaching a strange harbour at night. Entering a harbour by day is easier, but it will most probably be more difficult to identify the coastline. The best time to enter a harbour, therefore, is a little before dawn. At this time, you can identify the coast by the lights on shore, and then by the time you are well in port it will be daylight. If it is possible to arrange things this way, this, of course, is the ideal time. The different Admiralty Pilots contain many sketches of the coast which are a great help in identifying a landfall.

And so at last we have arrived at the harbour entrance and our fifth and final stage. All the information concerning the strange harbour should have been studied in the pilot or handbook and on the chart *before* and not while you make your entrance. You should know the depths of water and the direction and behaviour of the tidal stream. When approaching a strange harbour you must first make out the entrance, which you will be able either to see or else you can take a well-defined landmark to estimate its locality. The anchor should be ready for letting go instantly and you should have warps, fenders, and heaving-lines all ready on deck. So as to keep the yacht in full control when moving about the anchorage, it is a good plan to carry your mainsail right up to the time of anchoring. If you do not have a harbour plan on board, then look about the harbour, and if you see a place where boats of about the same size as your own are anchored together, it will most likely be safe for you to anchor there. But if you see no other yachts about, then take a lead line and sound yourself into an anchorage. The method of anchoring or mooring will differ in various harbours. In some harbours, such as Cherbourg, N. France, you lie with stern warps to a wall and a buoy ahead; or an anchor ahead as in

Cannes or Antibes, S. France. In other harbours, like Wey-mouth, S. England, you lie head and stern between two buoys. In still other harbours, such as Ramsgate, Newhaven, or Shoreham, etc., all in England, you will not have sufficient space to lie your own anchor, and you must lie alongside other vessels. Sometimes you moor head to a post and stern to floating jetty, as in Rotterdam, Holland. Sometimes you simply 'drop the hook' in a sheltered and peaceful anchorage. But wherever you are, especially if you are 'moored', be it in Cowes, Bombay, or Long Island Sound, don't forget to put out fenders for those who may come alongside!

Our passage is completed, but we have just one thing more to attend to. Our ship, like ourselves, needs a good wash down both above and below decks. Clean the salt from her decks and topsides and all the grime from her floorboards. You can now relax all the more over that glass of beer (gin, schnapps, vin de pays, manhattan?) ashore!

Now that we have made a passage, during which time we have of necessity been 'living on board', let us turn our attention to this aspect of the passage. Herein lies the main difference between a cruising boat and an open or half-decked boat. One of the main functions of the cruising boat is to keep her crew as comfortable as possible in all kinds of weather. Even in ocean racing, the closest to cruising, comfort below is of far less importance than speed and ability to sail close to the wind. There are many things to be considered in living aboard a small boat. Where to stow the bedding by day and how to keep it dry. How to keep the galley clean and free from fire hazards. A cruising yacht must be self-supporting, for as soon as she has dropped her moorings, she is almost completely cut off from shore. She must carry many varied things with her. Stowage is needed for sails, navigational instruments, charts, petrol, rope, fenders, food, fresh water, clothes, oilskins, shaving gear, wireless, books, bedding, boat-hook, flags, etc. Not only must she have good and sufficient gear and sails, but also the tools to repair them.

One of the great attractions of cruising is the feeling of escape and adventure that this self-reliance offers. The skipper must play many rôles: navigator, helmsman, signalman, shipwright, rigger, plumber, sailmaker, cook, doctor, and mechanic.

The basic requirements of a cruiser's accommodation are: good sleeping-berths, a properly screened and efficient toilet, enough space for the navigator to work, as good head-room as possible, proper stowage of clothes, including oilskins, good cooking arrangements, good feeding arrangements, and good ventilation arrangements.

You will discover that the more simple and plain your cabin, the more comfort you will ultimately have. You can, of course, fill it with double beds, an ice box, and a high-fidelity cocktail

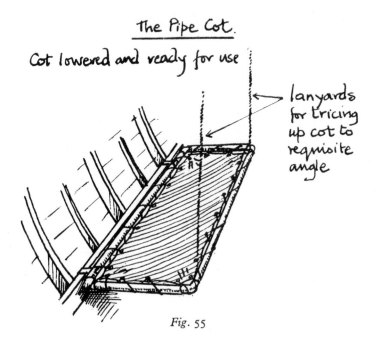

The Pipe Cot.

Cot lowered and ready for use

lanyards for tricing up cot to requisite angle

Fig. 55

cabinet—but, if you go to sea, you won't like it! The problem of berths is, of course, very important. Every built-in berth should have an adequate leeboard extending about a foot above the top of the mattress. You can then sink down behind it and feel very secure if the ship is heeling. Proper rest for the skipper is necessary for his own pleasure and for the welfare of the ship. He must turn in in a warm, dry, and comfortable bunk. A good width for a berth is 2 feet, as it gives enough room without using up too much space. A very good type of berth is the 'pipe cot', which consists of a frame of ordinary iron piping with

right-angle joints at the corners. Strong sailcloth is then fastened to this by means of a light line (hambro line), rove through
grommets in its edge at every few inches. (See Fig. 55.) Two
hook-shaped pieces of iron lashed to the ship's side support the
berth on the outboard side. The inboard side is triced up with
two strong lines reeving through ring-bolts in the deck-head.
Simply by tightening or slacking these tricing lines, the berth
can be adjusted so that it is horizontal for any angle of heel.
With a mattress on the canvas, a pipe cot can be more comfortable than most berths. Then there is the 'shelf' type berth.
Shelf berths by day form the backs of cabin seats and at night
they can be raised to any height merely by adjusting the lanyards as with a pipe cot. There is a lanyard at each inboard end
of the shelf berth which passes through a ring-bolt above it in
the deck-hand.

Yet another type of berth is the root berth. It is very good
and less unsightly than some others. The root berth is constructed with a strip of sailcloth stretched between the ship's
side and a metal tube running through the inboard hem of the
canvas. The tube is longer than the sailcloth and its ends can
be set in three different positions: a horizontal berth for use on
quiet seas; a berth with a bit more 'sag'; and for heavy seas, a
berth with a deep trough with the inboard side higher than
the outboard. There are a lot of cruising yachts designed with
quarter berths, which stretch aft from the cabin, go under the
deck, and often the cockpit seats.

A cruise can be spoiled if the second item on our list, plumb-
ing and sanitation, is not operating efficiently. There are several
good makes of water-closets available on the market. To have
the installation well carried out, there must be two holes in the
hull, one for supply and one for discharge. They must each be
a strong connection and each have a sea-cock that can be regu-
lated. Most agree that the best method is to pump in an amount
of water to flush the closet; then pump out by means of a pipe
which is carried up above the water-line and has an air-pipe in it.

The next subject in our list is space for the navigator. The
safety of the ship depends in a great measure on the work of
the navigator, so treat him well! Every yacht should have an
adequate chart table. As well as being large enough, it must be

flat. It must therefore be made of wood that will not warp. There should be sufficient stowage (if possible, flat stowage) for charts. The navigator should be able to work unencumbered if his work is to be satisfactory, and should have the following within his reach: dividers, parallel rules, binoculars, a number of hard pencils, a good indiarubber, a hand-bearing compass, a torch, a reliable watch, all the necessary navigational books, and a clear view of the barometer. It is helpful to have the chart table near the cockpit, so that the navigator can easily check bearings of lights, headlands, etc. It is also an advantage to have the chart table near the cockpit as there is more light and less movement in this part of the ship. A movable lamp on a long arm attached to the bulkhead is very useful in lighting any part of the chart.

There are few things more annoying than 'not quite' head-room. It is always desirable to have full head-room in a boat. If this is not possible, having sitting head-room. The in-between is of no avail. If only under a skylight or a dog-house roof you can manage full standing head-room, that will be sufficient.

Clothes must be stowed in places that you can be sure of remaining dry. A certain amount of hanging space is an advantage. There should be separate and adequate space for hanging oilskins.

Cooking arrangements in yachts are always a subject of controversy. There are two main conceptions regarding cooking arrangements. One holds that, since we spend much of our time eating, the galley must not only have sufficient space for the cooking gear, and enough elbow room for the cook, it must also be situated in a well-lighted part of the ship where there is least motion. That is, next to the cockpit, where it may also benefit from the advantages of a dog-house, giving even more light and head-room. The other theory contends that the galley, being an unsightly and smelly place, should be situated way up for'ard. Here it will be out of sight, and since the current of air in a ship is always from aft, forward, the smells will not be offensive.

Another problem in the cooking arrangements is what type of cooker to have. It is mainly a matter of personal choice. Many types of both slow-burning and pressure stoves are on the market. Calor gas cookers are labour saving, quick, and clean. However, there are some who contend that Calor gas is dangerous in a boat, as the gas, being heavier than air, sinks into the bilges, and having no smell, one is not aware of its presence. The gas is generally given a strong and definite smell and cancels out this objection. Many prefer the small, neat primus stove that burns vaporised paraffin. The slow-burning dependable type of oil stove is also preferred by some.

The galley should be arranged so that the cook has everything at hand without having to move from his position. His task will be easier if he can keep his pots on the stove while the ship is heeling over. The stove should therefore be slung in gimbals. To be able to cook properly when underway, it will, of course, benefit the cook to have a stomach of 'cast-iron'. While cooking in a stormy sea, the part of the body below the hips should be firm and 'as one' with the boat, and the top half of the body left free to pivot.

The actual feeding arrangements should be given as much consideration as the cooking. The type of saloon table you choose will depend mainly on your cabin arrangements. There are several types: a solid table that is fastened to the cabin sole, a swinging, weighted table, attached to the cabin sole, a table that swings from the deck-head, a folding table hinged to the mast or bulkhead. A table that does not swing should be fitted with portable slats, or fiddles, which fit into corresponding holes in the table. The table is then divided into several small compartments, where plates and glasses can rest with some degree of safety.

The comfort of the captain and crew is an extremely important factor in the success of any cruise. The cruising man must keep his inner garments dry if he is to enjoy his cruise, whereas the class-racing man won't mind getting soaked through. Except for the ocean racer, the racing man can look forward to a hot bath and dry clothes within a few hours. The cruising man, on the other hand, may have to stay 2 or 3 days at sea, enduring all kinds of weather. However, the cruising boat is usually drier, as it has more freeboard and shorter overhangs, whereas the racing yacht that races in rather sheltered waters will be very wet to sail to windward.

Let us first discuss the problem of keeping your change of clothes and your bedding dry below, which is even more important than keeping yourself dry. There is always the chance that the deck of any small yacht will develop leaks, especially in bad weather. If your decks are not canvased, it will not be very difficult to track down the leak, and you will most likely find that re-caulking will take care of the situation. However, if the decks are canvased, it is often very difficult to locate the source of the leak. For example, it may appear that there is a leak over the middle of the port berth, but the water is actually getting in where the canvas meets the covering board, way up for'ard, and then running along the deck under the canvas. Whenever there are such leaks, examine the deck very carefully. Examine, in particular, the covering board (the extreme outer plank of the deck on both sides of the yacht) and the margin, which rests on the carlines on each side, *i.e.* the deck plank on both sides of the yacht nearest to the cockpit coamings, the sides of the coach-roof, and of the hatches. The canvas is tucked under these planks in most canvas-covered decks, and when most of the paint has worn off, water will sometimes get into the seam and rot the canvas. Water will also frequently get in around the mast. To prevent this, when the mast is being stepped, put on an added coat of varnish for about a foot above the partners. Then lash a canvas coat around it and turn the coat down over the lashing and fasten it to the deck. Now give the coat a good covering of paint for added protection.

See that the decks don't get too hot and dry, since topside and deck leaks are often caused by expansion and contraction in the hot sun. It is wise to wash the decks down first thing each day.

Leaks will often occur in skylights and hatches. Hatches leak around their forward ends. By affixing a strip of rubber, you should prevent this. Putty the skylight panes quite frequently. Then give four good coats of varnish to the putty and all the woodwork.

Glass reinforced plastic decks and hatches, when well de-signed, go a long way to solving the leak problem here. The hatches can be a continuous part of the moulded deck. Wooden Trimming is often employed for purely aesthetic reasons. Some years ago, in a very leaky ocean racer, I experimented unsuccessfully with a canvas tent over each berth. The canvas kept the water out for a while, but in due course a drip could be started by merely touching the inside of the tent. I am referring to a lightly built racing boat, and it seems that, if one intends to do some stiff windward sailing in such craft, leaks must be accepted as being inevitable. You can avoid most of the leaks, of course, by not driving her too hard, but just jogging along is not likely to satisfy the proud owner of a fast little racing boat.

Now on to the problem of keeping yourself dry. There is much truth in the saying: it is far easier to stay dry than to get dry. It seems many people, once it starts to rain, postpone putting on their oilskins. I use the old seaman's word 'oilskins' here to cover the wide range of waterproof gear available today. The oilskins will keep them from getting any wetter, but they are already wet and cold underneath. If they are prone to seasickness, they are in just the position for such an attack. I am sure the reason why people postpone putting on their oilskins is that the majority of oilies are found to be hard to put on, as well as uncomfortable to wear. Make sure you have a proper oilskin locker in the ship. Comfort in wearing oilskins depends to a large extent on wearing the proper clothes underneath them. It is unnecessary to pile on sweater after sweater, and coat upon coat. As long as the inner garments are made of wool, the oilskins themselves will be quite sufficient as outer garments. Cotton is quite useless because it becomes cold when it absorbs moisture, whereas wool is much warmer. Oilies will not let moisture in, nor will they let it out. One is therefore inclined to sweat, and it is absorbed by whatever the inner garments may be. The best oilskins consist of two parts, a short coat and trousers. The coat should have plain, strong buttons and need not extend farther downwards than the hips. Avoid metal zip-fasteners as they soon deteriorate in the salt atmosphere. Your oilskin should have pockets. If not, wear a belt with pockets attached. There are always several things the yachtsman will want to have right by him, such as a knife, a marline-spike, or a torch. This applies especially at night when you won't want to bother the watch below. Your trousers should be long enough to cover the top of your sea-boots. Your boots should not fit tightly no matter what the length so that they will be easy to kick off in the case of emergency. Wear good warm socks under your boots. Put your boots on after the oilie trousers; otherwise, pushing the boots down through the trouser leg may tear the trousers. Another hint in this sea-attire business is not to leave part of the cuffs or collar projecting outside the oilskin cuffs and neckband, which should both button up tightly, otherwise, they will soak up water.

Regarding headwear, I don't believe anything can replace the sou'wester, which should have a good wide rim and an adjustable strap to fit under the chin. The question of wearing gloves is an arguable point. There are not many gloves that will last for long under the strain of hauling on ropes. I personally feel that it is only worth while wearing gloves in very cold weather, and few people cruise during the winter and in the summer it is rarely cold enough to warrant their use. Once again, I would point out that the term 'oilies', much in use when I first wrote this book, may be taken in this context to cover any good form of modern waterproof sailing clothing, of which there is a colourful variety available!

CHAPTER IX

YACHT RACING

ALTHOUGH there are many theories on how to win races, and many books on the subject by persons far better qualified than the writer to give advice on this difficult subject, yet I will be audacious enough to give here a few broad principles, in addition to a short outline of race organisation and the racing rules. Races are won or lost by very little things, by details. There is often only seconds between the first and second boats of a race. The crew of the second boat *might* have won—but they didn't. Now, why didn't they? Was it because the crew had been slow on the jib sheets when tacking? Was it the fact that the spinnaker had been hoisted in stops and the two stops at the head had stubbornly refused to break for a minute or two? Was it because the mainsail was not sufficiently stretched out along the boom by the outhaul to make it set well for the conditions at the time? Or, most worrying of all to the helmsman, was it on account of a tactical error? The answer is, it might have been any or all of these 'little things'. Even when the distance between two boats at the finishing line is as great as, say, 2 minutes, by avoiding little mistakes the second yacht might have been able to save a minute in an hour and, in a race lasting 3 hours, would have won by a minute. Just think! That means only a saving of one second a minute!

The experienced racing helmsman does not make these little mistakes. He starts the race with hull, spars, rigging, and sails in perfect racing condition. He 'stays with' his boat—driving her as hard as he can all round the course and giving the jib his full concentration. This is tremendously important. He makes as good a start as he possibly can. He uses racing tactics during the race, not only to improve his own position, but to hinder his opponent yachts and also to protect himself from their efforts to hinder him.

He is an opportunist, never missing a chance to take advantage of any little bit of luck which may come his way.

Now the main factor in race winning is probably good helmsmanship.

There are two essential factors in good helmsmanship. One is concentration. Unless you can keep your attention fixed on the task, you will not be able to steer a vessel in a race. The helmsman must always be alert for the slightest movement of the sails as they lift. He must notice at once any changes in the wind or any change in the tide. He must eye immediately any important rope which is out of order. In a small vessel especially the helmsman must be able to do this without detracting from his steering.

The other requisite for good helmsmanship is a light touch. A heavy-handed person will never make a good helmsman. Hands which are sensitive to vibrations and small changes of pressure are a great asset. We must learn to *feel* the tiller, and never grip it in light weather. It is important to realise that any vessel will be difficult to steer if your position is uncomfortable. As soon as your back or arms begin to ache, find another position, even if it means changing from the weather side of the tiller to the lee, perhaps for just a few minutes. On a calm day, try sitting to leeward and letting the tiller rest against the palm of your hand, pull it towards you using two fingers and a thumb, and while doing so look out for the first lift of the sails. As soon as this 'lifting' appears, you will be sailing as near the wind as the vessel will point. It is clear that if you add just a few degrees on to your acute angle to the wind, you will have to sail a greater distance in tacking back and forth to your windward mark.

Let us say we are sailing close-hauled and are sailing as close to the wind as the vessel will go. Now it is probable that the mainsail of our boat will begin to lift about a third of the way up the sail. We must be on the look-out for this, and if we are on the windward side we pull the tiller gently towards us, or if we are to leeward we push the tiller gently away from us.

We must practise getting to know the feel of wind on our face to help us note the flukes of the lightest puffs. A good helmsman is one who has become very sensitive and has acquired the art of 'anticipation'.

The wind is generally shifting a point or so all the time. It blows in curves and seldom in a straight line. These changes in the wind cause a 'free-puff' or a 'good slant' or, many times, a head-on buffet. It takes time to understand these vagaries in the wind, but eventually we learn to make the best of each one.

Let us assume that we are sailing 'full-and-by' (as near the wind as the vessel will point) on a rather squally day. Suddenly a head-on breeze comes up which shakes our sails. We immediately bear away and fill our sails. But when feeling for the wind a moment later, we may find that we are able to point higher than before the head-on breeze hit us. If we notice this right away, we get a lift up to windward which will do more than cancel out the heading off.

Now although the movements of the helm must be small when on a wind in a quick vessel, they must be enough.

You may at times be tempted to steer a course by another craft out on your weather bow, because she seems to be holding a better wind. This is a mistake. You are apt to be deceived by a vessel sailing to windward of you. She may be sailing along a parallel course to yours, but look as though she is pointing closer to the wind. You make an effort to 'pinch' your ship, *i.e.* sail too close to the wind. It is most important to have confidence in *your* sailing. As soon as you feel you are off the wind, luff gently and look for the lift of the sail. Check the luff quickly, and you can then be certain that you are sailing as near the wind as you will go.

Now, it is possible that the headsail will lift first, rather than the mainsail. In this case, you must test the sheets. The headsail sheet may need pulling in a bit, or perhaps the mainsheet is in too taut. It could also be that the sail sets badly and the set of sail wants checking up on; for example, the lead of the sheet and consequently the angle it makes with the sail, may be wrong. There is quite a difference, of course, between sailing in calm and sailing in rough water. The amount of helm required in different yachts varies considerably. Only through experience can you learn the correct amount. A yacht in rough seas may seem to be yawing much more than she actually is, and the beginner is apt to give more helm than is required. Watch these yaws carefully, especially with the wind on the quarter and a following sea. Your vessel may be moving up and down the waves taking the line of least resistance, and you will realise that all you must do is check the strongest of the rushes to windward and leeward. As I said elsewhere in this book, a vessel can often sail herself surprisingly well!

Now, let us assume that our vessel is running with the wind dead aft and is moving through the water in a 'cork-screw' motion. Here, a light hand on the tiller is quite useless. We must see that there is nothing in the way of putting the tiller hard down when necessary, as we must be quick to catch a luff and even quicker to avoid a sheer to leeward. The result, otherwise, would be a gybe and maybe the loss of our boom, or even our mast.

When sailing off the wind during a strong blow, in a 'hard-mouthed' vessel (one carrying a lot of weather helm), it is a good idea to ease out the mainsheet to let some of the wind out of it. This will mean the loss of driving power, but what is more important, it will take some of the strain off the rudder.

The best way to sail under all these conditions is, of course, a matter of experience in each particular boat. However, one must find some modification between 'jilling' the boat along in such a way to keep her dry and rushing her along so that her bows plunge into the water. The vessel should be eased into the sea. It is much better to ease the main sheet a little to keep her sailing more upright and increase her speed. This is so very clearly demonstrated in dinghy racing.

The helmsman can derive a great deal of pleasure in steering a good hard-weather vessel in a strong wind and rough sea, especially if sailing to windward. There are certain times during heavy weather when the helmsman should be able to steer on the lee side; for example, at the start of a race when it is extremely important to have a good view under his lee. He will need a clear vision also when rounding the weather side of a mark. It is often better to steer from the lee side in very light weather.

Finally, as to tactics. This is an enormous subject, and, as I have said, dealt with in a large number of excellent books by race-winning helmsmen. But perhaps I might briefly summarise here some tactical rules for the benefit of the beginner. By tactical rules I mean here ways in which you can embarrass your opponent in a race.

WHEN SAILING CLOSE-HAULED

(*a*) Tack either directly in front of your opponent to windward of him so as to blanket him.

(*b*) Tack in his lee forward of his 'wind-shadow' (wind-shadow is the area in the lee of a yacht where her sails 'blanket' the other vessel).

(*c*) Overtake him by sailing through his lee and give him your 'dirty-wind' (the wind spilled from your sails).

WHEN REACHING

(*a*) If you are ahead, give him your 'dirty wind'.

(*b*) If you are astern, try to get alongside and 'blanket' him.

WHEN RUNNING

Try and sail close astern of the yacht ahead, so as to 'blanket' him. In general: (1) avoid his 'wind-shadow', (2) avoid his 'dirty wind'.

Now modern yacht racing is carried out in accordance with definite rules, which are designed to make the contests fair by means of handicaps. Racing craft are classified and handicapped on a basis of their potential speed. We learned in an earlier chapter that the maximum speed of a yacht in knots is equal to 1·4 times the square root of her water-line length, and so we can see that the potential maximum speed is proportional to that water-line length. This maximum speed was achieved by racing yachts many years ago and despite the miracles of modern science it has never been exceeded. Naval architecture has, however, succeeded in getting the same speed with less sail area and a more 'sea-kindly' hull, largely through experiments in testing tanks. Racing yachts, therefore, are classified in accordance with size. In some classes yachts are handicapped in proportion to their measurements in accordance with a time allowance. In others, the yachts are of the same design and measurements, known as one designs, and race against one another without any time allowance.

The measurement rules vary all over the world, with small classes, but there are a number of international classes which are under the control of the International Yacht Racing Union, and whose object is to provide international racing; for example, the classes which usually race in the Olympic Games.

The history of how the racing rules developed from a simple fore-and-aft deck measurement rule, through the well-known formula, where the racing length was equal to the sum of the load water-line and the square root of the sail area divided by two, to the very complicated rules of the present day, such as the International Offshore Rule makes fascinating reading. But it is not part of this book to enter into this type of yachting history. Suffice to say that rules are essential. They must be fully understood by Race Committees as well as by the yacht owners taking part in races.

The following Extract has been taken from the Racing Rules of the International Yacht Racing Union as printed in the handbook of the Royal Yachting Association. This Association, which has kindly given permission for these extracts to be printed, is the body which controls racing in the British Isles and is the central organisation for yachtsmen of all kinds. Its address is Victoria Way, Woking, Surrey, and all the principal yacht clubs are members, as are a vast and steadily increasing number of yachtsmen. Of the Association's work, both legal and in the general assistance to the yachting public, no praise can be too high.

Fundamental Rule

Fair Sailing

A yacht shall participate in a race or series of races in an event only by fair sailing, superior speed and skill, and, except in team races, by individual effort. However, a yacht may be disqualified under this rule only in the case of a clear-cut violation of the above principles and only when no other rule applies.

PART I—DEFINITIONS

When a term defined in Part I is used in its defined sense it is printed in *italic* type. All preambles and definitions rank as rules.

Racing—A yacht is *racing* from her preparatory signal until she has either *finished* and cleared the finishing line and finishing *marks* or retired, or until the race has been *postponed*, *abandoned* or *cancelled*, except that in match or team races, the sailing instructions may prescribe that a yacht is *racing* from any specified time before the preparatory signal.

Starting—A yacht *starts* when, after fulfilling her penalty obligations, if any, under rule 51.1(c), (Sailing the Course), and after her starting signal, any part of her hull, crew or equipment first crosses the starting line in the direction of the course to the first *mark*.

Finishing—A yacht *finishes* when any part of her hull, or of her crew or equipment in normal position, crosses the finishing line from the direction of the course from the last *mark*, after fulfilling her penalty obligations, if any, under rule 52.2, (Touching a Mark).

Luffing—Altering course towards the wind until head to wind.

Tacking—A yacht is *tacking* from the moment she is beyond head to wind until she has *borne away*, when beating to windward, to a *close-hauled* course; if not beating to windward, to the course on which her mainsail has filled.

Bearing Away—Altering course away from the wind until a yacht begins to *gybe*.

Gybing—A yacht begins to *gybe* at the moment when, with the wind aft, the foot of her mainsail crosses her centre line, and completes the *gybe* when the mainsail has filled on the other tack.

On a Tack—A yacht is *on a tack* except when she is *tacking* or *gybing*. A yacht is on the *tack* (*starboard* or *port*) corresponding to her *windward* side.

Close-hauled—A yacht is *close-hauled* when sailing by the wind as close as she can lie with advantage in working to windward.

Clear Astern and *Clear Ahead; Overlap*—A yacht is *clear astern* of another when her hull and equipment in normal position are abaft an imaginary line projected abeam from the aftermost point of the other's hull and equipment, in normal position. The other yacht is *clear ahead*. The yachts *overlap* when neither is *clear astern*; or if, although one is *clear astern*, an intervening yacht *overlaps* both of them. The terms *clear astern*, *clear ahead* and *overlap* apply to yachts on opposite *tacks* only when they are subject to rule 42, (Rounding or Passing Marks and Obstructions).

Leeward and *Windward*—The *leeward* side of a yacht is that on which she is, or, if *luffing* head to wind, was, carrying her mainsail. The opposite side is the *windward* side.
When neither of two yachts on the same *tack* is *clear astern*, the one on the *leeward* side of the other is the *leeward yacht*. The other is the *windward yacht*.

Proper Course—A *proper course* is any course which a yacht might sail after the starting signal, in the absence of the other yacht or yachts affected, to *finish* as quickly as possible. The course sailed before *luffing* or *bearing away* is presumably, but not necessarily, that yacht's *proper course*. There is no *proper course* before the starting signal.

Mark—A *mark* is any object specified in the sailing instructions which a yacht must round or pass on a required side.
Every ordinary part of a *mark* ranks as part of it, including a flag, flagpole, boom or hoisted boat, but excluding ground tackle and any object either accidentally or temporarily attached to the *mark*.

Obstruction—An *obstruction* is any object, including a vessel under way, large enough to require a yacht, when not less than one overall length away from it, to make a substantial alteration of course to pass on one side or the other, or any object which can be passed on one side only, including a buoy when the yacht in question cannot safely pass between it and the shoal or object which it marks.

Postponement—A *postponed* race is one which is not started at its scheduled time and which can be sailed at any time the race committee may decide.

Abandonment—An *abandoned* race is one which the race committee declares void at any time after the starting signal, and which can be re-sailed at its discretion.

Cancellation—A *cancelled* race is one which the race committee decides will not be sailed thereafter.

PART IV—RIGHT OF WAY RULES
Rights and Obligations when Yachts Meet

The rules of Part IV do not apply in any way to a vessel which is neither intending to *race* nor *racing*; such vessel shall be treated in accordance with the International Regulations for Preventing Collisions at Sea or Government Right of Way Rules applicable in the area concerned.

The rules of Part IV apply only between yachts which either are intending to *race* or are *racing* in the same or different races, and, except when rule 3.2(b) (ii), (Race Continues After Sunset), applies, replace the International Regulations for Preventing Collisions at Sea or Government Right of Way Rules applicable to the area concerned, from the time a yacht intending to *race* begins to sail about in the vicinity of the starting line until she has either *finished* or retired and has left the vicinity of the course.

SECTION A—Obligations and Penalties

31—Disqualification

1. A yacht may be disqualified or otherwise penalized for infringing a rule of Part IV only when the infringement occurs while she is *racing*, whether or not a collision results.

2. A yacht may be disqualified before or after she is *racing* for seriously hindering a yacht which is *racing*, or for infringing the sailing instructions.

32—Avoiding Collisions

A right-of-way yacht which fails to make a reasonable attempt to avoid a collision resulting in serious damage may be disqualified as well as the other yacht.

33—Rule Infringement

1. ACCEPTING PENALTY

A yacht which realises she has infringed a racing rule or a sailing instruction is under an obligation either to retire promptly or to exonerate herself by accepting an alternative penalty when so prescribed in the sailing instructions, but when she does not retire or exonerate herself and persists in *racing*, other yachts shall continue to accord her such rights as she may have under the rules of Part IV.

2. CONTACT BETWEEN YACHTS RACING

When there is contact between the hull, equipment or crew of two yachts, both shall be disqualified or otherwise penalized unless:
either
(a) one of the yachts retires in acknowledgement of the infringement, or exonerates herself by accepting an alternative penalty when so prescribed in the sailing instructions,
or

(b) one or both of these yachts acts in accordance with rule 68.3, (Protests).

3. When an incident is the subject of action by the race committee under rule 33.2 but under no other rule of Part IV, it may waive the requirements of rule 33.2 when it is satisfied that the contact was minor and unavoidable.

34—Hailing

1. Except when *luffing* under rule 38.1, (Luffing and Sailing above a Proper Course after Starting), a right-of-way yacht which does not hail before or when making an alteration of course which may not be foreseen by the other yacht may be disqualified as well as the yacht required to keep clear when a collision resulting in serious damage occurs.

2. A yacht which hails when claiming the establishment or termination of an *overlap* or insufficiency of room at a *mark* or *obstruction* thereby helps to support her claim for the purposes of rule 42, (Rounding or Passing Marks and Obstructions).

SECTION B—Principal Right-of-Way Rules and their Limitations

These rules apply except when over-ridden by a rule in Section C.

35—Limitations on Altering Course

When one yacht is required to keep clear of another, the right-of-way yacht shall not so alter course as to prevent the other yacht from keeping clear; or so as to obstruct her while she is keeping clear, except:

(a) to the extent permitted by rule 38.1, (Same Tack—Luffing and Sailing above a Proper Course after Starting), and

(b) when assuming a *proper* course:
either
(i) to *start*, unless subject to rule 40, (Same Tack—Luffing before Starting), or to the second part of rule 44.1(b), (Returning to Start), or
(ii) when rounding a *mark*.

36—Opposite Tacks—Basic Rule

A *port-tack* yacht shall keep clear of a *starboard-tack* yacht.

37—Same Tack—Basic Rules

1. WHEN OVERLAPPED
A *windward yacht* shall keep clear of a *leeward yacht*.

2. WHEN NOT OVERLAPPED
A yacht *clear astern* shall keep clear of a yacht *clear ahead*.

3. TRANSITIONAL
A yacht which establishes an *overlap* to *leeward* from *clear astern* shall allow the *windward yacht* ample room and opportunity to keep clear.

38—Same Tack—Luffing and Sailing above a Proper Course after Starting

1. LUFFING RIGHTS
After she has *started* and cleared the starting line, a yacht *clear ahead* or a *leeward yacht* may luff as she pleases, subject to the *proper course* limitations of this rule.

2. PROPER COURSE LIMITATIONS

A *leeward yacht* shall not sail above her *proper course* while an *overlap* exists, if when the *overlap* began or, at any time during its existence, the helmsman of the *windward yacht* (when sighting abeam from his normal station and sailing no higher than the *leeward yacht*) has been abreast or forward of the mainmast of the *leeward yacht*.

3. OVERLAP LIMITATIONS

For the purpose of this rule: An *overlap* does not exist unless the yachts are clearly within two overall lengths of the longer yacht; and an *overlap* which exists between two yachts when the leading yacht *starts*, or when one or both of them completes a *tack* or *gybe*, shall be regarded as a new *overlap* beginning at that time.

4. HAILING TO STOP OR PREVENT A LUFF

When there is doubt, the *leeward yacht* may assume that she has the right to *luff* unless the helmsman of the windward yacht has hailed "Mast Abeam", or words to that effect. The *leeward yacht* shall be governed by such hail, and, when she deems it improper, her only remedy is to protest.

5. CURTAILING A LUFF

The *windward yacht* shall not cause a *luff* to be curtailed because of her proximity to the *leeward yacht* unless an *obstruction*, a third yacht or other object restricts her ability to respond.

6. LUFFING TWO OR MORE YACHTS

A yacht shall not *luff* unless she has the right to *luff* all yachts which would be affected by her *luff*, in which case they shall all respond even when an intervening yacht or yachts would not otherwise have the right to *luff*.

39—Same Tack—Sailing Below a Proper Course after Starting

A yacht which is on a free leg of the course shall not sail below her *proper* course when she is clearly within three of her overall lengths of either a *leeward yacht* or a yacht *clear astern* which is steering a course to pass to leeward.

40—Same Tack—Luffing before Starting

Before a right-of-way yacht has *started* and cleared the starting-line, any *luff* on her part which causes another yacht to have to alter course to avoid a collision shall be carried out slowly and in such a way as to give a *windward yacht* room and opportunity to keep clear, but the *leeward yacht* shall not so *luff* above a *close-hauled* course, unless the helmsman of the *windward yacht* (sighting abeam from his normal station) is abaft the mainmast of the *leeward yacht*. Rules 38.4, (Hailing to Stop or Prevent a Luff); 38.5, (Curtailing a Luff) and 38.6, (Luffing Two or more Yachts), also apply.

41—Changing Tacks—Tacking or Gybing

1. BASIC RULE

A yacht which is either *tacking* or *gybing* shall keep clear of a yacht *on a tack*.

2. TRANSITIONAL

A yacht shall neither *tack* nor *gybe* into a position which will give her right of way unless she does so far enough from a yacht *on a tack* to enable this yacht to keep clear without having to begin to alter her course until after the *tack* or *gybe* has been completed.

3. ONUS

A yacht which *tacks* or *gybes* has the onus of satisfying the race committee that she completed her *tack* or *gybe* in accordance with rule 41.2.

4. WHEN SIMULTANEOUS

When two yachts are both *tacking* or both *gybing* at the same time, the one on the other's *port* side shall keep clear.

SECTION C—Rules which Apply at Marks and Obstructions and other Exceptions to the Rules of Section B

When a rule of this section applies, to the extent to which it explicitly provides rights and obligations, it over-rides any conflicting rule of Section B—Principal Right-of-Way Rules and their Limitations, except rule 35, (Limitations on Altering Course).

42—Rounding or Passing Marks and Obstructions

1. ROOM AT MARKS AND OBSTRUCTIONS WHEN OVER-LAPPED

When yachts are about to round or pass a *mark*, other than a starting *mark* surrounded by navigable water, on the same required side or an *obstruction* on the same side:

(a) An outside yacht shall give each yacht *overlapping* her on the inside, room to round or pass the *mark* or *obstruction*, except as provided in rules 42.1(c), 42.1(d) and 42.4, (At a Starting Mark Surrounded by Navigable Water).

Room includes room for an *overlapping* yacht to *tack* or *gybe* when either is an integral part of the rounding or passing manoeuvre.

(b) When an inside yacht of two or more *overlapped* yachts either on opposite *tacks*, or on the same *tack* without *luffing* rights, will have to *gybe* in order most directly to assume a *proper course* to the next *mark*, she shall *gybe* at the first reasonable opportunity.

(c) When two yachts on opposite *tacks* are on a beat or when one of them will have to *tack* either to round the *mark* or to avoid the *obstruction*, as between each other rule 42.1 shall not apply and they are subject to rules 36, (Opposite Tacks—Basic Rule), and 41, (Changing Tacks—Tacking or Gybing).

(d) An outside *leeward yacht* with luffing rights may take an inside yacht to windward of a *mark* provided that she hails to that effect and begins to *luff* before she is within two of her overall lengths of the *mark* and provided that she also passes to windward of it.

2. CLEAR ASTERN AND CLEAR AHEAD IN THE VICINITY OF MARKS AND OBSTRUCTIONS

When yachts are about to round or pass a *mark*, other than a starting *mark* surrounded by navigable water, on the same required side or an *obstruction* on the same side:

(a) A yacht *clear astern* shall keep clear in anticipation of and during the rounding or passing manoeuvre when the yacht *clear ahead* remains on the same *tack* or *gybes*.

(b) A yacht *clear ahead* which *tacks* to round a *mark* is subject to rule 41, (Changing Tacks—Tacking or Gybing), but a yacht *clear astern* shall not *luff* above *close-hauled* so as to prevent the yacht *clear ahead* from *tacking*.

3. LIMITATIONS ON ESTABLISHING AND MAINTAINING AN OVERLAP IN THE VICINITY OF MARKS AND OBSTRUCTIONS

(a) A yacht *clear astern* may establish an inside *overlap* and be entitled to room under rule 42.1(a), (Room at Marks and Obstructions when Overlapped), only when the yacht *clear ahead*:

(i) is able to give the required room and

(ii) is outside two of her overall lengths of the *mark* or *obstruction*, except when either yacht has completed a *tack* within two overall lengths of the *mark* or *obstruction*, or when the *obstruction* is a continuing one as provided in rule 42.3(f).

(b) A yacht *clear ahead* shall be under no obligation to give room to a yacht *clear astern* before an *overlap* is established.

(c) When an outside yacht is *overlapped* at the time she comes within two of her overall lengths of a *mark* or an *obstruction*, she shall continue to be bound by rule 42.1(a), (Room at Marks and Obstructions when Overlapped), to give room as required even though the *overlap* may thereafter be broken.

(d) A yacht which claims an inside *overlap* has the onus of satisfying the race committee that the *overlap* was established in proper time.

(e) An outside yacht which claims to have broken an *overlap* has the onus of satisfying the race committee that she became *clear ahead* when she was more than two of her overall lengths from the *mark* or *obstruction*.

(f) A yacht *clear astern* may establish an *overlap* between the yacht *clear ahead* and a continuing *obstruction* such as a shoal or the shore or another vessel, only when at that time there is room for her to pass between them in safety.

4. AT A STARTING MARK SURROUNDED BY NAVIGABLE WATER

When approaching the starting line to *start*, a *leeward yacht* shall be under no obligation to give any *windward yacht* room to pass to leeward of a starting *mark* surrounded by navigable water; but, after the starting signal, a *leeward yacht* shall not deprive a *windward yacht* of room at such a *mark* by sailing either above the course to the first *mark* or above *close-hauled*.

43—Close-Hauled, Hailing for Room to Tack at Obstructions

1. HAILING

When two *close-hauled* yachts are on the same *tack* and safe pilotage requires the yacht *clear ahead* or the *leeward yacht* to make a substantial alteration of course to clear an *obstruction*, and when she intends to *tack*, but cannot *tack* without colliding with the other yacht, she shall hail the other yacht for room to *tack* and clear the other yacht, but she shall not hail and *tack* simultaneously.

2. RESPONDING

The hailed yacht at the earliest possible moment after the hail shall:—
either

(a) *tack*, in which case the hailing yacht shall begin to *tack* either:—

(i) before the hailed yacht has completed her *tack*, or

(ii) when she cannot then *tack* without colliding with the hailed yacht, immediately she is able to *tack* and clear her;

or

(b) reply "You *tack*", or words to that effect, when in her opinion she can keep clear without *tacking* or after postponing her *tack*.
In this case:—

(i) the hailing yacht shall immediately *tack* and

(ii) the hailed yacht shall keep clear.

(iii) The onus of satisfying the race committee that she kept clear shall lie on the hailed yacht which replied "You *tack*".

3. LIMITATION ON RIGHT TO ROOM WHEN THE OBSTRUCTION IS A MARK

(a) When the hailed yacht can fetch an *obstruction* which is also a *mark*, the hailing yacht shall not be entitled to room to *tack* and clear the hailed yacht and the hailed yacht shall immediately so inform the hailing yacht.

(b) If, thereafter, the hailing yacht again hails for room to *tack* and clear the hailed yacht she shall, after receiving room, retire immediately or exonerate herself by accepting an alternative penalty when so prescribed in the sailing instructions.

(c) When, after having refused to respond to a hail under rule 43.3(a), the hailed yacht fails to fetch, she shall retire immediately, or exonerate herself by accepting an alternative penalty when so prescribed in the sailing instructions.

44—Returning to Start

1. (a) After the starting signal is made, a premature starter returning to *start*, or a yacht working into position from the course side of the starting line or its extensions, shall keep clear of all yachts which are *starting* or have *started* correctly, until she is wholly on the pre-start side of the starting line or its extensions.

(b) Thereafter, she shall be accorded the rights under the rules of Part IV of a yacht which is *starting* correctly; but when she thereby acquires right of way over another yacht which is *starting* correctly, she shall allow that yacht ample room and opportunity to keep clear.

2. A premature starter while continuing to sail the course and until it is obvious that she is returning to *start*, shall be accorded the rights under the rules of Part IV of a yacht which has *started*.

Re-rounding after Touching a Mark

1. A yacht which has touched a *mark*, and is about to exonerate herself in accordance with rule 52.2, (Touching a Mark), shall keep clear of all other yachts which are about to round or pass it or have rounded or passed it correctly, until she has rounded it completely and has cleared it and is on a *proper course* to the next *mark*.

2. A yacht which has touched a *mark* while continuing to sail the course and until it is obvious that she is returning to round it completely in accordance with rule 52.2, (Touching a Mark), shall be accorded rights under the rules of Part IV.

46—Anchored, Aground or Capsized

1. A yacht under way shall keep clear of another yacht *racing* which is anchored, aground or capsized. Of two anchored yachts, the one which anchored later shall keep clear, except that a yacht which is dragging shall keep clear of one which is not.

2. A yacht anchored or aground shall indicate the fact to any yacht which may be in danger of fouling her. Unless the size of the yachts or the weather conditions make some other signal necessary, a hail is sufficient indication.

3. A yacht shall not be penalized for fouling a yacht in distress which she is attempting to assist or a yacht which goes aground or capsizes immediately ahead of her.

CHAPTER X

BAD WEATHER

BEFORE we go into the question of handling our vessel in bad weather, let us consider some elementary weather forecasting which any yachtsman should know. We can quite accurately predict changes in the weather by observing such things as the shape and movement of clouds, the colour of the sky at sunrise and sunset, or the behaviour of sea birds, animals, and fish. Then there is that essential part of the yacht's equipment, the barometer, which records all changes in the air pressure.

Two main types of pressure disturbances occur around the British Isles. The first is the anticyclone, the passing of which causes the barometer to fall and the clouds to change their shape. An anticyclone is a system of winds which move in a clockwise direction about an area of high pressure. It is a stable system bringing fair weather and is apt to last for a good length of time. The wind does not blow too hard and the air is rather dry. Frequently, there is a calm in the centre of the system. Here, in the centre, the air on the surface is damp and fog may be expected. The second main type of pressure disturbance is the depression, which is a low pressure system caused by a system of winds revolving in an anticlockwise direction round an area of low pressure. It travels generally in a northeasterly or easterly direction, bringing strong winds and rain, and moves rapidly. A depression gives several warnings of its approach: a falling barometer, 'mares' tails', the wind shifting in an anti-clockwise direction with the air becoming close, or the wind becoming stronger along with heavy rain; also, a halo round the moon, and low clouds banking up and steadily becoming denser.

The behaviour of the weather and the barometer in the following sequence of events is so consistent that as long as you know the shape, course, and speed of the system, you could very accurately predict any change in the weather.

When the centre of the depression passes directly overhead, the wind will suddenly shift in an anticlockwise direction (back) about 180 degrees, and eventually stir up an ugly-looking sea. If the centre passes to the south of the yacht, then the wind will have been moving to the right. As soon as the centre has passed, the barometer will start to rise, although the wind will still be backing. If the centre of the depression passes to the north of the yacht, the barometer will show very little change, but as the wind begins to back, it will show a slight rise. The force of the wind becomes stronger as you come nearer to the centre of the depression. The weather gradually becomes better once the centre has passed over. There will be clear periods with intermittent wind and rain, with the barometer rising steadily. If the wind shifts to the northeast, you can expect a fine period; or if it shifts to the northwest, you can also expect a fine spell. However, if the wind backs to the southward, and once again the barometer starts to fall, then you can expect another depression.

Now out in the open sea, the shape, course, and speed of the system will remain constant, making the job of forecasting a fairly simple one. However, we are most probably to be concerned with coastal weather conditions, and here these three factors do not remain consistent, owing to the presence of land. It is best for the yachtsman to try to do his own forecasting for the area where he will be sailing. He can do this by listening to the weather reports on the wireless, and then by observing local signs. The movements of the barometer will, of course, give him a good indication of the weather.

Let us study the barometer more thoroughly. First of all, a high barometer indicates fine weather; a low barometer bad weather. A steady barometer when the air is dry means a continuance of fine weather. Any rapid movement of the barometer will always be the forerunner of unsettled weather. Generally speaking, the barometer will fall for a southerly wind and rise for a northerly wind. When the air is warm, the wind is most likely to be from the southward, and if cold, from the northward. If the barometer has remained very low for a long time, the first rise generally means heavy winds, and can frequently mean northerly gales. A slowly rising barometer means settled weather, whereas a quickly rising barometer means bad weather. A rising barometer generally indicates less wind or rain, and a falling one means more wind or rain. Before and during a fine spell, the barometer will stay high and steady. If it is steady and the glass begins to fall with increasing dampness of the air, followed by wind and rain from the south, southeast, or southwest, then a depression is most likely approaching. If, on the other hand, the barometer is steady and the air becomes drier and the temperature falls, this will mean northerly winds and a dry period. The wind shifts round in the same direction as the sun under normal fair weather conditions, but if an easterly wind backs to the north or a westerly wind backs through south to the east, then bad weather can be expected. This is the approach of a depression coming from the westward. If the rain comes before the wind, then it will blow hard. However, if the wind precedes the rain, then it will neither blow as hard nor last as long.

One can generally expect rain with sea winds whereas land winds are dry. The prevailing wind in the British Isles is southwest.

Now, to give us additional information in our study of the weather, we can observe the different shapes of the clouds.

LOWER CLOUDS

Strato-cumulus—Rolls of heavy dark clouds covering the whole sky with occasional blue patches showing through. Generally seen in winter, it means wind but not rain.

Nimbus—The rain cloud. A dark heavy mass of cloud with no definite shape. If broken up into small clouds it is known as 'Fracto-nimbus'.

Cumulus—Thick white woolly clouds with clearly defined, flattish lower edges. A fair weather formation. If rather oily in appearance, and growing in size towards evening, a change in the weather may be expected.

Cumulo-nimbus—Heavy masses of cumulus rising high with a heavy black base of nimbus. This means thunder and heavy squalls, lightning, and rain.

Stratus—A layer of cloud somewhat like fog, not resting on the ground. If broken up by winds, it is known as Fracto-stratus.

UPPER CLOUDS

Cirrus—White feathery clouds ('mares' tails'). If they remain steady and isolated, good weather will continue. If they assume a regular formation, gradually covering the whole sky, this means bad weather.

Cirro-stratus—A thin white sheet of cirrus completely covering the sky. If of no definite shape and the weather is fine, it will continue. If, however, the formation starts by being cirrus and becomes a regularised formation, bad weather will follow.

A halo round the sun or moon in these conditions also means bad weather.

Cirro-cumulus—A collection of white masses of cirrus formed in groups or lines. This is the 'mackerel' sky of sailors. The cirrus, if isolated, mean fine weather will continue; if they fill the sky and come close together, bad weather can be expected.

Alto-cumulus—A large type of cirro-cumulus, arranging itself in tightly packed lines or waves, and completely covering a large part of the sky.

Alto-stratus—A sheet of grey cloud with a bright patch indicating the sun (or moon).

A fair period followed by cirrus or cumulus clouds high up and passing through the sky in a different direction from the lower clouds and existing wind, indicates a shifting of wind in the direction from which the high clouds come. Any small dark clouds indicate rain. Small, light grey moving clouds mean wind, and hard, clearly defined clouds or a hard, dark blue sky is a warning of wind with possible rain.

Still another way to judge the weather conditions is by observing the sea birds who remain near the land whenever bad weather is approaching; also porpoises will swim to windward and jump out of the water.

We now know that by listening to the wireless weather reports (full details of these are given in *Reed's Almanack*), by studying the movements of the barometer, the direction of the wind, and the colour of the sky at sunset and sunrise, we can quite accurately forecast the weather at sea and plan our passage.

You have learned to handle your yacht extremely well under normal conditions, but the big test of your seamanship comes along when you must manoeuvre in bad weather. You should always go to sea fully prepared for bad conditions so there is no danger of your being 'caught out'. No one enjoys bad weather. It is wetting, uncomfortable, and cooking becomes quite a difficult task. It is not very pleasant to get drenched while shifting jibs on a wildly pitching forecastle. But when all is over and you have arrived safely in harbour, you will feel real satisfaction with your own seamanship, and great affection for the little craft which has looked after you so staunchly.

Spend a little time observing the wind before getting under-way. The strength of the wind should always be estimated in relation to the size of your yacht. A two-reef breeze for a small boat may be a full sailing breeze for a large yacht. Whenever the wind is before the beam, it is quite apparent when it increases, but when the wind is abaft the beam, it is more difficult to notice. If the wind appears to be increasing, it is best to arrange for a heavier blow. If the wind is lessening, you will realise you need not bother to take in a reef that you will have to 'shake out' almost at once. One is inclined to over-estimate the power of an on-shore breeze and to under-estimate the power of an off-shore breeze. The sea will appear calm when the wind is blowing off the land, and will appear disproportionally rough when the wind is blowing on-shore. Sea breezes are steady, whereas land breezes are generally puffy or squally as the wind is broken up by land masses and shore objects. Before reefing for a land breeze, time the puffs or squalls, and if there are long intervals between each one, by luffing up or starting the sheet just as each squall catches you, you can probably manage without having to reef. If, on the other hand, the squalls occur at frequent intervals, then it is wisest to reef.

If you have carefully planned your passage with the possi-bility of having to shelter, and if you have listened to weather forecasts and studied the barometer, you should never, under normal cruising conditions, run into bad weather for which you are unprepared.

As I have said, it is difficult, when sailing before the wind, to estimate any increase in the force of the wind. If you see that the wind is increasing by the state of the sea, the best way to esti-mate the wind's strength is to turn the boat so as temporarily to bring the wind ahead, or at any rate on the beam. Sail for a moment on a close reach. If the wind is driving the yacht over more and more so that she is staggering along at too great an angle, then it is clearly time to reef, but the question is one reef or two? Let us assume that our boat has the ordinary point reefing, because this is slightly more complicated than roller reefing. Now we can see that the sky looks like wind, the glass has dropped, and, moreover, we know that shortly we must alter course and sail close-hauled. It is, therefore, best for us to take in two reefs at this stage and set the small jib. It will be harder to do it later.

If you are not pressed for time, rather than reef underway, it is easier in a small yacht to lower the sails and drift while taking in the reefs. But if there is not enough sea-room, you will have to keep moving. With another hand aboard, you can lower the mainsail and sail under headsail. Another very good method is to heave-to. Then haul the jib to windward with the weather sheet, and haul in the main sheet and lash the helm almost amidships. Now top the boom up with the topping lift so as to take the weight off the mainsail. As you lower the head of the sail you tie down the cringle in the luff at the first reef. Rig an outhaul through the reef cringle in the leech, and pass it over a sheave in the first reef bee block in the outboard end of the boom. Haul it hand tight and secure it to a cleat on the boom. It is quite possible to reef underway, and while sailing in a long race you would do so. Whatever method you employ, when the luff reef cringle has been tied down to the boom, you take the leech between the first reef cringle and the clew, roll it up tightly, and put it on the top of the boom. Now, taking a line, tie down the cringle in the leech to the boom. Both this line and the outhaul are holding the cringle in the leech to the boom. You now have the luff and leech reef cringles tied down to the boom. Take the middle of the part of the sail between the foot and the first reef, roll it up, and tie in the reef points with reef-knots. You will have to pass one line of each point underneath the sail, but do not tie the points round the boom, tie them round the rolled-up sail. It is easy to make the mistake, when tying in one reef, of tying a point in the first reef to a point in the second reef. As a precaution, take both ends of the reef point and pull them alternately. A pull on one side should be felt immediately on the other; if not, you have two different points. We have assumed that it is necessary to tie in a second reef, so we repeat the process, but this time we must tie the reef in on the starboard side, since the first reef was tied in on the port side. The leech outhaul will be passed through a second bee block, nearer the mast than the first, and all the points will be tied in on the opposite side of the sail. We will, of course, have to use different outhauls and different lines for the luff and leech cringles. If you have to tie in as many as two or three reefs, the lowest batten will have to be removed from the sail. A third reef must be tied in on the opposite side to the second reef. It is generally best when tying in reef points to begin at the luff and work aft.

Now that we have tied two reefs in the mainsail, we can ease off the topping lift and set about taking in (handing) the jib and hoisting in its place the smaller jib. We bring the second head-sail to the fo'c'sle and while the first headsail is still hoisted, snap the hanks or spring hooks onto the fore-stay *underneath* the lowest spring hook of the first jib. (It is often the case that to leave enough room on the fore-stay for all the hooks of the second jib you must unsnap the lowest hook of the first jib.) Once all the hooks are on, unshackle the tack of the first jib. If the boat is fitted with a tack downhaul, slacken away and then unshackle from the tack. Now shackle on the tack of the second headsail. If the boat is not fitted with a tack downhaul, the tack will most likely be shackled on to a ring-bolt in the deck, or on the stem-head. Now lower away the jib halliard, if you take the halliard off the cleat on the mast and bring it for'ard, you can then gather in the jib as it comes down, the sheets having been cast off or eased. It is best to have only one on the fo'c'sle in a small yacht, but should there be two of you, one can lower away and the other gather in the jib, at the same time quickly casting off the spring hooks. When the jib is lowered, unshackle the halliard from the head and shackle it onto the head of the second jib. The jib sheets must then be unshackled from the clew of the first jib and shackled onto the clew of the second. If there is no other member of the crew, you will do this your-self, once you have lowered and unhooked the first jib and shackled the second jib onto the halliard. Then hoist away and make the halliard fast round the cleat on the mast. If there is a tack downhaul, set it up, and carrying the first jib with you, go astern and trim the sheets. Stow the first jib (bag it if it is not wet), and the vessel is now ready to carry on under her reduced canvas.

This operation is greatly simplified on some modern yachts which are equipped with twin fore-stays. In this way a second headsail may be hanked on and hoisted at the same time as the first headsail is lowered. However, twin fore-stays are another of those yacht club fireside subjects of controversy!

When shaking out a reef, just reverse the process of tying one in. Starting at the middle point, you untie the reef points. Once you have done this, cast off the luff hold-down. Then cast off the leech hold-down and then the leech outhaul. The reef points must be untied before the luff and leech hold-downs, otherwise you are more than likely to tear the sail. After you have shaken out a reef in a gaff-rigged boat, lower the peak into a horizontal position before hoisting sail again, and whatever rig your boat has, you should hoist very carefully after shaking out a reef, in case there are any points still tied. Remember what we learned about the balance of the sail-plan. You will have to change jibs if you have two reefs in the mainsail, and if there are three reefs in the mainsail, you may have to change again. If you do not have a smaller jib, you may find that the yacht will balance better without any jib at all. The drawback here, however, is that the mainsail loses efficiency the moment the headsail is lowered. Generally speaking, though, the smallest jib (storm jib) should balance even a trysail.

So far we have talked about point reefing. But many modern craft employ a handy and efficient method of reefing the mainsail by simply rolling it round the boom. This method requires strong gear. After setting up the topping lift, the halliards are eased slowly, and while you lower the sail, you roll it round the boom, by turning the latter with a handle that turns a worm gear (see Fig. 56).

If the wind increases to such an extent that you consider it necessary to reduce canvas further, you will be forced to set the trysail and (if you carry one) storm jib. Observing how she is

ROLLER REEFING.

① Worm Gear

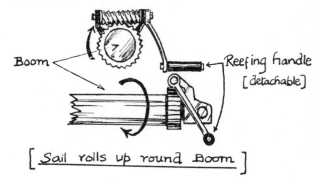

Boom

Reefing Handle
[detachable]

[Sail rolls up round Boom]

② Pawl and Ratchet

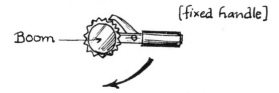

Boom ——

[fixed handle]

③ Drum and Wire

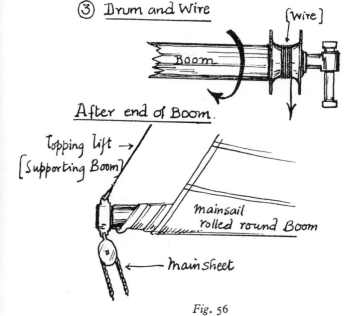

[Wire]

Boom

After end of Boom.

Topping lift →
[Supporting Boom]

mainsail
rolled round Boom

mainsheet

Fig. 56

behaving, we trim sheets and tiller accordingly, so that the vessel lies in the most comfortable position.

Both the storm jib and trysail are made of heavy canvas and have heavy bolt ropes and fittings to stand up to strong winds. The trysail may have a small gaff but it is more likely to resemble a Bermudan sail (see Fig. 57). It is a loose-footed sail and has no boom. The sheets of the trysail are double sheets. To bend the trysail, first lower the jib so that the yacht will not pay off to leeward while the mainsail is off her. Set up the topping lift, and then lower and furl the mainsail, and, using gaskets or tiers, tie it firmly to the boom. Lower the topping lift and ease the boom down into its crutch, and lash it securely. If there is no proper crutch, ease the boom down to the deck. Next cast off the main halliard from the head of the mainsail and shackle it to the head of the trysail. The trysail may have parrel lines and ash parrel balls (see Fig. 57) or it may have slides on the luff that will run up the usual mast track. Fit the slides in the track and then hoist the trysail. In the case of parrel lines, as each parrel line comes close to the foot of the mast, they can be fitted while you hoist. Trysail sheets are sometimes shaped like purchases—a double whip or luff and are most often led through stout blocks on each quarter. On the tail of the standing block is a hook which must be fastened onto a ring-bolt on each quarter. Once you have hoisted the sail, trim the sheets. If you have a storm jib aboard, which is a very small jib made of heavy, tough canvas like the trysail, you should now hoist it in the same way as you hoisted the No. 2 jib.

If running before a big sea, it is essential to steer very cautiously. Each time any dangerous-looking seas threaten astern, you should put the helm up to meet them exactly stern on, taking care not to gybe. If conditions worsen, you may very well decide to heave-to.

When heaving-to in such conditions, you should reeve a line through the cringle in the clew of the jib and make the two ends fast. This line is called a preventer and is used to hold the jib secured in case the sheets carry away. It should not be as taut as the jib sheet itself. If you have no such line and the jib sheets should part, the sail will violently flap about and is not only difficult but often dangerous to handle. Some water will

The Trysail

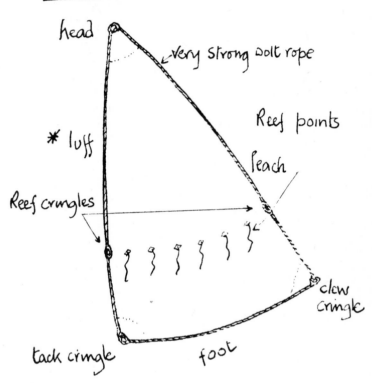

head

very strong bolt rope

Reef points

* luff

leach

Reef cringles

clew cringle

tack cringle   foot

* Luff is secured to mast by means of
either slides which run in the track
on the mast, or by parrel lines.
with parrel balls ⟶

Fig. 57

probably come aboard, so it is wise to put more lines round anything large like the dinghy and make certain that everything on deck is firmly lashed down.

Every yachtsman will at some time have to make the decision as to whether he should shelter or carry on, and it is helpful to remember the following: if you have quite enough sea room and you are doubtful of the harbours under your lee, then stay at sea. You may not be comfortable, but you will be safer at sea than if you tried to enter an unknown harbour. With sea room and a sound yacht and gear, you will definitely be safe riding out the gale at sea. If, on the other hand, you are certain the nearest harbour to leeward has deep water and can be entered no matter what the state of the tide, then you should be quite safe in entering. It is wisest not to enter harbour against ebb tide, and never enter if there is a bar to cross. It is always difficult, judging the strength of the wind at sea.

Wind force in weather reports is generally measured and referred to by numbers and is called the Beaufort Scale.

As you can see, the yachts referred to in column (2) are fishing smacks, larger than the average yacht of about 7 or 8 tons. The latter could keep sailing up to about force 8, and would then most likely heave-to. It is not safe to heave-to above force 8. It is fairly easy to tell when it is unsafe to lie hove-to. The force of the wind and the curling of the seas increase rapidly and toss the yacht about. The crests of the waves will become bigger, she will have at times an alarming angle of heel, and more and more water will come on deck. The first thing you must do, in this case, is to hand the sails, and the yacht will then most likely lie broadside on to the seas. Since water will come aboard and into the cockpit, a yacht with a large open cockpit should not sail where she might be exposed to such weather. However, today there are many yachts with the excellent device of a self-draining cockpit, which will empty itself. You should now put the sea anchor over the side. A sea anchor should form part of the yacht's equipment, as it is of invaluable use at times like this. Furthermore, even though the sea anchor will only work properly under certain conditions, no matter what kind of craft you possess, she should carry one. For instance, a modern ketch or yawl will ride to a sea anchor very

Beaufort number	Description of Wind (1)	Specification of Beaufort Scale		Limits of Speed Nautical Miles per Hour. (4)	Probable Height of Waves (in metres)
		For Coast Use, based on Observations made at Scilly, Yarmouth and Holyhead. (2)	For use on Land, based on Observations made at Land Stations. (3)		
0	Calm.	Calm.	Calm; smoke rises vertically.	Less than 1	—
1	Light air.	Fishing smack just has steerage way. (1)	Direction of wind shown by smoke drift, but not by wind vanes.	1–3	—
2	Light breeze.	Wind fills the sails of smacks, which then move at about 1–2 miles per hour.	Wind felt on face; leaves rustle; ordinary vane moved by wind.	4–6	0·15
3	Gentle breeze.	Smacks begin to careen and travel about 3–4 miles per hour.	Leaves and small twigs in constant motion; wind extends light flag.	7–10	0·60
4	Moderate breeze.	Good working breeze; smacks carry all canvas with good list.	Raises dust and loose paper; small branches are moved.	11–16	1·0
5	Fresh breeze.	Smacks shorten sail.	Small trees in leaf begin to sway; crested wavelets form on inland waters.	17–21	1·80
6	Strong breeze.	Smacks have double reef in main sail. Care required when fishing.	Large branches in motion; whistling heard in telegraph wires; umbrellas used with difficulty.	22–27	3·0
7	Moderate gale (2)	Smacks remain in harbour, and those at sea lie to.	Whole trees in motion; inconvenience felt when walking against wind.	28–33	4·0
8	Gale.	All smacks make for harbour if practicable.	Breaks twigs off trees; generally impedes progress.	34–40	5·50
9	Strong gale.	High waves. Spray affects visibility	Slight structural damage occurs (chimney pots and slates removed).	41–47	7·0
10	Storm.	Very high waves. Visibility affected.	Seldom experienced inland; trees uprooted; considerable structural damage occurs.	48–55	9·0
11	Violent storm.	Exceptionally high waves. Visibility affected.	Very rarely experienced; accompanied by widespread damage.	56–63	11·30
12	Hurricane.	Sea white with driving spray. Visibility virtually nil.	—	above 64	13·50

(1) The fishing smack in this column may be taken as representing a trawler of average type and trim. For larger or smaller boats and for special circumstances allowances must be made.

(2) In statistics of gales prepared by the Meteorological Office only winds of force 8 and upwards are included.

well with the mizzen set. If a yacht is of the old straight-stemmed type, with a deep forefoot, she will ride to a sea anchor all right without a riding sail. If the yacht is a modern sloop or cutter, she will not ride so well to a sea anchor, because she has less forefoot to get a grip on the water.

Now to consider how to use the sea anchor. First bring it up on deck with its tripping line bent on. If stout coir rope, which will float, is used for the anchor warp, it will not be necessary to buoy the sea anchor. To take the chafe of the anchor warp in the fair-lead, we will need some hessian or strips of old canvas. Now bend the warp to the anchor. Secure the inboard end of the tripping line and throw the anchor over the weather bow. Pay out enough warp to prevent a sudden jerk coming on it and fasten it securely inboard and secure the tripping line. Then wrap the hessian or strips of old canvas round that section of the warp which will be chafed in the fair-lead. The tripping line should be strong. Some believe that it is better to use a short line attached to the sea anchor, and which can be retrieved with a boat-hook when the time comes for its use, because of the chafing done by the tripping line to whatever it touches while the gale conditions last.

To get the sea anchor aboard, when conditions have improved sufficiently for you to make sail again, you should haul the yacht up to it by the warp and the tripping line, which being made of coir is floating and easy to retrieve with a boat-hook. Unless you use a tripping line of some sort to capsize the water out of the sea anchor, you will not be able to get it aboard.

Supposing your vessel will not ride to a sea anchor properly, and having taken in all canvas, you are lying 'a-hull' (lying with no sail set and no sea anchor out). In due course, you may find that the force of the waves is endangering the hull or that too much water is coming aboard and that it is no longer safe to remain in this position. Now is the time to 'run before it'. First put a lashing round the lower half of the jib and hoist the head a few feet. If you assist the yacht with the helm, she will then pay off gradually and will slowly begin to move ahead. Her stern will stand up to the breaking seas far better than her side, since she can now retreat more easily. Never let the yacht run at too great a speed when running before any sort of breaking sea. If the yacht is moving ahead more slowly than the waves, they will pass underneath her, but if she is running too fast, a big wave will break over the stern and into the cockpit. This is called getting 'pooped'. To keep her speed down you can tie bundles of fenders, old rope, spars, etc., to the outboard ends of warps which you pay out over the stern, and tow.

The boat's speed may also be checked by means of the sea anchor. It should be towed about 5 fathoms, or 30 feet (1 fathom =6 feet) astern on both warp and tripping line, with the latter taking the strain. Every time a big sea comes astern, the tripping line is quickly slackened and the warp being tight the anchor begins to operate, checking the boat until the wave has passed beneath. The tripping line may then be hauled on to capsize the sea anchor and the yacht carries on. This use of the sea anchor is a good way of keeping the yacht moving as fast as is safe when running for shelter. A yacht skipper should be familiar with the normal distress signals to be displayed by a vessel requiring assistance from other ships or from the shore:

EXTRACT FROM THE REGULATIONS FOR PREVENTING COLLISION AT SEA.

DISTRESS SIGNALS

1. The following signals, used or exhibited either together or separately, indicate distress and need of assistance:

(a) a gun or other explosive signal fired at intervals of about a minute;

(b) a continuous sounding with any fog-signalling apparatus;

(c) rockets or shells, throwing red stars fired one at a time at short intervals;

(d) a signal made by radiotelegraphy or by any other signalling method consisting of the group . . . — — — . . . (SOS) in the Morse Code;

(e) a signal sent by radiotelephony consisting of the spoken word 'Mayday';

(f) the International Code Signal of distress indicated by N.C.;

(g) a signal consisting of a square flag having above or below it a ball or anything resembling a ball;

(h) flames on the vessel (as from a burning tar barrel, oil barrel, etc.);

(i) a rocket parachute flare or a hand flare showing a red light;

(j) a smoke signal giving off orange-coloured smoke;

(k) slowly and repeatedly raising and lowering arms outstretched to each side;

(l) the radiotelegraph alarm signal;

(m) the radiotelephone alarm signal;

(n) signals transmitted by emergency position-indicating radio beacons.

2.   The use or exhibition of any of the foregoing signals except for the purpose of indicating distress and need of assistance and the use of other signals which may be confused with any of the above signals is prohibited.

3.   Attention is drawn to the relevant sections of the International Code of Signals, the Merchant Ship Search and Rescue Manual and the following signals:

(a) a piece of orange-coloured canvas with either a black square and circle or other appropriate symbol (for identification from the air);

(b) a dye marker.

CHAPTER XI

ROPEWORK AND SHIP'S HUSBANDRY

IN this chapter, let us study how to tie some of the more commonly used knots, bends, hitches, and splices that have been used from time immemorial as being each one the best for its own particular purpose. Before looking at the knots themselves, though, let us consider first the various type of rope that seamen use.

Rope consists of a number of fibres which are twisted into yarns. The twist is always right-handed. Then a number of yarns are laid up left-handed into strands. The actual rope is made from these strands, by laying them up either right- or left-handed. Hawser-laid rope, for example, is the ordinary type of rope laid up right-handed with three strands, whereas shroud-laid rope is four-stranded and laid up left-handed. Cable-laid rope is made up of right-handed hawsers laid up together left-handed. It is used for large warps, tow ropes, etc., and, therefore, only found in large vessels. Nylon rope may often be eight or sixteen plaited. Nylon has come to stay. It has completely proved its strength, reliability and economic value. It is very strong and has an attractive appearance. Cotton line of American and/or Egyptian cotton was often used on board racing yachts.

Manilla is good, strong hemp of pleasing appearance, grown in the Philippine Islands. It is whiter and slightly better in quality than Italian hemp, though the latter is also good. A similar Commonwealth product is sisal, although it is much cheaper and less reliable than hemp. Coir or grass line is a light, wet-resistant rope made from coconut fibres. It is extremely good for kedge warps, lifebuoy lines, etc. Hemp (Italian, generally) may be used for lanyards or the bolt ropes of sails, and when used in this way is usually 'tarred' with Stockholm tar.

I have avoided lengthy explanations of the following knots I have drawn, as I believe it is easier to learn to tie a knot from a drawing. I have included a few bends, hitches, splices, etc., as well as some of the fancy knots, mats, plaits, etc., because, although many of them have no practical use, they are decorative; they are fun to do, and are a traditional part of the seaman's art, handed down from the days of old square riggers, like the one in which John Masefield's 'Dauber' sailed:

The Reef Knot.
[to join two ropes of the same, or nearly the same, size]

The Figure of Eight.

Overhand or "Thumb."

The "Granny"
[the WRONG way to tie a Reef Knot!]

HITCHES

1. simple Half Hitch.

2. Clove Hitch.

3. Round Turn and Two Half Hitches.

seizing

4. Fisherman's Bend

Hitches on Hooks.

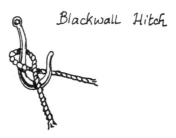

Blackwall Hitch

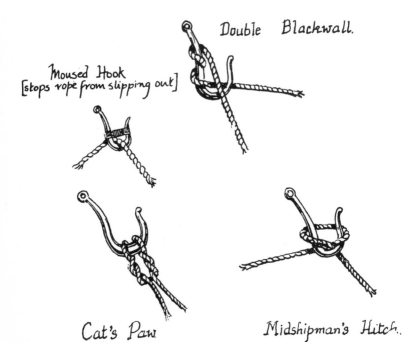

Double Blackwall.

Moused Hook
[stops rope from slipping out]

Cat's Paw

Midshipman's Hitch.

Two methods of joining two ropes
of different sizes :—

① Carrick Bend.   ② Hawser Bend

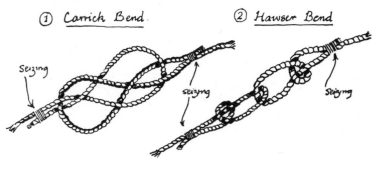

Seizing   seizing   Seizing

Timber Hitch   Stopper Hitch

[For towing a spar]

Rolling Hitch

[will not slip along a spar]

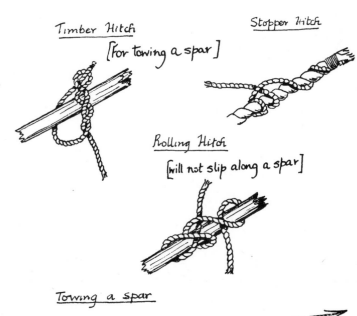

Towing a spar

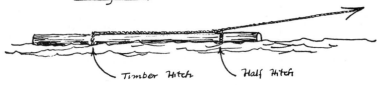

Timber Hitch   Half Hitch

The Sheepshank

[For shortening a Rope]

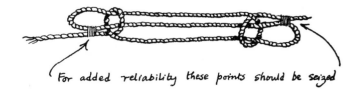

For added reliability these points should be seized

The Sheet Bend.

[For Bending a Sheet to an eye-splice, another rope or a cringle.]

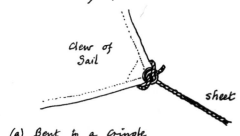

Clew of Sail

sheet

(a) Bent to a Cringle

(b) Bent to another rope.

The Bowline.

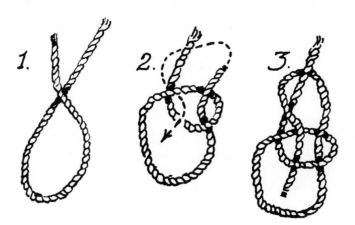

1. 2. 3.

Running Bowline.

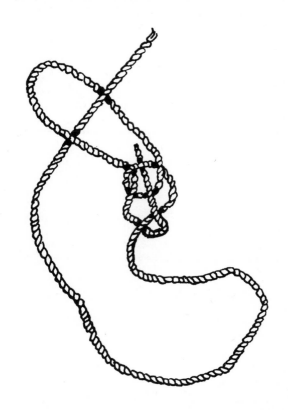

Bowline on a Bight.

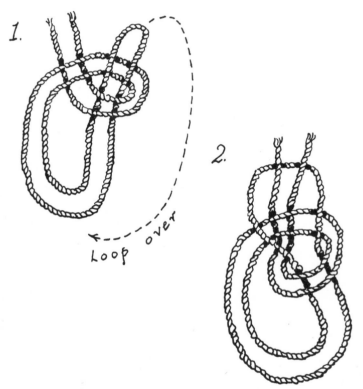

1.

LOOP OVER

2.

[This is a very useful knot for hoisting a man aloft. One bight goes under his arms, the other bight under his legs.]

SPLICING

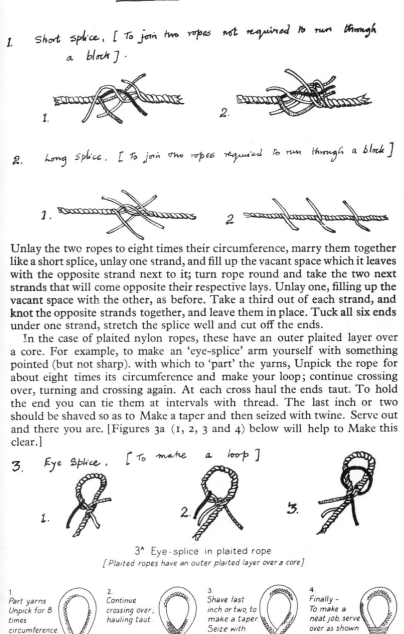

1. Short splice. [To join two ropes not required to run through a block].

   1.   2.

2. Long Splice. [To join two ropes required to run through a block]

   1.   2

Unlay the two ropes to eight times their circumference, marry them together like a short splice, unlay one strand, and fill up the vacant space which it leaves with the opposite strand next to it; turn rope round and take the two next strands that will come opposite their respective lays. Unlay one, filling up the vacant space with the other, as before. Take a third out of each strand, and knot the opposite strands together, and leave them in place. Tuck all six ends under one strand, stretch the splice well and cut off the ends.

In the case of plaited nylon ropes, these have an outer plaited layer over a core. For example, to make an 'eye-splice' arm yourself with something pointed (but not sharp). with which to 'part' the yarns, Unpick the rope for about eight times its circumference and make your loop; continue crossing over, turning and crossing again. At each cross haul the ends taut. To hold the end you can tie them at intervals with thread. The last inch or two should be shaved so as to Make a taper and then seized with twine. Serve out and there you are. [Figures 3a (1, 2, 3 and 4) below will help to Make this clear.]

3. Eye Splice. [To make a loop]

   1.   2.   3.

3ᴬ Eye-splice in plaited rope
[Plaited ropes have an outer plaited layer over a core.]

1
Part yarns
Unpick for 8
times
circumference.
Make loop

2.
Continue
crossing over,
hauling taut.

3.
Shave last
inch or two, to
make a taper.
Seize with
twine.

4
Finally –
To make a
neat job, serve
over as shown
here ⟶

Synthetic rope can be prevented from unravelling by the simple expedient of lighting the end with a match. This fuses the ends solid. It is not as simple as that, however, not all ropes are synthetic and not all situations allow for the easy striking of matches! It is essential to learn the traditional methods of whipping as illustrated here.

WHIPPINGS

1. Plain Whipping.

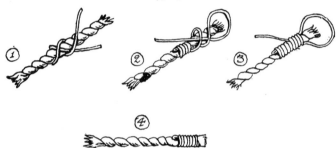

2. Sailmakers Whipping.

tied with a Reef Knot

3. West Country Whipping.

4. Snaked Whipping.

ROPES END KNOTS.

The Wall Knot

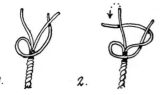

1.   2.   3.   4.

The Crown Knot

1.   2.   3.   4.

The Manrope Knot

[First make a Wall, then a Crown and follow both round]

1.   2.

The Mathew Walker

1.   2.   3.

SOME ORNAMENTAL WORK.

Putting a Turks Head on a Spar or tiller

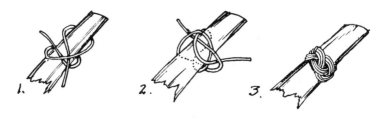

Putting Coach Whipping on a Spar

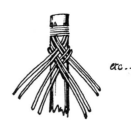

etc....

Square Sennit

"You want to know square sennit? So fash. Look!
Eight foxes take, and stop the ends with thread.
I've known an engineer would give his head
To know square sennit......."

Dauber. John Masefield.

etc....

So much for bends and hitches. Now to consider sails. Look after your sails! Attractive sails add greatly to a boat's appearance and the more effective her sails the better she will perform. Keep your sails clean and dry. The sailmaker puts three roaches or curves along the edges of the Bermudan sail, and four in the case of the gaffsail. The edges are stretched straight when the sail is bent to the boom and hoisted. They give a curvature to the sail which makes the necessary aerofoil shape.

A sail should be dry before it is furled. Do not stow ship and let the sails dry out with a reef in. The sails of a very small boat can be unbent and taken ashore every night. In larger boats where the mainsail is left bent on, it should be carefully furled and covered with a waterproof sail cover. There are several ways to dry sails: by sailing on them; by hoisting them loosely at anchor, shaking out all reefs first; or by taking them ashore and hanging them over a clothes line or in a warm, dry attic.

During the past thirty years there has been a revolution in sail-making. Whereas previously sails would be made from canvas and liable to mildew, nowadays they are made from synthetic fibres, Terylene, nylon, etc. Because these synthetic sails do not mildew, there is a temptation to stuff them into their sail bags, wet, any old how! They resent such treatment as can be seen when on being taken out of their bags later, they emerge creased and crumpled. And these creases can be surprisingly difficult to get out. So treat your sails with respect.

Although it is quite possible to carry out minor repairs to sails oneself (indeed any seaman should be able to), at the end of the season it is a good plan to send sails to a sailmaker for washing, drying and a proper overhaul (and, if required, winter storage). When you are folding sails for storage yourself, roll or fold them with as few creases as possible. If you should find that your sails have got bad creases in them do not try and iron these out yourself.

The better care you take of your sails, the longer they will last. A cruising boat's sails should last about eight seasons, and light weather sails, like the spinnaker, ghoster, etc., should last much longer. A racing boat's sails will have to be renewed much more frequently, especially in a highly competitive class.

As well as your sails, take care of your boat's hull, which can easily be changed from something beautiful to a dirty travesty of the gleaming thing which left the fitting-out slipway. The hull gets scarred in a number of ways. Always be careful when bringing the dinghy alongside. Have a fender of thick coir rope or, better still, of rubber, all round. The anchor also can scar the hull. Lash it down when it is on deck to prevent it moving around when in rough waters. When you weigh, wash off the mud before you pull the anchor aboard. Take care not to hit the bow with one of the flukes as you haul it clear of the water. Be careful when coming alongside other yachts or wharves. Always have plenty of fenders out. Look out for craft coming alongside you. Always have fenders on your vacant side. Unless you are properly fended, another craft may come alongside and is quite likely to scar you.

An enemy of all wooden craft is dry rot. It is a fungus that spreads quickly and ruins the wood. There are two precautions for dry rot: a good coating of paint and good ventilation. All the wood should be kept covered with enough coats of paint which have been put on when the wood was completely dry. The boat must have sufficient ventilation and sun and air must be able to get inside her. Examine the hull and cabin for places where stale air can collect. Make sure that air can flow through the boat, ventilating all the corners. Regardless of which way the wind is, the current of air in a ship is from aft forward. There is but one thing to do once dry rot has set in. You must have expert advice and act *immediately*. By practising immediate surgery, removing the affected wood, and any wood that may be affected round it, you will save hundreds of pounds. Be certain it is properly seasoned wood which is put in to replace what was removed. A job of this kind should be done by a reliable firm of yacht builders.

Worms bore into and eat wood and are another cause of hull trouble. Most often found in the British Isles is the gribble worm. The teredo is worse, but preferring the warmth, is found mostly in the tropics. A good anti-fouling will control the worm situation. Anti-fouling is poisonous paint with which the bottom may be coated. Although it is not easy to get the anti-fouling into the rudder trunk (and the centre centreboard case in centreboard boats) where worms generally get their start, it can be done, and is essential. One defence against worms and marine growth is to put copper sheeting on the bottom of the ship. It is advisable, though expensive, for a ship which is to sail for any length in the Mediterranean or tropical waters. An easier method is to use copper paint. According to some, this is just as effective.

I hardly need point out that while there may be much to be said on both sides in the argument of wooden *versus* reinforced plastic hulls, the latter's immunity to worm is a great advantage. Glass fibre is also immune to rot provided it is made of the glass as laid down in Lloyd's specification Of course 'fibre-glass hulls are not 'weed' proof and antifouling against this is required.

You should wash down the topsides of your boat with fresh water quite often. The salt deposit spoils the glow of enamel paint, and only fresh water will remove it.

During the winter months you can lay up your boat ashore, covered or in the open with her own canvas cover, or in a mud berth. Whichever you do, it is well worth the extra expense to lay up for the winter with a good yard. In such a yard, if the yacht is hauled out, they will see that she is well supported, or 'cradled' at several points along the bottom and held in a firm position.

When the yacht is hauled out and laid up, everything that is removable should be removed, stored, and labelled. An inventory should be made out and you should have a copy. All wire rigging should be removed, examined, and well greased before storing. Running rigging and blocks should be removed and the blocks cleaned. Remove pins and sheaves, grease them, and put them back. The mast should be stored in a shed, and, like the hull, supported at enough places to prevent it, too, from sagging. Floorboards should be taken up. Remove all ballast and clean out the bilges. Store the ballast in a dry place. The sails should be washed in fresh water, completely dried, and stored. A good sailmaker is likely to do a better job for a reasonable charge. If the boat has a cabin, the hatch and portholes should be left open. All lockers and inside doors should also be left open.

In a mud berth the yacht makes a hole in the mud in which

she sits at low water, while being afloat at high water. It is best to avoid crowded yacht yards, for in a strong wind at high water they will do damage by bumping against one another. If the yacht yard you have selected wishes you to keep your yacht in a mud berth, make sure she is firmly moored and well fended off with outsize fenders. Some say this type of laying up, by keeping the hull wet, keeps it cooler in the possible hot weather of early spring, and prevents the heat from opening the seams. This is mainly a geographical consideration, of course.

When the time comes to fit out again everything should be carefully examined for rot, worms, decay, etc. In particular, the centreboard and rudder trunks, the dead wood and rudder post, and the garboards should be looked at. There is usually no need to have the keel bolts tested, but if you have any doubt, get the yard to remove them and inspect their condition. It is usual for the yard to step the mast, and set up the standing rigging, but reeving running rigging can be done by you. I list paying and/or recanvasing decks as a job for the yard, for it is a long, tiresome, and tricky job. It can be done by the amateur, but depends on his time and money. No one wishes to spend all the holiday time fitting out. Some yacht-owners like to do their own painting and varnishing. Painting is a long process but you can save a great sum in man-hours by doing it yourself. You will greatly add to your boat's appearance and gain much satisfaction from the work you have done, and it is *not* a simple job to do it well. At the same time, it is only fair that the yard should have some fitting-out employment from your boat, since they have housed you all winter. In fact, there are some yards which will not allow the owner to do any work on his yacht if they house her. You should investigate this when enquiring for terms in laying up, if you want to do some of your own fitting-out work. It is only fair to both you and the yard. Whatever else you arrange, I would suggest you let the yard do the anti-fouling. It is a tedious job. However matters have been simplified nowadays by the introduction of new types of antifouling (such as T.B.T. made by the International Paint Company) which (instead of having to be immersed in the water within 24 hours of being applied to the hull, which was the case previously) can be left for up to six weeks before the vessel need be launched.

If you have planned to do the painting, you must first decide if the topsides are to be burnt off and painted, or washed, rubbed down, and painted. If you wish to change the colour of your yacht from red or blue to white, burn off. Also, if many layers have accumulated and the paint is old, it is best to burn off. It is a long job, requiring much patience, and wisest to let the yard do. Only burn off when it is really necessary.

When selecting a colour for the hull, remember that white looks attractive, will keep the sides cool, wears well, and will not show salt-water stains. However, it will show every other mark. Black will attract and hold the heat and show salt-water stains, but with certain types of craft it looks very smart. A dark yacht appears small, whereas white gives the illusion of size. There are many makers of yacht paints and varnishes, and advice should be taken when selecting paint, from the yard which is to do the work. Great strides have been made in this, as in other fields of ship's husbandry, and modern paints and varnishes include polyester resins and plastic finishes, which are very hard-wearing and generally excellent.

A job which many yacht owners do is varnishing the bright work or at least some of it. If the wood under the varnish has become stained, it will be necessary to use varnish remover and a scraper and to scrape right down to bare wood. Otherwise, it is only necessary to rub it down. If it is necessary to scrape off, you first apply the varnish remover, using a brush. Work only a small area at a time. Let the varnish remover stand for 4 or 5 minutes before starting to scrape. After scraping, wash down with turpentine, and bleach any black spots in the wood with a strong solution of bleaching acid. When this has been done, rub down with sandpaper. Then give one coat of varnish. Let it dry, and once more rub down with sandpaper. Give another coat of varnish and rub this down lightly when dry. Finally, give the top a coat of varnish.

If, however, it is not necessary to scrape off, you simply wash the bright work, rub down with sandpaper, and then carry on giving two or more coats as desired, rubbing down in between. Always varnish on a fine dry day when there is little wind.

CHAPTER XII

AUXILIARIES AND DINGHIES

Two controversial matters provide the subjects for this chapter. The first, whether a yacht should have an auxiliary engine, and as a corollary, how much use should be made of it; and the second, whether or not a small yacht's dinghy should be considered primarily as a means of getting ashore which can be stowed on deck or whether it should be considered as a lifeboat capable of carrying the whole crew in a case of emergency, in which case it would most probably have to be towed. Let us take the engine controversy first.

There are many who feel very strongly against the 'mechanical topsail'. However, it must be admitted that there are indeed many advantages in having an engine. For example, you can use it to hold the boat head to wind when reefing or to run up to the anchor when weighing it during a fast-running tide. It is useful in difficult moments in crowded anchorages, and if pressed for time when arriving in harbour, you can enter on the motor, and by the time you reach the anchorage, can have the sails furled and covered and the deck squared up. To have an engine aboard is to have at least one really good additional member of the crew!

But what of the disadvantages? First of all, there is the danger of the motor making the yachtsman lazy. Realising how easy it is to enter and leave all anchorages under power, it may gradually become a habit. But one day the motor may fail. Our yachtsman has by now forgotten much of his seamanship and so finds himself in difficulties! Another serious disadvantage in having an engine is the smell of petrol below decks which appears to be incurable. A diesel engine will, of course, smell less than a petrol one. An engine in a yacht should take up as little as possible of the available space, but should also be large and powerful enough to combat a foul tide, to claw off a lee shore, and so on. There are quite a large number of makes of engine on the market which combine these requirements. It is generally a mistake to use a converted car engine, because although the engine may operate perfectly in a car on dry land, it may not stand up to the harder wear, the far less frequent maintenance, the salty atmosphere, general dampness, rain, etc., at sea. In fact, most marine engines are miraculous in the way in which, having weathered the strain at sea and having been completely forgotten for nearly six months, they will still operate when the call comes and operate very well at that!

It should be realised, when it comes to the consideration of the size of an engine, that power follows the law of diminishing returns. For example, a boat of a certain size and shape is only capable of a certain speed. For example, a yacht which has a 4 horse-power engine will drive at 5 knots, will go only 6 knots if driven by an 8 horse-power engine. Or suppose a boat has a 12 horse-power engine which will drive her at 6 knots. If this engine were replaced by an engine of twice the horse-power, the yacht's speed would probably be increased by only one knot, and this speed would be increased very little even if an engine of far greater horse-power were installed. The skill and experience of an expert is required in the selecting and installing of a marine engine and its propeller shaft, fuel tanks, reduction gear, exhaust pipe, etc., and for these and other reasons it is always wisest to take professional advice when installing an engine. A propeller has been likened to a screw turning in wood. Indeed the term 'screw' is often used. The blades of a propeller are twisted in opposite directions to one another, forming an angle called the pitch. The ship's speed through the water must be in a direct ratio to the revolutions per minute of the motor. The propeller shafts of most of the small motors in use today revolve at a great number of revolutions per minute. If a ship has a certain maximum speed and the number of revolutions are exactly the right amount to drive the ship through the water at that speed, then there would only be a slight wastage or 'slip'. However, if the shaft was revolving at a much greater speed, there would be quite an appreciable slip. It is for this reason that most small engines are fitted with a reduction gear, which ensures that the propeller revolves at a slower speed while the motor itself runs at a high speed. A small engine can, therefore, give a yacht quite enough power by means of the use of reduction gear. This is a great help in cutting down the weight and running costs of your engine.

When installing an engine in a yacht, an important point to consider is whether the propeller shaft should project through the stern post or through one of the quarters. The advantage of the central installation is that by being placed rather low in the yacht, its weight adds stability. However, it has the disadvantage of making it necessary to have a hole in the deadwood and/or rudder. This hole is far more of a hindrance to the yacht than the propeller itself. The water flowing along the ship's bottom and along the deadwood is suddenly and simultaneously released from both sides when it reaches the hole, and consequently a whirlpool must be ploughed through by the leading edge of the rudder. This is the reason why so many prefer the quarter or bilge installation. The minimum of resistance is encountered with the 'feathering propeller' (the blades of which can be twisted so that the propeller has no pitch and presents little resistance to the water) or the 'folding propeller'.

The bilge installation produces a more pronounced kick, when going ahead, away from the side from which the propeller projects, and it is difficult turning in the opposite direction. The centre installation enables you to turn to starboard or to port, both more quickly and more easily, because the engine delivers a stream of water against the *rudder* on both sides. The stream of water in a bilge installation, however, is not directed against the rudder, with the result that the rudder will begin turning the hull only after the yacht has gathered way. Since a central propeller is deep in the water, it will not jump out when the weather is lively. But in the bilge installation, when the yacht is heeling over away from the side from which the propeller projects, the latter may come out of the water and race, which, of course, can do harm to the engine. To present the least possible resistance to the water, a two-bladed propeller can (by marking the shaft) be turned so that the two blades being up and down are concealed behind the deadwood. It will be obvious then, that there are many pros and cons and there is not as yet a completely satisfactory solution, though some designers strongly advocate certain methods by which to cope with the problem. One way is to place the propeller above the rudder and thereby do away with the hole in the deadwood. The theory here is that since the engine will in all probability be used in calm waters or in harbour, there is no chance of it racing out of the water. Another variation is to install a bilge installation and place it near enough to the rudder that it can be low down and close to the keel. An external strut projecting from the hull would not be necessary, as is frequently in quarter installations. Another plan is to cut the hole entirely in the deadwood; and still another is to cut the hole entirely in the rudder. More yacht club arguments!

Let us turn now to the question of the position of the exhaust pipe. This should be fitted in such a way that it is always above the water level at the average angle of heel. Since marine engines are cooled by sea water, the hole through which a pump draws water must, of course, be sited below the water level at the average angle of heel. The water which cools the engine will generally pass through the water-cooling system around the motor and is emitted through the exhaust opening. Be certain that the water-cooling system is working whenever the motor is running. The majority of engines in small yachts are located below the cockpit, and sometimes project into the main saloon. If possible, this should be avoided. Make sure your engine is well protected from the rain, and at least once a week during the season, run it for a few minutes to keep it dry and in good working order. Finally, when laying the yacht up, it is wisdom to have the engine removed and properly stored! And now to our second controversy—the dinghy.

Let us consider a small craft, say, a 5-tonner, and see what type of dinghy will suit her best. We can choose from several different types, but all in all the best type of dinghy is the ordinary type with stem and square stern, and with a hard bilge and flat floors. There is the pram dinghy. These are often built in glass re-inforced plastics; the bows tending to be more rounded than those of wood. They are strong, buoyant and light.

In fact, looking at craft around the coast, one sees that the most common type of dinghy carried on the decks of 5-tonners is the 6 or 7 feet pram dinghy. Then there is the collapsible type of dinghy, which is, of course, more easily stowed than the other types. However, these are not usually sturdy enough for doing real duty as a lifeboat in the case of an emergency.

There should be a fender all round the gunwale of a yacht's dinghy, in order to prevent it marking or harming the parent (or other) ship(s) when alongside. A length of 3-inch coir (grass line) is very good for such a fender. Rubber is better still, but expensive.

When you are running before a sea, and towing your dinghy, tow on a long line so that it does not run up on the waves and hit you in the stern. But if you are sailing close-hauled, especially if it freshens a bit, tow the dinghy close up to the stern.

For towing purposes, the dinghy should have a ring on the forward side of the stem near the water-line. If you tow your dinghy in bad weather, make certain that all movable gear is well secured, and always tow with two painters in case one parts.

The dinghy should be easy to row even when filled with water and carrying passengers, and should therefore have buoyancy tanks that will keep her afloat. It is helpful to be able to scull over the stern. A small notch cut in the centre of the transom will be necessary. An outboard motor will certainly simplify the dinghy work, but it is difficult, and frequently impossible, to stow in a small craft. The correct way to row and scull a dinghy must be carefully learned. You can generally tell the novice when he is rowing by the lack of power in his strokes, by the height he lifts his oars out of the water, and by the way his elbows stick out when he rows. The oars should not be dipped a long way into the water. The method of sculling is shown on the next page. This is merely a question of knack, but will take a little time to perfect.

If you find your dinghy half-full of water when you are on your moorings, don't try and get into her. Bail out as much water as possible, working from the yacht, and when you do step aboard the dinghy, finish the job with care. If you want to bail the dinghy while under way, put fenders out and bail from the yacht's deck.

SCULLING

A DINGHY OVER THE STERN

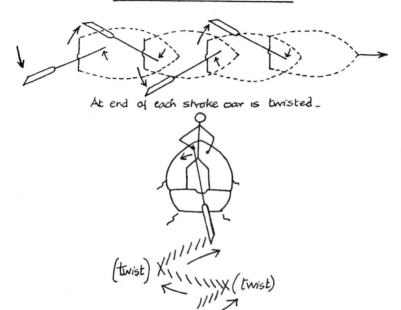

At end of each stroke oar is twisted.

(twist) X (twist)

It is advisable to have the name of your yacht marked on the dinghy, since dinghies are frequently borrowed and it also greatly increases your chances of retrieving your dinghy in the sad event of her getting adrift!

CHAPTER XIII

THE DESIGN OF POWER YACHTS

IT would seem that the steam yacht, luxuriously appointed and manned by a large paid crew, has had its day. However, the total combined tonnage of power craft afloat has never been greater, but this tonnage is made up of a number of relatively smaller craft of varying sizes and widely varying design. Since a large craft is simply an extension and a development of a small craft, let us consider here the principles involved in the design and lay-out of the type of small craft that are to be found in estuaries and rivers the world over.

Of course, the cheapest and smallest type of vessel to which a power unit can be attached is the open dinghy. You can provide motive power either by means of a small inboard engine such as the $1\frac{1}{2}$ horse-power Stuart Turner, an excellent small two-stroke engine, or by means of an outboard motor, clamped to the dinghy's transom. Proceeding up the scale of size, we come to the half-decked type of power boat known as a runabout or small motor launch. Although it is possible to construct a canvas hood over an open motor launch, to provide occasional sleeping accommodation when cruising in an estuary or river, yet if your means will stretch a little further, considerably more comfort and a greater resultant cruising range may be obtained from what has been dubbed a 'pocket-cruiser'. To give some idea of size, a pocket cruiser could vary from 14 feet to 20 feet overall length, and have accommodation for two and sitting head-room below decks. Apart from financial considerations the type of vessel you buy will, or should, depend on the kind of motor boating you intend to do and the nature of the waters in which you will be doing it; for example, in the matter of the draught of your boat you will be faced with just such a decision. If you will be venturing to sea at all, or even messing about in a

SOME TYPES OF POWERCRAFT

large open estuary, it is very important that your boat should have a certain amount of draught for stability. If you will be sailing, however, in a sheltered river, then too much draught can be both unnecessary and extremely troublesome. Again, the question of beam must be considered. A boat with broad beam will not roll too much and will give plenty of room to work on deck. On the other hand, beam can be overdone and too much proportionate breadth only results in an extremely uncomfortable motion at sea. As a general guide the length of a small boat should be about three times her beam.

The design of any craft calls for a great deal of knowledge, experience, and skill. As a general principle boats are built either with round-bilged (or round-bottomed) hulls, chine-bottomed or V-shaped hulls. The latter type of bottom is virtually standard for fast boats, and the old objection to it, namely, that the round-bottomed hull was much stronger, has been removed through the use of reinforced plastics (G.R.P.) and of synthetic bonding and marine plywood. It is, of course, impossible to design a boat which will please everybody. The man whose primary interest is to get from A to B as quickly as possible will have to make sacrifices, particularly regarding space below, as the larger heavier engines and fuel tanks will encroach upon the living accommodation. Alternatively, the man who wants a small flat with all modern conveniences below will have to make some sacrifice of speed and seaworthiness. The classified advertisement section of any of the motor yachting periodicals such as, for example, the *Motor Boat and Yachting* will show that there is always a wide variety of second-hand craft from which to make a choice. We have already seen in Chapter III, how essential it is, before finally deciding to buy a boat that takes your fancy, to employ a surveyor to make sure that she is sound and properly constructed.

Let us look for a minute at the broad principles of construction as they apply to a small motor boat. Let us imagine that we are having a small boat built from the design of a naval architect. The different sections of the boat are drawn out in full scale, moulds are then cut to the shape of these sections. Meanwhile the keel of our boat has been made and laid out on the ground. To this keel are fitted our moulds. Then the fore-part of the boat, known as the stem, is fitted to that end of the keel by means of a scarfed joint which is reinforced with bolts of galvanised iron or, much better, of copper. Running the length of the boat above the keel and fastened to it, is the hog, and a piece of wood known as the bow knee is then fitted to join the hog to the stem. So much for the stem. Now at the stern, we have a flat-shaped section of wood, known as the transom. The transom will most likely be fastened to a stern post, which in its turn is fastened to the hog by a stern knee. Now comes the ribs of our boat, called the timbers. These are made of wood, steamed and bent into the required shape. Frequently the timbers in the widest part of the boat, the centre, curve down from one gunwale over the top of the hog up to the other gun-wale, but in the narrower, sharper part of the boat near the stem, and also sometimes near the stern, the timbers have to be fitted in two pieces running in each case from hog to gunwale.

It is to these timbers that the planking or skin of our boat is fastened. I have described it already in the earlier chapter, so I will refresh the reader's memory, by saying that the three principal types of wood construction are the carvel, the clinker, and the diagonal methods of construction, and, of course, nowadays one finds a great deal of plywood chine construction, not to mention fibre glass and other synthetic materials, all excellent in their respective ways. The method of resin-glass construction has already been touched on in Chapter II. Here, for the purpose of understanding construction and design, we are dealing with wooden construction of the traditional type. Half-way up our ribs, running from stern to stem, are two bilge stringers, these give strength to the hull.

Additional strength to the hull, and especially the ribs, is given by sturdy timbers cut with the grain of the wood, called floors. These floors are frequently made of metal. They join the timbers to each other across the hog. In a motor boat, or for that matter any boat with a motor, they form support for the engine bearers, because their function is to receive the entire thrust of the engine and distribute it evenly over the hull bottom. In the case of a single engine it will be installed in the centre line, that is to say, parallel with the keel of the boat. The propeller shaft itself will run parallel with the keel through a hole bored in it. In the case of a twin-engined vessel, one engine is installed on one side of the keel and the other on the other, the shaft from each passing through a shaft-log. This shaft-log is supported by a bracket fixed to the outside of the hull. These cross strengtheners need to be tough, particularly in the case of diesel engines, and while talking of strength it is important that particularly strong bolts be used to attach the engine to its bed. Between the bearers which support our engine there should be fitted a metal drip tray to catch the oil which invariably leaks from the engine. This drip tray should be readily removable so that it can be emptied at regular intervals and so keep the bilge free from oil. The boat is guided by means of the rudder, fastened at the top to the stern post or transom, and at the bottom in the case of many small powered boats to the keel by means of a bracket.

So far, we have got an open boat with an engine (or two) and a rudder to steer her. Now we must put on the decks. To do this, deck beams are dovetailed to the gunwale and secured by bolts or side screws. These transverse beams, slightly curved, support the planking laid fore and aft. This planking is generally tongued and grooved and subsequently kept covered with canvas set in white lead and painted. Speed boats and fast runabouts frequently have fine planking laid edge-to-edge and splined with thin strips of wood of a contrasting colour. It is rather rare nowadays to find laid and caulked decks in small motor craft.

Let us now look at another point of small-boat construction: the type of construction in which the boat is planked with marine plywood, glued and screwed by sections into position. Modern marine plywood is excellent for its job. It is flexible, easily bent into shape, has a good finish for taking varnish and paint, it is light, and at the same time very strong. By clamping plywood sheets together and cutting them with a saw, two panels can be cut out together, thereby saving both time and expense, an important point these days. In this kind of construction, joints are made by the use of synthetic glue. A hardener is spread on one surface and glue, such as, for example, 'Aerolite 300', is spread on the other. The moment the two surfaces are clamped together the glue will begin to set.

A word now about accommodation. As we said earlier, where speed is of little importance the smaller engine and smaller fuel tank will allow for more room inside our boat. Again, the purpose for which our boat is intended will affect our accommodation; for example, a craft which is going to operate exclusively in the relatively sheltered conditions of a river can with safety be given a higher cabin top, or higher topsides, and consequently better head-room than a similar hull which is going to be taken to sea. This problem of accommodation, particularly that of the very small cruiser, has been studied by our modern designers and some extremely ingenious lay-outs have resulted. If you pause for a moment and consider the shape of the interior of a boat and the fact that fuel tanks, fresh-water tanks, and some form of water closet have to be fitted, in addition to bunks, cupboards of various kinds, and a folding table, you will soon see that the designer of one of those modern rabbit-hutches called flatlets has an easy task by comparison.

In the case of small boats, estuary, and river craft, there is little opportunity for variety in the basic lay-out. The cockpit will be open and in it will be the engine casing. Aft of the cockpit will be the petrol tank and at the forward end of it, the wheel. The accommodation will probably be entered by means of a hinged door, usually centrally placed. In the cabin will be two settee berths with probably a folding table between them. Sometimes the toilet is through a second door that leads right to the forward part of the ship, sometimes it is situated in a compartment to port or to starboard. The galley or cooking space will be situated to port or to starboard. It is advisable that this should be in the most central part of the boat, as even the toughest 'sea cooks' will agree that the less motion when cooking the better. In the cabin will be found lockers and shelves. Stowage of gear is always a problem in a small boat. Food and other hard stores may be stowed in the lockers underneath the settee berths. These lockers are unsuitable for clothes as, being only just above the bilges of the ship, they tend to be damp. It is, of course, possible to use the bilges themselves to stow tins of food in, but this is not entirely a good idea. A friend of mine who did this found that not only did his tins rust in the dampness of the bilges, but all the labels came off, with the result that he never knew whether his appetite was going to be assuaged by stewed plums or Irish stew till he opened the tin! Cooking will probably be by paraffin, like the Taylor stove or primus stove, or by petrol or by Calor gas. Calor gas is really more suitable for larger boats than the one we are considering at the moment, as the stowage of the Calor gas cylinder or container presents quite a problem in a small boat. It cannot be repeated too much that certain precautions must be taken when using Calor gas in a boat. The golden rule is when the stove is not in use, turn off the gas by the tap at the cylinder itself as well as by the tap on the stove itself. The installation of cylinder and stove must be properly carried out with proper gas-tight joints wherever necessary. The reason for these precautions is that Calor gas or bottled gas, being heavier than air, sinks into the lowest part of the ship, that is to say, the bilges. If allowed to leak in any quantity it can form in the bilges a highly combustible and extremely dangerous element. A dropped lighted match or cigarette, or an errant electrical spark and you may find yourself navigating the Styx!

So far we have been talking about the smallest practical type of motor cruiser, that is to say, about 18 to 20 feet length overall (see Fig. 58). I should perhaps point out here that the overall length does not differ greatly from the water-line length in motor boats as their overhangs are very much less than that of sailing yachts. Progressing now to a somewhat larger vessel of, say 25 feet in length, we find that we can do quite a bit more with the accommodation. For example, a third bunk or two bunks can be arranged in the after part of what was before the open cockpit. The lay-out below will be basically the same, but everything will be a little bit larger. The galley will be larger. Stowage space, cupboards will all be better. And, a very important point, in a craft of this length it should be possible to obtain standing head-room, that is to say, 6 feet head-room in the centre of the cabin, whereas in the smaller boat there would not be standing head-room anywhere below. This question of head-room is, of course, a matter of taste. Personally, I have always found it a great convenience to take off or put on my trousers in a standing position, let alone the satisfaction of being able to stretch out fully when standing. As I said, it is a matter of taste.

To continue with the lay-out possibilities of our 25-foot boat, let us assume that we are going to accommodate three persons. We can have our steering position in the centre of the boat. This means to say that the cockpit will be admidships and will separate the two cabins. Abaft the cockpit will be a sleeping

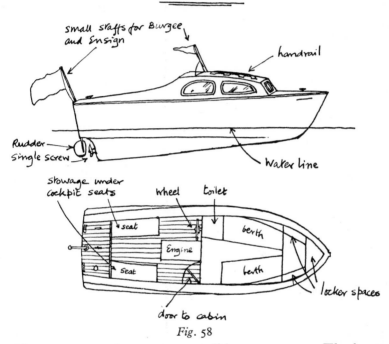

Fig. 58

cabin to accommodate one or possibly two persons. The larger cabin, which will be the forepart of the ship, will contain not only the saloon with two settee berths, but the toilet compartment and the galley space, and it will probably be possible to work in at least one full-length hanging cupboard, a great boon. However, some people prefer to have the cockpit right aft. In this case, both cabins will be forward. One will have two settee berths and the other possibly two bunks or one and a small hanging cupboard. Between the two will probably be the galley to one side and the toilet compartment to the other. In both the lay-outs I have mentioned there is generally a small space in the fo'c'sle which is used as a boatswain's store. In the larger galley the cooking arrangements can, of course, be more ambitious. In a boat of this size it is perfectly feasible to have a bottle-gas cooker, and bottle-gas cooking stoves can be bought in sizes from single ring stoves to a full-size domestic cooker. Probably for a boat of this size, though, a model with two rings and a grill underneath would be sufficient. In the case of a paraffin stove a two-burner stove again should be enough. It is worth recording here an advantage which the paraffin stove has over the bottle gas. It is that the paraffin stove, like the well-known primus stove, may be slung, if it is a single burner, in gimbals which permits it to remain upright whatever angle of heel the ship may be taking. In the case of larger paraffin stoves, the stove is usually gimballed so that it swings athwart ships only, and this, of course, is possible with bottle gas, and, of course, the larger the boat the more stability and the less the necessity for gimbals. Again, in our larger boat we will probably find that the toilet is of the kind which flushes the effluent into the water outside. This I personally regard as a great advantage, although it means having a hole in the bottom of the ship, which some people object to. Smaller craft, like the one we were discussing earlier, have to make do with a chemical type of toilet like, for example, the 'Elsan', which is perfectly clean and hygienic, but I personally consider inconvenient.

Cabin lay-out is extremely important. First and foremost there must be comfortable, dry sleeping accommodation for each member of the crew. The second and third essentials are adequate cooking gear and proper sanitary accommodation, about which we have already spoken. Fourthly, there must be comfortable sitting room for every member of the crew. A back rest is essential here. The minimum head-room is 3 feet over the top of the cushions which form the seat. The seat should be a minimum of a foot high and a cushion makes it approximately 14-15 inches. This is a comfortable height. Finally, each sitting position should be properly illuminated. A table of some sort is a necessity, and there should be as many lockers as possible. Fresh water can be carried in tanks or in special tins. It is best to have a tank fitted with an efficient pump that can discharge the water in the vicinity of the galley. If the boat is going to be used in the spring, or late autumn, or both, and certainly if she

30 foot L.W.L.
Single Screw
(Petrol) 80 b.h.p.

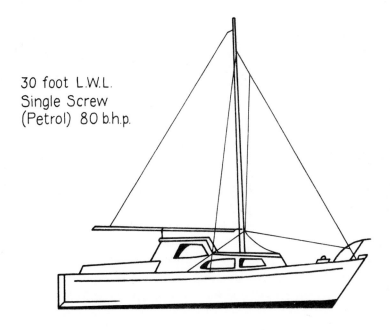

40 foot L.W.L.
Twin Screw
(Diesel)
40 b.h.p. each

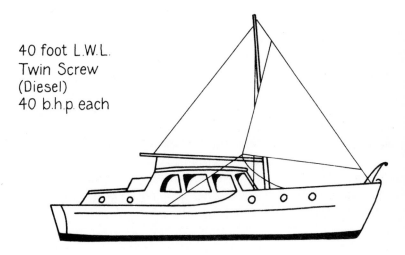

Fig. 59 Two typical examples of steadying sail on motor yachts

is in commission during the winter though (with most people this is unlikely), some sort of stove is an essential. There are many types on the market, working with a number of fuels. The owner can choose which one he prefers, but it is important to remember that it is dangerous to use any form of stove whatever without good proper ventilation.

In the sailing yacht section of this book I dealt fully with rot and worm but a word here will not come amiss. The great precaution against rot is good ventilation. Air must be able to pass freely through the length of the boat, particularly in the bilges where foul air is most likely to collect. Rot is generally found in places where water can lodge, and therefore it is most important to see that water cannot get under deck canvas or behind panelling, for example. The great precaution against marine worms is anti-fouling, that is to say, the poisonous paint which should cover the underbody of the ship. The worm most commonly found in English waters is the gribble. If you are going to cruise in warmer latitudes like, for example, the Mediterranean, you will meet with a worm called the teredo, who bores in much the same manner as the gribble but with rather more determination. Some woods, like teak, offer extreme resistance to marine borers, and of course reinforced plastics and metal craft are a complete answer. If either rot or worm is discovered soon enough, its spread can be stopped by chemical preservatives. This is certainly true of worm, but personally speaking in the case of rot, I would always advocate cutting out the rotten part and the wood round it and replacing with sound wood. The amount of wood round that should be cut out for safety can well be left to the boatbuilder who is doing the job. But I know of one boatbuilder who says you should remove wood up to a radius of 12 inches round the affected part. So much, then, for design and lay-out; let us now look at the motive power of our vessel.

It is of great advantage to a motor cruiser intended to operate offshore that she should have some form of sail to steady her. The amount of sail she will need and can set will vary with her size (see Fig. 59).

CHAPTER XIV

ENGINES AND THEIR INSTALLATION

BEFORE we consider types of engines and installation, I think it may be of use to consider how an engine works. I apologise immediately in advance to those readers for whom all this is boring reiteration of something they know far better than I. But, personally, when I bought my first boat I knew very little about engines indeed, and I think it possible, even in this mechanical age, there may be many like me.

First of all, what is an engine? Well, one definition is that it is a machine which turns heat into movement. Now in the case of a four-stroke petrol engine, petroleum spirit is combined with air to make an explosive mixture which is then ignited by a spark, and the resultant explosion forces a piston along a cylinder. The piston turns a crankshaft and so produces the movement which in turn causes the propeller to revolve and so drive the ship (see Fig. 60).

The petrol and air must be mixed together in the correct proportion to make the explosion when ignited. This is done by the carburettor. The carburettor is supplied with petrol by means of a pump or by simple gravity. The petrol enters what is called the float chamber. This is so called because in it is a small metal float, which rises up the chamber as the level of the petrol rises. The object of this float rising is that when it reaches a certain height it shuts off the supply of petrol into the chamber until that chamber has been emptied. Now, that petrol has somehow got to get itself into the cylinder by means of a jet. A petrol engine has one or more cylinders, and a piston which moves up and down inside each one of them. This piston fits extremely tightly, and as it is forced through the cylinder a vacuum is formed. It is this vacuum which sucks the petrol through the jet. The cylinder is connected to the carburettor by a pipe called the induction pipe, which sucks the petrol into the jet chamber from the carburettor and so through the jet into the cylinder in the form of a spray. Air drawn from outside the engine mixes with the spray and forms an explosive mixture.

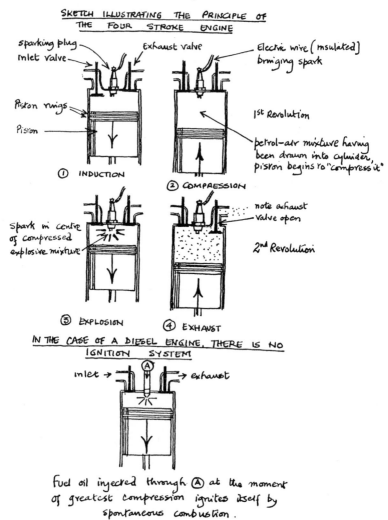

SKETCH ILLUSTRATING THE PRINCIPLE OF THE FOUR STROKE ENGINE

sparking plug
Inlet valve
Exhaust valve
Electric wire (insulated) bringing spark

Piston rings
Piston

1st Revolution

petrol-air mixture having been drawn into cylinder, piston begins to "compress it"

① INDUCTION

② COMPRESSION

Spark in centre of compressed explosive mixture

note exhaust valve open

2nd Revolution

③ EXPLOSION

④ EXHAUST

IN THE CASE OF A DIESEL ENGINE, THERE IS NO IGNITION SYSTEM

inlet →   → exhaust

Fuel oil injected through Ⓐ at the moment of greatest compression ignites itself by spontaneous combustion.

Fig. 60

Now, the richness of this mixture is controlled by the throttle. The stronger the mixture the greater the force of the explosion, the greater the rapidity with which the piston is forced down the cylinder and the greater the speed of the engine, and, in turn, the speed of the boat. It is easy to see from this illustration how the speed of our boat is controlled by the throttle.

Continuing our illustration: there is a spring-loaded inlet valve, driven indirectly from the engine-shaft, which cuts off the petrol-air mixture when the piston has reached the end of the cylinder. We now have a mixture of petrol and air in the cylinder. Our piston now commences its journey back along the cylinder, compressing the volatile mixture of petrol and air into a highly explosive state. When the piston has reached the top of the cylinder and the combustible vapour mixture is at its greatest pressure, a spark is applied to bring about the explosion.

This spark is supplied by a sparking plug, which is let into the top of the cylinder. Now how does the spark happen to arrive at the sparking plug just at the moment it is required? The spark is produced by an electric current. At the bottom end, that is to say, the end of the sparking plug which is inside the cylinder, are two metal points, set at a gap of about 0·025 inches. The points are right in the centre of the explosive mixture. The spark is produced by causing an electric current to leap across the space between the points at a pressure of several thousand volts. A small dynamo, driven by the engine, generates an electric current of from 6 to 12 volts. Somehow this low-tension current must be transformed into a high-tension current of several thousand volts in order to cause our spark. This is done by passing the low-tension current through what is called a coil. The coil consists simply of long lengths of very thin insulated wire. From the outlet end of this coil our (now) high-tension current is led to another piece of electrical machinery called the distributor. It is the function of the distributor to send out the spark to one sparking plug after another. Inside the distributor is a rotating contact arm, known as the rotor arm. As our piston approaches the end of its stroke and the compression in the cylinder is reaching its maximum, the rotor arm is making contact with a small metal stud. Running from the stud to the required sparking plug is a cable which carries the high-tension current to that plug at the very moment that the spark is required to ignite the explosive mixture in the cylinder.

The spark does not, as a matter of fact, arrive exactly at the same time as the piston reaches the top of its compression stroke but slightly before. The reason for this is that the explosion of the mixture in the cylinder is not instantaneous, and the slight delay makes it possible for the maximum pressure to be built in the cylinder before the explosion. This is what is called advanced ignition. The mixture, once ignited, causes tremendous pressure and forces the piston hard down the cylinder transmitting this force to the shaft of the engine and so to the propeller.

Finally, on its fourth stroke, the returning piston pushes away the burned gases through an exhaust valve which is operated in a manner similar to the inlet valve we spoke of earlier, and from where they are discharged into the atmosphere by means of an exhaust pipe.

What we have just followed in some detail is the cycle of operation of a four-stroke petrol engine. However, in small boats with small inboard engines, and particularly with outboard engines, a type of engine known as the two-stroke engine is commonly found. In the two-stroke engine each outward movement of the piston combines the two actions of induction and explosion, and each inward movement of the piston combines the two actions of compression and exhaust. Two-stroke engines work on a mixture of petrol and oil, commonly called petroil. The proportion of petrol to oil, in petroil, is about half to one pint of oil to each gallon of petrol. In this way a two-stroke engine is self-lubricating. A two-stroke engine does not run as efficiently as a four-stroke, and certainly not at low speeds; but it will be readily seen that it is a much cheaper engine, both to maintain and produce, and it has the further dual advantages of lightness and simplicity (see Fig. 61).

While we are on this question of lubrication, let us see for a moment how this essential part of an engine works. Except for those engines which run on petroil, lubrication is achieved by a continuous circulation of a very thin film of oil through the working parts of the engine. This film of oil separates the working surfaces of the engine. If it should be allowed to fail, the engine would be permanently damaged. The engine drives a pump located near the bottom of the sump which causes the oil to circulate. This sump should always be kept adequately full of oil, by reference to a line indicated on the dip-stick.

Almost all inboard engines have an oil-pressure gauge fitted, whose function is to indicate the pressure at which the oil is circulating through the engine system. The colder the engine the higher will this pressure be, but the normal working pressure should be about 40 lb. per square inch. Slight variations of

THE TWO STROKE ENGINE

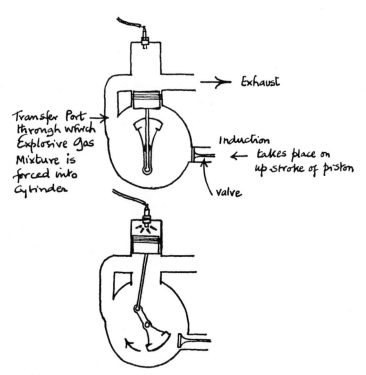

Transfer Port through which Explosive gas Mixture is forced into Cylinder

Exhaust

Induction takes place on up-stroke of piston

valve

the two stroke completes operation in one revolution of the engine

Fig. 61

this pressure are quite unimportant, but a sudden and large variation is evidence that something serious is wrong, and the engine should be stopped at once or trouble will result. It should be emphasised here that pressure indicated on the oil-pressure gauge does not necessarily mean that oil is reaching all parts of the engine that it should. The only way of finding out if there is sufficient oil in the sump is by using the dip-stick. In addition to the oil lubrication system, engines must be cooled either by air or water. Most motor boats are fitted with engines cooled by water. Water is drawn by pump through a water inlet in the bottom of the hull below the water-line. From there the water is pumped through water jackets surrounding the cylinder. From there it continues on its way, cooling the exhaust system of the engine until it is finally expelled over the side into the sea, sometimes through the exhaust outlet itself, sometimes through a pipe alongside.

Cooling water should be filtered where it comes through the bottom of the hull at the intake. There should also be a filter in the oil sump, and while on the question of filters, make sure that the fuel is filtered properly before, and after, entering the tank. The place for the fuel tank is usually aft, the opening for filling the tank being let into the deck flush with it, and enclosed with a screw cap operated by a key. Fuel tanks are made as a rule of galvanised iron or brass.

So far we have been considering petrol engines, but mention should be made of the paraffin engine and also of the diesel engine, this latter being a type of engine for which many people have a preference. The paraffin engine works on the same principle as the petrol engine, with the difference that it makes use of a paraffin vaporiser. The engine is actually started on petrol, and when the vaporiser becomes hot the engine switches over to a vaporising oil fuel or kerosene. The vaporiser works on the heat of the exhaust. Compression is somewhat less than a petrol engine, being reduced to prevent pre-ignition, and the carburettor jet is a little larger than that of the normal petrol engine.

The third type of engine we mentioned, the diesel engine, works on the principle that if you compress air sufficiently it will of itself generate enough heat to ignite fuel oil. The cycle of working operation is the same as we have studied in the four-stroke petrol engine earlier. But with the diesel engine there is no carburettor, and the induction stroke simply draws air into the cylinder. The air is then compressed, and at the moment of highest compression a small amount of fuel oil is injected at the top of the cylinder. Because of the heat of the compressed air this ignites at once, whereupon power and exhaust strokes follow in the same manner as a four-stroke petrol engine. A diesel engine is a good deal heavier, at the same time stronger than a petrol engine; it is also a good deal more expensive.

We have been talking all this time of inboard engines. Let us pass now to the outboard motor. In outboard motors we find as a rule the two-stroke engine with either one or two cylinders. There are a number of four-stroke outboards but it is more usual to find the two-stroke. To start an outboard motor, the fly-wheel at the top of the engine is turned, usually by the simple means of pulling a cord, but in the larger makes they can be started electrically. The fly-wheel magneto produces the spark. Beneath the cylinder a vertical shaft descends to the water, where the propeller is fixed at right angles to it and is turned through a bevel gear. The exhaust is discharged under water, and outboard engines are generally water-cooled. They are self-lubricating. In the case of larger outboard motors, a clutch is fitted so that the propeller can be stopped turning without having to shut off the engine, but the small outboards have no clutch and when you want to take the way off the boat you have to stop the engine. Also, there is no reverse gear, so if you want to go astern the motor must be turned 180 degrees so that the propeller faces forward. The engine is turned by means of a handle like a tiller, and by this means you steer the boat. There are many makes of outboard motor on the market. Certain firms have made a speciality in the development of inboard-outboard engines, in an attempt to combine the advantages of the eleva-table screw unit of the outboard with the greater engine protection and accessibility of an inboard. They have had a marked success in small power craft and are very popular.

Let us now consider how an engine transmits movement to the propeller, and how the propeller, in its turn, transmits movement to the ship. The propeller shaft is controlled by means of a gear lever. This lever has three positions, forward, neutral, and reverse or astern. There is no variation in the forward gearing. Speed is increased or decreased by means of the throttle lever, as we have seen. Propellers are either right-handed or left-handed. If two engines are fitted, one engine should turn with a right-handed rotation and the other with a left-handed rotation, so that the propellers turn away from the centre line of a yacht. A yacht so fitted is extremely manoeuvrable. It is very important when the engine is fitted that the tail shaft and the propeller are properly lined up. If they are not, a lot of vibration will result which will strain the stern gland and the hull and in due course produce leakage. The stern gland is a gland filled with grease that joins the tail shaft and the propeller shaft. Care should be taken to grease it fairly regularly either by hand or mechanically. Now let us consider how the propeller itself drives the boat through the water. To do this we must understand what we mean by two technical terms, diameter and pitch. The diameter of a propeller is the diameter of the circle covered by the tips of the blades. Pitch is a little harder. Pitch is the depth of screw. Imagine for a moment that the propeller is a solid screw turning in a block of wood. If we turn our screw with a screw-driver one complete revolution, the amount by which it advances is the depth of the screw, that is to say, the pitch. Now the ratio of pitch to diameter is extremely important, because on this depends the efficiency of the propeller.

This illustration of screwing a screw into a block of wood is rather misleading, because the propeller does not really cut through a solid mass, but through moving liquid. This means that it will slip a bit and some of the propulsive force will be lost. Exactly how much of this is lost depends on the type of boat, her underwater shape, and to some extent the number of revolutions per minute the propeller is doing. To increase the engine revolutions for more power by limiting the speed at which the propeller is revolving, one employs what are known as reduction gears. The choice of the right propeller for a boat is extremely important, because a bad propeller will waste a surprisingly large amount of the efficiency of the engine. In some cases where no astern gear is fitted, a reversible propeller may be employed. With reversible propellers the blades are turned into reverse by a cam. In the same way the blades may be turned just slightly so as to vary the pitch.

Now we have seen that the thrust of water from the blades of the propeller of an outboard engine steers the boat in the direction away from that thrust, but in larger boats, with one or more inboard engines, the direction of the thrust is constant, and change of direction is, of course, obtained by means of the rudder. There are two sorts of rudder, the ordinary rudder and the balanced rudder. The ordinary rudder has the head of the stock hung in a bearing; the balanced rudder is fitted in cases where the keel extends right up to the stern post. In this case the blade extends fore and aft of the stock, and that part of the blade forward of the stock being considerably less than the part aft. Movement is given to the rudder by means of a tiller or a quadrant, that is to say, an arm to which cables from the steering wheel are attached. With the tiller, of course, the boat can be steered by hand direct, or a wheel can be fitted and cables from this led through sheaves to the tiller on either side. This has the advantage of enabling one to steer the boat either by wheel or by tiller. It is a *sine qua non* that the steering cable should be easy to get at, because a wise skipper gives it fairly frequent examination.

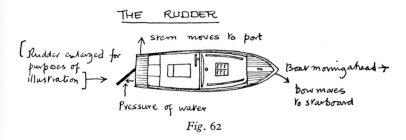

THE RUDDER

[Rudder enlarged for purposes of illustration] →

Stern moves to port

Boat moving ahead →

bow moves to starboard

Pressure of water

Fig. 62

Now let us go a little more thoroughly into how the propeller and the rudder actually work. Let's start with the rudder. Imagine that our boat is moving forward, and the rudder has been put over to starboard. As the yacht moves ahead the water presses on the fore side of the rudder, and so pushes the stern of the boat to port. It is the stern rather than the bows which moves when the rudder is operated. We can see then that by altering the angle of the rudder we alter the course of the vessel (see Fig. 62). Assume now that our boat is going astern. The water will now be pressing on the after-side of the rudder, and so if the rudder is put to starboard the stern will be pushed to starboard, and the bows will therefore swing to port. As a matter of fact, when the vessel is going astern the rudder does not have much power, even when the propeller is turning, because the only force acting on the rudder comes from the water flowing past it, instead of being forced onto it by the propeller. It is important to remember this when going astern.

The effect of the rudder is, of course, greater when the vessel is moving ahead than when she is stopped. When the propeller begins to turn in the ahead direction, a column of water is projected against the fore side of the rudder. Now at once we have an effect which is extremely useful when manœuvring a boat. When the boat has no way upon her this force from the propeller, being very great, tends to kick, as it is termed, the stern in the opposite direction to the rudder.

Now let's have a look at the effect of the propeller. There are, as we mentioned earlier, both right-handed and left-handed propellers. If you were standing behind a vessel looking at her stern, the right-handed propeller would be the one revolving in a clockwise direction when driving the ship ahead, and vice

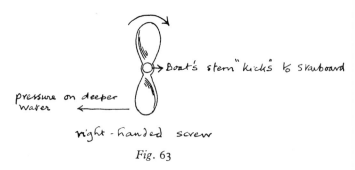

THE PROPELLER

A propeller gives a boat an initial kick sideways

Boat's stern "kicks" to starboard

pressure on deeper water

right - handed screw

Fig. 63

versa. Let us assume that we are looking at a right-handed propeller revolving in such a way as to drive the vessel ahead. It is a two-bladed propeller and we can see as we watch it revolving why it is that the stern is pushed sideways when the propeller begins to revolve. The water in which the propeller is revolving is considerably denser, that is to say, has greater density, the deeper you go, and it is quite clear from this illustration that the bottom blade is pushing against a more solid mass than the top blade. Let us suppose, for example, that only the bottom blade is in the water. Because of the shape of the blade, pressure is exerted on the water in a sideways direction as well as a forward direction, but the sideways pressure of the bottom blade is greater than that of the top, and therefore the stern of the ship is pushed away to starboard (see Fig. 63).

This pushing to starboard is called transverse thrust. We have seen that it has little effect when the boat is moving ahead, apart from causing the stern to veer a little away from the thrust, and when the boat is moving at any appreciable speed it pretty well completely disappears. However, when the engine is going astern the effect of transverse thrust is much more important. Supposing our propeller is revolving in an anticlockwise direction. As before, the bottom blade is exerting a greater pressure than the top, and so the stern is pushed away to port. Now the difference here is caused by the fact that the hull of the ship comes into play. The bottom blade is forcing the column of water upwards and forwards towards the bow. This body of water pushes on the starboard side of the hull ahead of the propeller, and therefore in turn pushes the stern to port. Now you see we have two forces acting in the same direction, and so the effect is very marked. But once again as the boat gains sternway the effect decreases.

To sum up then, with a right-handed propeller turning so that our vessel is going ahead, the stern will kick to starboard. If the propeller is reversing so that the vessel will go astern, then the stern will kick to port. In the case, of course, of a left-handed propeller the opposite effects will obtain. So much then for engines, rudders, and propellers. Let us consider in the next chapter how we can use them to make our powered vessel do our bidding.

CHAPTER XV

THE HANDLING OF A MOTOR YACHT

LET us now use our knowledge gained of the behaviour of a boat, as a result of the interplay of the rudder and screw, to turn that boat round in the smallest possible circle. This is one of the things which any motor-boat owner should be able to do, as it is frequently necessary to do this in crowded anchorages or narrow rivers. Very well, then. Our imaginary ship has no way upon her; she is stationary. We put the rudder hard-a-starboard, and our engine, which is running in neutral, will drive the ship ahead as soon as we move the gear lever. Our ship has a right-handed propeller; we remember therefore that when the engine is put astern the stern will kick to port, etc. We have put our rudder hard-a-starboard; we now move our engine ahead. This has the effect of kicking the stern to port and our boat begins to gather headway. Now here we must be on the alert. As soon as the boat begins to move ahead, put the engine astern leaving the rudder still to starboard. What happens now is this: the transverse thrust of the propeller, as we have seen before, will kick the stern to port. The fact that the rudder is over to starboard makes no difference because the ship is not moving astern. We must watch this, because as soon as she begins to move astern at all, we again move the gear lever into the ahead position. As we have seen, this continues to kick the stern to port, our helm being hard-a-starboard. So we repeat this movement, alternatively astern and ahead, and if we do it properly we will find that we will turn our boat completely round about her pivoting point. If the propeller had been left-handed, we would, of course, have put the rudder to port, so as to kick the stern to starboard when the engine was ahead, and the transverse thrust would kick it in the same way when we put our engine astern.

So much, then, for turning a right-handed screw ship in her

own length to starboard. Supposing now we wish to turn to port. This is not quite so simple, but it is not difficult. We put the rudder hard-a-port and ,move the engine ahead. This will have the effect of kicking the stern to starboard, and our boat will move slowly ahead. While the stern is still swinging we watch it carefully; we put the engine astern. This will stop our ship moving ahead, and will also check the swing of our stern. Watching carefully to see when our stern's motion stops, as soon as it does so we put our rudder amidships. Our boat will be beginning to gather sternway, and when this happens we put our rudder hard-a-starboard. This will overcome the transverse thrust and the result will be that the stern will move to starboard. Now, put the engine in neutral, put the wheel amidships, and put the engine ahead. Remember to put the rudder amidships before the engine is put ahead, otherwise the stern will be kicked the wrong way.

Let us now analyse what we have done in this manoeuvre. First we put the rudder to port, the engine ahead; then we stop; then we put our engine astern and our rudder amidships. When our ship begins to move astern, we put our rudder to starboard; we stop again; we then put our rudder amidships, our engine ahead and, as soon as the propeller starts to turn, the rudder to port. It sounds a good deal more complicated on paper than it is in practice, and when you have done it once or twice it will seem very simple and at the same time give you a delightful sense of self-confidence in your ability to handle your boat.

Assume now that we are in a narrow stretch of water and a moderately strong ebb-tide is running. We want to turn to starboard. Our boat has a single right-handed screw. Now, how do we do it? It is a good general rule that in any stretch of water with land on either side the tide runs more strongly in the middle than at the sides of the water. We will leave out for the moment the question of eddies, which are counter currents running along one side in the opposite direction to the main stream of tide. Let's assume for our illustration that we are moored near the left bank. We want to turn short round to starboard. In other words, we want the bows to go to starboard and the stern to go to port. We have seen that with a right-handed propeller the stern will kick to port with the engine going astern, therefore

EFFECTS OF CURRENT AND USE IN TURNING.

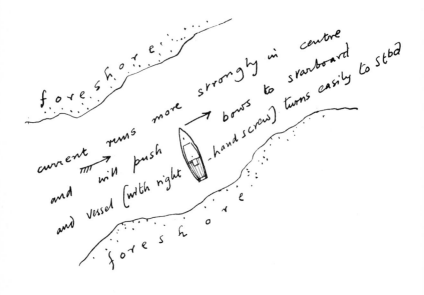

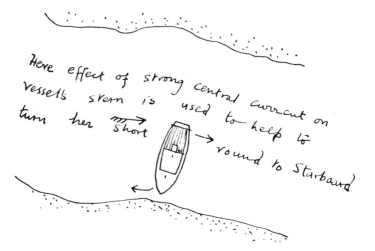

Fig. 64

by giving the stern a kick to port and bringing the bows round to starboard, we will bring the bows into the centre of the stream of water where the tide will complete the turning process. Of course, if the tide were flooding and we wanted to turn to starboard as before, we should turn our ship on the other side of the piece of water. In other words, we want to put our bow in the slacker water and our stern in the stronger water (see Fig. 64).

Now it is unusual, at any rate in British waters, that manœuvres are carried out in the absence of any wind, and therefore we must take into consideration the effect of wind on our vessel. Motor craft are affected very much by wind as regards surface drift. Their freeboard is usually higher than that of a sailing vessel, while their draught is usually considerably less, and they have, therefore, less grip on the water. The upper structure of a motor boat acts rather like the sails of a sailing boat; for example, if you have a long stern and high bows, those high bows will act like a jib, and your bow will tend to blow away from the direction of the wind. The opposite will apply if you have large upper-works built right aft; the boat will then behave like a sailing boat with a mizzensail set but no jib, the stern will move away from the direction of the wind. A boat which has both high bows and a lot of superstructure forward will turn away from the direction of the wind very quickly. Also some motor-craft have very, very little draught forward compared with their draught aft, and this increases the tendency for the bows to fall away from the wind. To give an illustration: we know that with a right-handed screw with the engine going astern the stern will tend to kick to port. Now supposing that we have time to check this by putting the rudder over to starboard; this will, other things being equal, eventually cause the ship, the stern of the ship that is, to move to starboard. Now suppose that a strong wind is blowing and our vessel has the high bows and high superstructure forward of which we were speaking; she is now like a sailing boat with the jib set, and the wind will blow her bow to starboard and will, if it is strong enough, overcome the effect of the rudder. This is an illustration of how, had there been no wind, the helmsman, by putting his rudder to starboard, could have achieved what he wanted.

In the case we have quoted, when a strong wind is blowing, however, he will not achieve his object because of the design of his ship and he must think again. It is, of course, impossible to lay down rules governing the movements of ships under all conditions, and I simply quote these few instances in order to point out how a vessel underway is affected by four separate things: her propeller or screw, her rudder, the wind, and the tide.

Now that we have seen something of how a boat with a single screw behaves, let's turn our attention to twin screws. Boats with twin screws generally have them arranged so that the two propellers turn outwards. I say generally because occasionally one comes across inward-turning screws. By outward-turning screws I mean that the starboard screw is a right-handed propeller and the port-hand screw is left-handed. In other words, when the ship is going ahead the top blades of the propellers are moving away from the centre line of the ship. Now, when we were discussing our right-handed screw, the first manœuvre we considered was to turn her short round to starboard. This manœuvre, although not difficult, becomes very much more simple when carried out in a twin-screw ship. Are we ready, then? Right! Slow ahead port engine, slow astern starboard engine. Now, we know from our previous discussion that the effect of the port engine going slow ahead will be to push the port side of the ship forward, and the effect of the starboard engine going slow astern will pull the starboard side of the ship astern. Consequently our ship will turn with her bow going round to starboard. Generally speaking, this would be sufficient in itself to turn our ship round pretty short, but it is found as a general rule that the propeller which is going ahead has more driving power than the one going astern, and the result of this is that the ship starts to gather a little headway. If this happens it will, of course, increase her turning circle so that unless something is done to counteract this effect she will not have sea room to turn. So what we do is this. We put our starboard engine half astern, instead of slow astern. This overpowers the port propeller, which is still going slow ahead. The ship will in fact slowly begin to gather sternway; when she does this we put the starboard engine back to slow astern, and in this way we can keep a check on the effect of the port engine giving our vessel too much headway and so increasing our turning circle. Once you have done this two or three times, you acquire a confident and pleasant feeling of command of your ship. This is the time-honoured way of turning a twin-screw ship short round, be she of 7 or 700 tons. To turn short round to port is just as easy. Slow ahead starboard engine, slow astern port. Here the converse procedure applies. We keep the speed of our starboard engine constant, varying the speed of our port engine to keep control over our turn. Furthermore, just as we used the effect of the tide in a single-screw ship, so can we with a twin-screw ship.

Now that we have learnt to turn our ship round and taken some note of the effect on her of wind and tide, we had better go a step farther and secure her to a mooring buoy in midstream. We will assume that we have a right-handed single-screw vessel, with a moderate forward draught. Now we are under way. There is no tide and we are approaching the buoy with the wind ahead. Only experience will teach you to know how far your ship carries her way. That is to say, how far she will move ahead once the gear lever has been put into the neutral position and the engine is no longer driving the propeller. As you approach the buoy, you put the engine into neutral when you think that you are close enough to the buoy for the ship to be able to reach her comfortably but without too much way on. The last thing we want to do is to ram it. In the bows on deck there will be a fair lead through which we will lead the mooring rope of our buoy. There should be a fair lead on either bow. Now we steer our ship to the buoy, but we don't steer straight for it, we steer so that it will lie slightly on the starboard bow. As we get up to it we put the engine astern. The object of this is twofold. The first object is to take the way off so that we remain stationary by the buoy. Remember that there is no tide. The second object of our touch astern is to kick the stern to port, so that the bow falls off a little to starboard. Now this brings both wind and buoy just on the port bow. In other words, we have the buoy between our bows and the wind. The object of this is to prevent our bows being blown over the top of the buoy. It is now a simple matter to reach over the bows with a boat-hook and bring the buoy on deck, hauling the buoy rope through the fair lead and then to make fast. Always remember when approaching a buoy in this manner that when you take the way off the ship, and I'm speaking of a right-handed screw ship, the effect is going to be twofold, because not only will your ship be stopped but her stern will kick to port, and therefore you must position your boat in such a way that this inevitable kick to port will not cause the bows of your vessel to move too far from the buoy so that you cannot reach it.

Now supposing that our ship has high bows and a shallow draught forward. With her shallow draught, as we have discussed elsewhere, she will have very little grip on the water, and as soon as the wind is not dead ahead she will fall away from it. This tendency will be increased by reason of her high freeboard forward. These circumstances alter the case. It will now be best for us to approach down wind. In this case we must consider very carefully the effect of the wind in driving us ahead. In other words, we will have to put our engine astern in plenty of time to prevent us being carried well past the buoy. Of course, if we had a twin-screw vessel it would be quite simple to hold our ship steady by the buoy while the buoy rope is being secured by keeping both engines going slow astern. However, in the case of a single-screw it must be remembered as always that the stern will kick to starboard or to port according to whether we have a right- or left-handed propeller, and once again we must position our bows accordingly. If, however, there is a tide running we will have to decide which is the stronger, the tide or the wind. If the former is the stronger, we must approach against the tide, making due allowance, in positioning our bows, for the wind's effect. If the wind is the stronger, the latter will be the factor that must govern our behaviour, as in the previous two paragraphs.

These, then, are the fundamental principles of securing to a buoy. But supposing that there is no buoy? In this case we must anchor. Now anchoring involves quite a bit more thought, because in addition to the purely technical procedure of stopping our ship and letting go our anchor and veering the necessary amount of cable, we must also consider the locality in which we are proposing to do this. One may reasonably assume that in the case of a buoy, that buoy has been laid with due thought to prevailing winds, strong tidal streams, and sea-room. We may also reasonably assume that there will be sufficient length of mooring chain for the rise and fall of the tide at all stages. But in the case of anchoring ourselves, all these matters must be given consideration, and the chart or harbour plan carefully studied in making our choice of anchorage. With regard to the general principles of anchoring, the amount of cable that should be veered, etc., this question we have already considered fully in an earlier chapter, and I will try and avoid repetition so far as I can. However, there are certain aspects which apply particularly to power craft, and if I repeat myself I hope the reader will be indulgent.

Having chosen our anchorage, and the spot where we wish to drop our anchor, we must decide as before whether the effect of the wind is going to be greater than the effect of the tide, or vice versa. If the tide is the stronger, we turn our ship into it, and let us assume for purposes of this illustration that this is the case. We know the depth of water from the chart and we have decided in view of the fact that the anchorage is a little exposed to veer five times the depth of water. (Normally, three times would be sufficient.) Now the anchor to be let go must be that of the weather bow, so that the ship's bow will blow away from it and not across it. We are now approaching our anchorage and we lower our port anchor through the fair lead in the bows, not so that any part of it is touching the water but so that it is all ready for letting go. We put our engine into neutral, and, as we slowly reach the appointed place, we put our engine astern. We are not in this case concerned with positioning our bows about a buoy, but nevertheless with our right-handed screw ship our bows will go to starboard as the ship comes astern. This is what we want, because we want both wind and tide to be on the port bow when we let go our port anchor. Now we let go our anchor and put our engine into neutral. As the cable runs out, the marks on it should be counted and the cable snubbed or made fast at the appropriate mark. In earlier chapters of this book we have seen how by bearings of objects on shore we can test whether or not our ship is dragging her anchor. If the anchorage is a little exposed, and one anchor does not seem sufficient to hold her, the ship should be given a sheer by putting our rudder to

Giving a Sheer with the helm

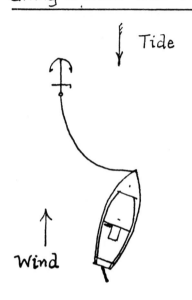

Tide

Wind

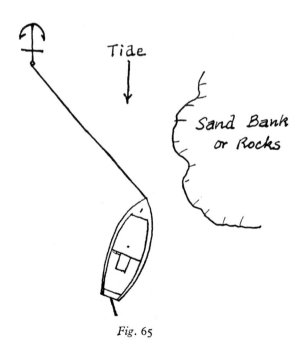

Tide

Sand Bank
or Rocks

Fig. 65

starboard (see Fig. 65). This will cause the tide to bring her
bows over to starboard and enable us to let go the starboard
anchor. This method of anchoring the ship with two anchors is
known as mooring and is used not only under the conditions
we have just described, but in harbours where space is very
limited, there are no mooring buoys available, and where there
is insufficient room for a ship lying to a single anchor to swing
either when the tide turns or under the influence of the wind. A
ship moored in this way will pivot when she swings about her
bow and swing in approximately her own length.

Now, to moor our ship correctly is not the same as letting go
a second anchor to hold our ship in the way that was described
a few sentences back. That might be regarded in fact as a temporary measure, and indeed when the tide turned the starboard
anchor would probably have to be weighed or one of the cables
would foul the other anchor. The proper way to moor a ship is
as follows. Approaching the anchorage chosen against the tide,
we run on beyond the place where the bows will finally be
resting when moored. If we are going to veer 15 fathoms of
cable, then we run beyond our chosen spot for about that
distance. When this distance is reached, we put the engine
astern, and, as soon as our boat has gathered sternway, we let
go one anchor; that is to say, the port anchor (see Fig. 66).
Continuing gently astern we veer our port cable until we have
out 30 fathoms of cable, or twice the amount that we will finally
be riding to. At this point we let go our starboard anchor. We
heave in on our port cable and veer our starboard cable until
we have 15 fathoms on each cable. As soon as this point is
reached, both cables are made fast and our ship can be considered as moored. Our two anchors will be in line, or should
be, with the direction of tide, or if there is no tide, the wind, or
in other words a line drawn from one anchor to the other should
point directly either towards, or away from, the tide.

Now we must make sure that our ship swings opposite ways
at each turn of the tide. The reason for this is, that if she swung
the same way each time, the cables would get successive turns
round each other. We can usually ensure that she swings in
opposite directions by giving her a sheer with the rudder,
putting the rudder to port, say, at one turn of the tide and to

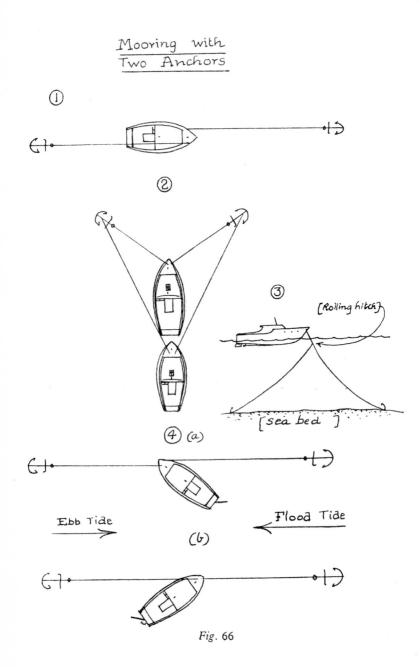

Fig. 66

starboard at the next. Should it come on to blow in an athwart-ships direction, that is to say, at right angles to the line between our anchors, the two cables and anchors will come under considerable strain and it is possible that the anchors may drag. This can be avoided by veering as much cable as there is room for in the way of sea room astern of our ship. The more acute, or less, the angle between the two cables, the safer will our ship be, and the more undisturbed will be our enjoyment of that well-earned pink gin in the saloon! When the time comes to weigh anchor, we start by heaving in first that anchor to which the ship is not riding.

We have now considered anchoring, mooring, and securing to a mooring buoy, but there will be many occasions when we do none of these three things. I refer, of course, to the occasions when we moor alongside a wall or jetty. Let us consider this in three separate sections: how to come alongside, how to secure our vessel once alongside, and, thirdly, how to leave.

If there is no wind it makes the task of coming alongside very much easier. For example, if as we approach the harbour wall of our choice, we have a fairly strong following wind, this raises in its turn the following problem. The wind would tend, as we approached the quay, to catch our port quarter, and blow our stern out to starboard with the result that we would be approaching the quay at right-angles, a highly undesirable state of affairs, if we were not driven hard into the quay itself. The principle involved here is the same as that when approaching a buoy when the wind is strong, that is to say, the quay or jetty should be approached up-wind. We must turn our vessel round and head her bows as much as possible into the wind.

If, of course, the wind is ahead when you enter harbour, there is no need to turn round, as your ship is already head to wind. In this case it is simply necessary to angle the boat towards the jetty and in the same way as approaching a buoy, stop our propellers turning by putting the clutch into neutral in sufficient time for our boat to lose her way as she comes abreast of the quay. Just before her bows reach the quay we put our engine astern and the transverse thrust of the propeller will kick the stern to port. This will in fact bring her parallel to the jetty where it will be a simple matter to moor her ahead and astern.

COMING ALONGSIDE

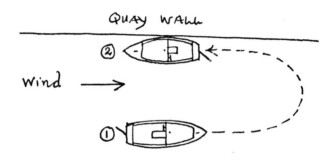

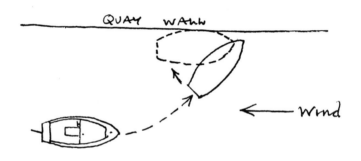

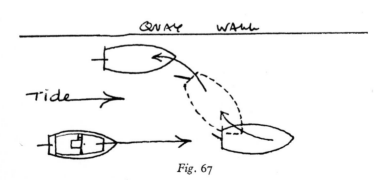

Fig. 67

It must be remembered that not only will the shape of your vessel affect her performance; in other words, as we saw before, if she has high bows she will behave like a yacht with a jib set; but also we must take into consideration such factors as the height of the tide or of the jetty. The wind may be blowing quite strongly off the jetty, but if it is a high jetty and we are approaching it at rather low state of the tide, it will blanket the wind as we approach. If, on the other hand, the jetty is low and does not in any way blanket the wind, then with our high-bowed vessel as we approach we will find that the wind will tend to blow our bows away to starboard, and therefore we should counteract this effect by approaching the jetty at a bolder, less acute angle. Similarly, if the wind tended to be blowing our bows onto the jetty, not only will the jetty provide no blanketing effect—and we must bear in mind the effect of the wind all the time—but we must remember, too, to approach the jetty at a very slight angle, and in this case the transverse thrust to port as we put our engine astern will assist us in keeping our bows away from the quay until our crew has managed to place a fender between our bows and the quay wall. I make this last remark in the full knowledge that the experienced skipper will already have seen that fenders are set along the side of his ship which is approaching the quay. Even so, it is always wise to have somebody standing in the bows in circumstances like these with an additional fender, and this applies particularly in the case of power boats which frequently have a flare in the bows. When coming alongside in tidal waters and where there is a wind blowing, it will be necessary for the boat's skipper to judge whether the tide or the wind is going to have the most effect on his ship, or possibly what effect their combination will have. In all these cases, as a simple rule of thumb, it is fair to say that you should head your vessel into whichever is the stronger, wind or tide.

So far, we have been considering a single-screw ship. Just as a twin-screw ship is easy to manœuvre in midstream or when approaching a buoy, so the position of a second screw makes coming alongside a good deal simpler. By that I do not mean that it is necessarily simpler in operation; it isn't, but on the other hand the second screw gives the skipper a measure of confidence and control that seems to simplify the operation.

Let us, then, take an example. We are approaching our jetty, it is slack water, so we do not have to bother about the tide, and the wind is ahead. We are therefore approaching the quay at a moderate angle, and when we judge that our boat has sufficient way to bring her to the quay, we put our gear lever into neutral. Now as we come up to the quay we put our outboard propeller, that is, the propeller away from the quay, slow astern. The reason we do this is as follows. First of all we want to take way off the ship completely, and stop our ship by the quay. Secondly, the effect of our outboard propeller going slow astern will be to bring our stern into the quay so that we can moor ship. If we put both our engines astern this would merely have the effect of stopping the ship without bringing the stern in. This might not matter so much in a very small boat, but in a larger vessel it would make it very difficult, if not impossible, to get a stern line onto the quay, and in any way the method of using the outboard propeller slow astern is the correct way to do it. Of course, you can go half astern or full astern, if in excess of zeal to arrive alongside you have been approaching the quay like a bull at a matador. Let's take a second example. Supposing there is some tide and it is lee going, that is to say, it is running in the same direction as the wind. We are, in other words, heading into it. We can now make use of the tide to bring in our stern. We approach the quay at the same angle, but this time we stop our way by putting both engines slow astern. This stops our bow just at the jetty and we can moor our ship ahead. As soon as tide takes effect and the strain comes on our head rope, the stern will come in and mooring aft will be a simple matter. You can, if you like, assist your vessel to do this latter with the rudder. To bring this about it is only necessary to remember that the effect of a running tide on the rudder of a moored vessel is the same as if that vessel were moving through the water. In other words, if we are lying starboard side to the quay our rudder should be put to port. The same principles that apply to a sailing vessel approaching a jetty with a very strong wind blowing onto that jetty apply to motor vessels. If the wind blowing onto the jetty is so strong that you have reason to fear that damage to your ship will result, and if you have sea room to do it, you should let go the weather anchor a couple of ship's lengths from the quay or more if you have more sea room, and then, once your ship has got her cable, you veer astern on it, keeping it taut. In order (assuming once again that we are coming alongside port side) to cant our bows in towards the quay so that we may get our head-rope out, we keep our starboard engine going slow ahead. When the bow is near enough to the jetty for us to get the head rope out and secured, the starboard engine may be stopped. The stern will then swing in towards the quay. This you must watch carefully, because if it swings in too rapidly damage to your ship may result. The swinging in movement may be checked by putting the starboard engine ahead for short bursts.

It would be both tedious reading and an insult to the reader's intelligence to give all the numerous examples of the varied effects of wind and tide working together and in various degrees and angles of opposition when manœuvring ships alongside in this fashion. Like everything else to do with boats, once the general principles have been appreciated, only experience of actually carrying out the manœuvres under different circumstances can give you confidence in handling your boat. It is indeed surprising how many different combinations of wind and tide, visibility, etc., there can be, but no one will grumble at that, for surely it is this endless, fascinating variety that makes boat handling so rewarding.

Now that we have learnt to approach a quay, let us now direct our attention to the method by which we are going to secure ourselves to it, in such a way that our vessel will be perfectly safe under all normal conditions of tide and weather. Look at Fig. 68. You will see that there are no fewer than six ropes joining our vessel to the quay. These ropes are, reading from forward to aft: the head rope, the fore breast rope, the fore spring, the after spring, the after breast rope, and the stern rope. This boat is really well moored, but why do we need so many ropes? To answer this, let us consider the functions of the various ropes. The duty of the head rope and stern rope will be obvious. They are the first ropes which are secured. Now the two springs A and B in the figure are equally important. We are lying, we will assume, head to tide. The tide will be trying to carry our ship astern, strain will come on the head rope and will also come on the after spring. Now the after spring will tend to pull the stern towards the quay, but the tide flowing between the stern of the ship and the quay will force it out again. The spring then will be keeping the ship in the right position relative to the quay. But now, what happens when the tide turns? The answer is,

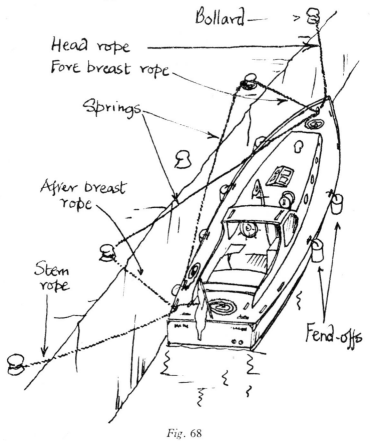

Fig. 68

precisely the same except this time the strain will come upon the fore spring. Now it may be that this combined action of springs and tide will force our vessel too far from the quay; this is where the breast ropes come in. If the head rope and stern rope are short ropes and are made fast at no very great distance in front of the bow or abaft the stern of the ship, breast ropes may very well be unnecessary, but it is wise policy to leave the head rope as far forward and the stern rope as far aft as is conveniently practicable. Of course, if there were no tide and no great strength of wind, neither springs nor breast ropes are really necessary, but even so springs at any rate provide a welcome additional measure of security.

I can visualise the reader saying to himself, this is all very well, these taut ropes holding our vessel well in to the quayside; what happens when the tide falls? Surely the boat will remain suspended in mid-air by the mooring ropes? Well, this is the main reason why springs, head ropes, and stern ropes should be secured as far ahead and astern of the ship as possible, because then they will not need tending as the tide rises and falls, because the distance between the bollard on the quay and the fair lead or point where the rope is made fast on the vessel will remain very much the same, whereas if the mooring ropes are made fast ashore close to bow and stern, they will have to be eased as the tide falls and taken in as it rises. This, in fact, is what you have to do in the case of breast ropes; there is no alternative for it. As the tide falls or rises it is well to check not only the mooring ropes but also fenders between yourself and the quayside. Make sure that they are not caught or getting damaged. If the quay wall is very dirty and oily, and you wish to avoid getting this mess on your nice white canvas fenders, put two large fenders over the side and sling a spar, or plank, outboard of them. The spar will then rub against the quay and keep your fenders clean. This method is particularly useful when lying alongside a wall which, as one quite often finds, has big buttresses or baulks of timber running from the top of the quay to the sea-bed, and spaced at regular intervals of, say, about 6 feet, sometimes considerably more. In cases like this it is virtually impossible to keep one fender between one of these baulks and the ship's side, and the only way to keep your ship fended is to use the spar method. In this way one spar can be made to span two of the baulks.

We have approached a quay and moored ourselves to it. Let us now learn the correct way to leave it. If our ship is lying in a tideway, we can use the tide to enable us to pass clear ahead or astern of other vessels which may be lying near us. If, for example, there is a boat lying close astern and we wish to get away from the quay bows first, we can use our after spring to cant the bows out into midstream by letting go the breast rope and fore spring and easing away on our head rope, the tide pushing on our bows will cause them to swing out to starboard as the after spring causes the stern to swing in towards the quay. Somebody should be standing by in the stern, incidentally, with a fender. If there were no tide, or it was slack water, you would put the engine slow astern and this would act in the same way as the tide by putting a strain on the spring and pulling the vessel's stern into the quay and bringing the bow out in consequence. When the bow is out far enough we cast off head rope and stern rope and finally cast off spring and put our engine ahead, initially putting our rudder a little to port so as to kick our stern clear of the quay. If we were manœuvring with a twin-screw ship, we would use the outer screw and put our rudder slightly to starboard. It is almost always advisable never to use the inside screw when lying alongside, because in many twin-screw vessels the propellers project beyond the ship's side and in any case there may be ropes or other objects lying near the inboard propeller.

Supposing there is a ship lying close ahead of us, we have more room astern and therefore the best way will be to leave the quay stern first. The problem now is to get our stern out in the same way as we got out the bows. To do this we use the fore spring. We cast off the stern rope and put our engine slow ahead, this brings the strain on the fore spring and pulls in our bows. Before we put the engine ahead we should put our rudder a little to port. Now the spring pulling the bow in will cause the stern to come out, and in addition the wash from our screw, driving against the rudder, will also help to bring the stern out. As soon as the stern is out far enough, we put our engine into neutral, cast off our spring, and put our engine astern. If we were doing the same manœuvre with a twin-screw vessel, we would put our outer engine ahead, leaving the rudder amidships; this would kick the stern out.

Now if the ship was lying in a tideway we could use the spring to get the stern out, provided, of course, that the ship was lying stern to tide. The tide flowing between the port quarter of the ship and the quay will force the stern out. In this case, care must be taken to check the movement of the stern with either the stern rope or an after breast rope, otherwise it may swing out too far, especially in a strong tideway and get out of control. Because of the fact that a boat's bows curve round much more than her stern, the fore spring exerts considerably greater leverage than the after spring. It is worth while remembering this when you have the alternative choice of leaving either ahead or astern, but where, because of craft lying two or three abreast ahead and astern of you, or because of a strong on-shore wind the greater leverage of the fore spring will be a considerable advantage. Of course, if the wind is off-shore it makes the task of getting the ship out from the quay that much easier.

We have been talking of the use of mooring ropes in leaving a quay, but it should be remembered that frequently there is no need to use the springs at all. For example, imagine we have a single-screw ship lying alongside port side to. Now we are not going to use our spring and we are going to leave stern first. We put our rudder hard-a-port and our engine slow ahead. The wash from the screw will act on our rudder to kick the stern out. Watching carefully, as soon as the stern is sufficiently far out, we put our engine astern and our rudder amidships. As our ship has a right-handed screw, we allowed our stern to come well clear of the quay before putting our engine astern, remembering the initial kick to port. And by the same token, if we had been lying starboard side to, we could put our engine astern after casting off our ropes, because the thrust from the propeller in this case will kick our stern away from the quay.

Very often there is nobody on shore to let go ropes when one wants to leave, particularly if one is leaving in the very early hours of the morning to catch a tide. In this case the ropes can be secured in such a way that they may be slipped from the vessel herself. This is quite simple to arrange; one end of the mooring rope being secured on board, the other being taken ashore round a bollard or through a ring on the quay, and brought back on board again. When you want to leave, all you have to do is to let go one end and haul on the other. Make sure, though, that the end that is going to be hauled through the ring on the quay is clear of loops, knots, etc., or it will catch in the bollard at the most embarrassing moment. Do I hear the reader asking what on earth would he be doing with knots and loops

A "MOTOR - SAILER"

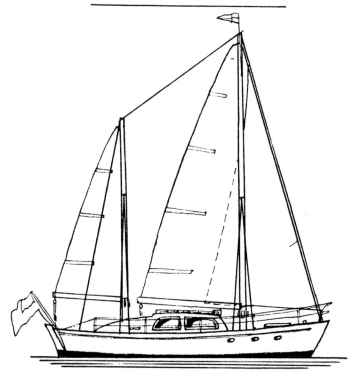

An excellent type of motor-sailer, having sail area of about 800 sq feet on a waterline length of about 40 feet, and at the same time, possessing a powerful engine of 100 b h p, capable of driving this fine ship at 9 knots.

Fig. 69

in his mooring ropes? Well, I apologise, but it does sometimes happen!

Before concluding this section on power yachts I would like to call the reader's attention to the motor-sailer: a type, formerly despised, but which is fast gaining great favour (see Fig. 69). After all, a good motor-sailer can combine the best of both worlds—the ability to run to a planned schedule coupled with the ability to sail and give the peace and the satisfaction of sailing. There are many to whom this form of compromise—and it is a compromise—appeals.

CHAPTER XVI

FIRST AID, SEASICKNESS, AND THE MEDICINE CHEST

THE wise skipper, no matter how far afield he plans to go, will be prepared for the time when one of his crew will need first aid and need it immediately.

The following is a list of some of the more usual problems and their proper first-aid treatment: they are by no means comprehensive. A cruising yacht should have on board a book on practical first aid. A very good one is Bruce's *First Aid to the Injured*, which is used as the handbook of St. John's Ambulance Association.

1. *Splinters*

The hands should first be washed well in disinfectant water. Clean the surrounding skin with iodine. If you can get at the splinter with tweezers, it should be easy to extract it. You may find you have to snick at the skin until you can get a hold of the splinter with the tweezers. Only use a knife or needle for this if they have been boiled for at least 20 minutes. After extracting the splinter, dress the wound so as to keep the dirt away from it. A deep and very stubborn splinter may need hot fomentations to be 'worked to the surface'.

2. *Minor Cuts*

Wash any cut in antiseptic and apply iodine. If a large cut this might be very painful and cause an iodine burn. Then put on a lint dressing and bandage it or fix it with plaster.

3. *Deep Cuts*

Treat a bad cut very carefully and promptly. First wash the cut very thoroughly with plain warm water. Then dissolve a soloid of sublimate of mercury in a pint of warm water and again wash very thoroughly in this solution. The person dressing the wound must wash his hands well in disinfected hot water. He should then use surgical sewing silk to sew up the wound with an interrupted stitch. The surgical needle must be sterilised by letting it boil for a good 20 minutes. After the wound has been stitched, it should be swabbed with a solution of sublimate of mercury, as before, and covered with a gauze pad, and bandaged. Keep the limb raised if the wound continues to bleed.

4. Burns and Scalds

Remove any clothing near the burn—but do not remove clothing stuck to the skin. (To comply with this, you may need to cut seam stitches with a knife.) If the skin is not broken, put flour on the affected area and leave. Or you may apply carron oil or olive oil on a gauze pad or Nikalgin thickly on a piece of gauze. Bandage very lightly.

If someone's clothing catches fire, he should immediately throw himself on deck, rolling over and over to check the flames until he receives help. If practicable, a better way is to wrap a rug or blanket round the burning part and exclude the air. The most important thing to remember to do with burns is to exclude the air as soon as possible.

5. Sun Burn

Applications of calamine lotion night and morning will usually give relief. In bad cases, you should apply Nikalgin jelly.

6. Stings

Wasps and other troublesome insects do manage to find their way aboard. A fresh raw onion cut across the root will produce a milk-like fluid. Apply this direct to the stung part, and then a clean piece of ordinary soda should be gently rubbed over the same place.

7. Boils

A bad boil is usually treated by hot fomentations. Soak a piece of boric lint in boiling water, wring it out and apply to the boil hot. Cover the lint with a piece of oiled silk and bandage. A little cotton wool will be a further help to keep the heat in. Plaster strips, where suitable, may be used instead of a roller bandage.

8. *Constipation*

This is a frequent ailment aboard ship, owing partly to the lack of exercise. Two grains of calomel will relieve the situation.

9. *Sore Throat*

Gargling with a solution composed of a teaspoonful of carbolic acid in half a pint of warm water will greatly relieve the discomfort of a sore throat.

10. *Food Poisoning*

First make the patient sick. To make him or her drink a large amount of salt water or mustard and water is one way of doing this. Afterwards a good dose of Andrew's Liver Salts or Epsom Salts should be given.

11. *Drowning*

There are several different stages in drowning and appropriate treatment for each:

If the patient does not seem to have suffered at all from being immersed, remove clothing immediately; dry well; put on dry clothes; give a hot drink and rest.

If the patient is suffering from temporary exhaustion, remove clothes, dry, put to bed between warmed blankets (if necessary massage to promote circulation). Then give a hot drink (beef tea, etc.) and rest, and, if possible, go to sleep.

If the patient is suffering badly, but is still breathing, remove all tight-fitting clothing, lie down on deck and turn on his or her side. Smelling salts will help normal breathing.

Where the breathing has stopped is, of course, the most serious stage. Again loosen tight clothing and lay on deck, but in this case the patient should be face downwards, the head slightly inclined to the right. The patient should be handled very carefully and not forced into a position, but you must not let him or her lie face upwards. Clear the mouth of any slime and start artificial respiration as follows: kneel astride the patient facing towards the head. Placing your hands on the small of the back, spread the fingers out over the lower ribs with the thumbs almost touching. Then lean steadily forwards putting your weight on your hands, and exert a downward pressure on the patient. In this way you are driving air (and water, if any) from his lungs. Then swing back, releasing the pressure quickly. This should make him or her inhale. Keeping your hands in position on the small of the back, repeat this every 4 or 5 seconds in a regular rhythm. You are actually effecting a breathing motion in the lungs like that caused by natural breathing and you must continue for as long as necessary until natural breathing is brought back. Make certain the natural breathing has been restored before you stop the artificial respiration. Then turn the patient face upwards and try to promote circulation by massage. The blood-stream should be massaged upwards towards the heart along the inside of the legs and arms and on the back, massaging every time towards the heart. Next warm the patient by applying hot-water bottles or heated flannels to the arm-pits, the soles of the feet, and the pit of the stomach. Apply a hot linseed poultice to the chest to ease pain in breathing.

When the patient appears to be fully restored to life, remove the clothes and dry thoroughly, again rubbing towards the heart. Wrap the patient in warm blankets and put to bed in a *well-ventilated* room or cabin. Test if the swallowing ability has returned by giving a teaspoonful of warm water. If so, give some weak, warm brandy or beef tea. Encourage the patient to go to sleep. Keep constant watch should the breathing fail again. If it does, resume artificial respiration immediately.

Remember that you must not start operations by putting the patient into a hot bath, as it could be very dangerous. Remember also never to start off by giving the patient stimulants.

We have now considered all the more common ailments. Remember in all serious accidents to send for a doctor as soon as possible, for First Aid, as its name implies, is a number of prompt measures, pending professional assistance.

We now come to that distressing malady—seasickness. Most doctors agree that seasickness is mainly a disorder of the nervous system. Experience and familiarity with the sea will bring about an amount of tolerance, varying considerably. Seasickness has been said to be divided into two phases: 'In the first you think you are going to die, in the second you are afraid you aren't!' The contributory causes of seasickness are many and varied; apprehension, coldness, tiredness, the motion of the ship, the smell of petrol or paraffin, indigestion—all these play a part in inducing this cruel maritime affliction. But do not be disheartened, much can be done to alleviate the distress! Firstly, remember that prevention is *far* better than cure. Avoid greasy food, acids, and over-indulgence of any kind for a few days before going to sea, and you will find that it makes a great difference.

When at sea, take Eno's Fruit Salts to avoid constipation.

I would recommend the drugs Avomine or Dramamine as the best anti-seasickness preparations. Other cures are Quells and Mothersill, both of which work on some people. Some are also helped by taking two 10-grain tabelts of Chloretone before sailing and may safely take a further 10-grain capsule some hours later.

Some drugs, like Avomine or Dramamine, work on *some* people when they are actually feeling sick, but it is always wisest to take them *before* you feel sickness coming on.

In a mild attack, eat dry foods—biscuits, cold chicken, also glucose barley sugar. If possible, stay in the open and try and turn your attention to work of some sort. In a bad attack, lie down with head low, keep warm, and eat dry foods as above, even though it may be a big effort to do so.

Finally, the yacht's Medicine Chest.

It is a question of personal preference and experience as to what the medicine chest should contain. The following list of items should furnish a good basis:

Cotton wool	Boracic crystals
Gauze dressings	Soloids of Sublimate of Mercury
Dressings for burns	Aspirin tablets
Two or three triangular	Alka Seltzer tablets
bandages	Eno's Fruit Salts
Boracic lint	Calomel
Splinter tweezers	Epsom salts or Andrew's Liver
Scalpel	Salts
Surgical scissors	Avomine (obtainable in Great
Thread and needles	Britain)
Safety-pins	Dramamine (obtainable in the
Sticking-plaster	U.S.A.)
Elastoplast or similar dressings	Surgical needle and sewing silk
Hot-water bottle	Castor oil
Iodine	Olive oil
Disinfectant (Lysol, etc.)	Calamine lotion
Zinc ointment	Oiled silk

Bicarbonate of Soda
Quinine tablets
Brandy
Chloretone (in 10-grain capsules)
'Quells' tablets (another seasick-
ness remedy)

Medicine glass
Roller bandages
Finger-stalls
A small tin of Antiphlogistin,
and last, but by no means
least, a clinical thermometer!

CHAPTER XVII

FLAGS, SIGNALLING, AND FLAG ETIQUETTE

In accordance with a very old custom, every yacht which cruises should 'wear' at least two flags, a burgee and a national flag, sometimes called an 'ensign'.

For example, the national flag of British merchant vessels is the 'Red Ensign'. This dates from the year 1707. A vessel which is used only for pleasure and not profit is classified as a merchant ship under the British Merchant Shipping Act of 1894 and permitted to wear the Red Ensign, if registered in conformity with the provisions of the Act. Yachts which are not registered with the Board of Trade are not 'legally' British vessels and therefore not entitled to wear the Red Ensign. However, there are in the Act a number of conflicting orders, and it is not likely that an unregistered yacht would be barred from flying the Red Ensign. It is fair to say, therefore, that any yacht can fly the Red Ensign.*

In Great Britain, a number of yachts fly a 'special' ensign. This will be the ensign of a yacht club which has the right to apply to the Admiralty on a yacht owner's behalf for a warrant for that owner to fly a special ensign from his yacht. This may be a plain blue ensign, a blue 'defaced' ensign, or a red 'defaced' ensign. An ensign which has a device or heraldic symbol near the outward edge (the 'fly') is termed 'defaced'. The White Ensign, the ensign of Her Majesty's fleet, may be flown only by members of the Royal Yacht Squadron, whose headquarters is at Cowes Castle, Cowes, England.

There are various regulations regarding the right of a yachtsman to fly one of these special ensigns. The Navy List contains

* Generally speaking, the mercantile flag of a country is the one which is worn by yachts.

the names of clubs which possess the privilege, but membership of such a club does not mean that you have automatically obtained the right to fly the special ensign. Every member of such a club must apply through the club's secretary who will know the proper form in which to apply to the Admiralty. If he is a member of two or more such privileged clubs, he must apply separately for each special ensign he wishes to fly.

Should a warrant holder cease to belong to the club through which he has obtained the warrant, or if he should sell the yacht for which the warrant was issued, in each case the warrant must be returned to the Admiralty.

The special ensign may be worn only when the owner is on board the yacht. However, it need not be hauled down if the owner is ashore for just a short time, or in any case in the vicinity of the harbour, as he is still considered to be in control of the yacht. Whenever the special ensign is not flown the Red Ensign should be substituted.

Finally, when a cruising yacht either enters, leaves, or anchors in a foreign port, she must, under the Merchant Shipping Act, wear an ensign. Moreover, she must wear an ensign when entering a British port if she is over 50 tons register. The Commanding Officer of one of Her Majesty's ships can order a yacht to hoist ensign. No yacht is ever permitted to hoist the Union Flag (the 'Union Jack'). From the ensign let us pass to the burgee, the triangular flag of a yacht club. All members fly it from the main masthead. But first it must be mentioned that the following special flags, however, are worn by the flag officers of the club:

Commodore—Swallow-tailed flag.
Vice-Commodore—Swallow-tailed flag with one ball in the hoist.
Rear-Commodore—Swallow-tailed flag with two balls in the hoist.

All yacht clubs have their own burgee with their own heraldic device. When an owner belongs to several clubs, he may find it a problem deciding which club's burgee he should fly. In this event, priority is given to the senior club. The Royal Yacht Squadron has precedence over all others, the privileged clubs over the ordinary clubs, etc. It is polite, of course, when in the harbour of a club of which the yacht owner is a member, to wear that club's burgee.

When in harbour the senior officer present (generally, the duty officer of the local yacht club) will, by example, show the correct time for burgees and ensigns to be hoisted or hauled down. They are hoisted when colours are 'made'; that is, in summer (from 26th March to the 20th September) at 08.00 hours, and in winter (from 21st September to the 25th March) at 09.00 hours. They are hauled down at sunset. When a yacht is at sea, the ensign may be flown between sunrise and sunset, and the burgee kept flying all night.

In addition to an ensign and a burgee, a yacht may occasionally wear a house flag, a racing flag, a prize flag or ensign of a foreign country, and flags of the International Code. It is quite rare to find a house flag today. It is the particular flag of the owner, and entirely to his choosing whether he flies one or not. The only rule governing its colour, size, or design is that it must not be similar to any other design, and it must not conflict with any Admiralty or Board of Trade Regulations. In Fig. 70 we see that the house flag is flown at the fore masthead in schooners, at the starboard yardarm in single-masted ships, and at the mizzen masthead in yawls and ketches. However, if a yacht is flying the White Ensign, she does not wear a private flag.

A racing flag is hoisted instead of the burgee, if the yacht is taking part in a race, and, when colours are made at regattas, may be hoisted in place of the burgee. Racing flags, like house flags, have no restrictions as to design, but are usually of rectangular shape.

Prize flags are flown at the end of a day's racing to indicate successes. They are flown from the masthead, all bent upon one line (generally on the main halliard). The 'first' prize is usually a silk miniature of the racing flag. The 'second' and 'third' prize flags are red and blue pennants with the figures 2 and 3 printed in white.

Flags of the International Code enable the yachtsman to signal in an easy and amusing way, and communicating at sea by use of flags is rather a satisfying experience. However, stowage of these flags can be quite a problem. One plan is to have labelled flag pockets sewn in a roll of canvas. It is generally too

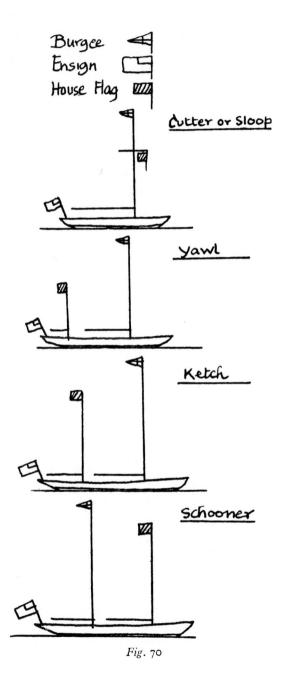

Burgee

Ensign

House Flag

Cutter or Sloop

Yawl

Ketch

Schooner

Fig. 70

awkward for the small yacht to carry the usual flag locker, which contains each code flag in its own labelled pigeon-hole. For economical and other reasons, many yachtsmen do not carry a full set of code flags, but only those flags which would be needed more often:

INTERNATIONAL CODE OF SIGNALS

SINGLE LETTER SIGNALS

The most *important Code Signals* of all—the *single letter signals*—consist of *Very Urgent* signals or those in common use. Seamen should know these by heart, so that there may be no hesitation in acting on them.

The following may be made by any method of signalling, but those marked * when made by sound may only be made in compliance with the International Regulations for Preventing Collisions at Sea, Rules 34 and 35.

$(\cdot -)$	A	I have a diver down; keep well clear at slow speed.
$(-\cdot\cdot\cdot)$	B	I am taking in, or discharging, or carrying dangerous goods.
$(-\cdot-\cdot)$	C	**Yes** (affirmative or 'The significance of the previous group should be read in the affirmative').
$(-\cdot\cdot)$	*D	**Keep clear** of me—I am manoeuvring with difficulty.
$(\cdot)$	*E	I am altering my course to **starboard.**
$(\cdot\cdot-\cdot)$	F	I am **disabled.** Communicate with me.
$(--\cdot)$	G	I **require a Pilot.** When made by fishing vessels operating in close proximity on the fishing grounds it means: 'I am hauling nets'.
$(\cdot\cdot\cdot\cdot)$	*H	I **have a Pilot** on board.
$(\cdot\cdot)$	*I	I am altering my course to **port.**
$(\cdot---)$	J	I am on **fire** and have dangerous cargo on board; keep well clear of me.

† Signals 'K' and 'S' have special meanings as landing signals for small boats with crews or persons in distress. (International Convention for the Safety of Life at Sea, 1960, Chapter V, Regulation 16.) Single letter R has so far *not* been allocated a signal meaning as this already has a meaning in Rule 15 of the Collision Regulations.

(— · —)	†K	I wish to **communicate** with you.
(· — · ·)	L	You should **stop** your vessel instantly.
(— —)	M	My vessel is **stopped** and making no way through the water.
(— ·)	N	**No** (negative or 'The significance of the previous group should be read in the negative'.) This signal may be given only visually or by sound. For voice or radio transmission the signal should be **'No'**.
(— — —)	O	**Man overboard.**
(· — — ·)	P	**In Harbour** (Blue Peter) All persons should report on board as vessel is **about to proceed to sea.** (Note: To be hoisted at the foremast head.) **At Sea.** It may be used by fishing vessels to mean: 'My nets have come fast upon an obstruction'.
(— — · —)	Q	My vessel is **healthy** and I request free pratique.
(· — ·)	R	
(· · ·)	†*S	My engines are going **astern.**
(—)	*T	Keep clear of me; I am engaged in pair trawling.
(· · —)	U	You are **running into danger.**
(· · · —)	V	I **require assistance.**
(· — —)	W	I **require medical assistance.**
(— · · —)	X	**Stop** carrying out your intentions and watch for my signals.
(— · — —)	Y	I am dragging my **anchor.**
(— — · ·)	Z	I **require a tug.** When made by fishing vessels operating in close proximity on the fishing grounds it means: 'I am shooting nets'.

With a little experience almost anyone can become quite efficient at the Morse code. Whether in communication with other craft or sending messages home via Lloyd's signal stations, being able to signal in this manner is a great asset at sea. The type of gear you use will depend on your pocket. A large signalling torch is adequate, though a signalling lamp with a key is better. The best of all is a signalling lamp, like the Aldis lamp, but they are expensive.

I list below the letters, numerals, and special signals of the Morse code:

A · —	N — ·	1 · — — — —
B — · · ·	O — — —	2 · · — — —
C — · — ·	P · — — ·	3 · · · — —
D — · ·	Q — — · —	4 · · · · —
E ·	R · — ·	5 · · · · ·
F · · — ·	S · · ·	6 — · · · ·
G — — ·	T —	7 — — · · ·
H · · · ·	U · · —	8 — — — · ·
I · ·	V · · · —	9 — — — — ·
J · — — —	W · — —	0 — — — — —
K — · —	X — · · —	
L · — · ·	Y — · — —	
M — —	Z — — · ·	

Call for unknown ship, etc. · — · — · — · — · — etc.

Answering sign, etc. — — — — — — — etc.

Space sign · ·   · ·

Break sign — · · · —

Erase sign, etc. · · · · · · · · · etc.

Repeat sign · · — — · ·

Ending sign · — · — ·

From (DE) — · · ·

Correct — · — ·

Repeat back — — ·

Message received · — ·

Cannot read you due to bad light · — —

Full stop · ·   ·   · ·

When calling up another ship by Morse, make the call sign which is a succession of A's until you see that the ship is answering you with a succession of T's. When answering another vessel, make a succession of T's, until the calling ship ceases to call. The calling-up ship will probably make the 'From' sign (letters DE) once she has received your answering T's. This is most likely to be followed by her signal letters, or perhaps by her name. Then you, as receiving ship, should send this back followed by DE and your own name or signal letters, which will be repeated back by the first ship. Each repeat back should be acknowledged by the letter C, indicating 'Correct'. The ship

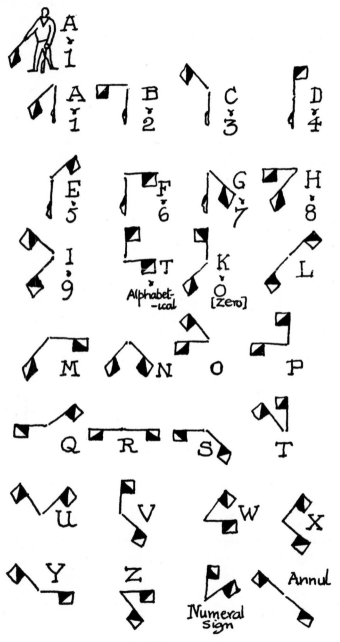

Fig. 71

signalling will then make the 'Break' sign (BT), which indicates that the text of the message is about to be sent. The receiving ship repeats back the 'Break' sign and then the transmitting ship makes one more 'Break' sign and begins the message. If the message is in plain language, when each word has been correctly received, the receiving ship should answer with a T. If the receiving ship does not answer with a T, then the transmitting ship should repeat the word until she receives a T. Once the message has been finished and acknowledged by the receiving ship, the sender should make the ending sign, AR. The receiver should then acknowledge with 'R' (message received).

Also useful to know is the semaphore code, a quick method of signalling by day to other yachts, merchant vessels, warships, and shore stations. (See Fig. 71). The easiest way to learn the semaphore alphabet is by thinking of the letters in terms of circles, such as: A to G is the first circle, H to N (*omitting* J) is the second, O to S the third, T, U, Y, and 'annul' is the fourth, 'numeral', J (or 'Alphabetical'), and V is the fifth, W and X is the sixth circle, and the seventh and last is Z. In the first circle A to C are made with the right arm, and E to G with the left. The letter D is made with whichever is convenient to the sender. In the second circle, and in the remaining circles, the right arm remains at a stationary position while the left arm makes the movements. *Never* bend your elbows when signalling. Your arm, wrist, and hand flag should form one straight line, and when changing from one sign to another, the arms should be kept straight. You can use for signalling any two brightly coloured flags on short hand staffs. Let us now pass on to marks of respect.

When you plan to visit a foreign port, be certain that you have aboard the national ensign of the country and hoist it at the crosstrees when in harbour. It is an act of courtesy which will always be appreciated. If you carry a complete set of flags aboard, you can 'dress ship over all' on any ceremonial event.

When you pass a vessel to which you wish to pay respect, you should salute by slowly lowering your ensign to the 'dipped' position, which is two-thirds of the distance the flag is hoisted. The ship you have greeted will dip her ensign in acknowledgment. The yachts that should be saluted, apart from warships, are: royal yachts and flag officer's yachts.